Offla's Children
–A family Memoir

Helena Wilson / Liz Ban / Paul Ban

First published 2020 by Helena Wilson, Liz Ban and Paul Ban

Produced by Independent Ink
independentink.com.au
Copyright © Helena Wilson, Liz Ban and Paul Ban 2020

The moral right of the author to be identified as the author of this work has been asserted.

All rights reserved. Except as permitted under the *Australian Copyright Act 1968*, no part of this publication may be reproduced, stored in a retrieval system, or transmitted in any form or by any means, electronic, mechanical, photocopying, recording or otherwise, without prior written permission from the publisher. All enquiries should be made to the author.

Cover design by Daniela Catucci
Edited by Alison Arnold
Internal design by Independent Ink
Typeset in 12/17 pt Adobe Garamond by Post Pre-press Group, Brisbane
Cover image: supplied by Helena Wilson, Liz Ban and Paul Ban

 A catalogue record for this book is available from the National Library of Australia

ISBN 978-0-6489749-0-1 (colour paperback)
ISBN 978-0-6489749-3-2 (B&W paperback)
ISBN 978-0-6489749-1-8 (epub)
ISBN 978-0-6489749-2-5 (kindle)

Disclaimer:
Every effort has been made to ensure this book is as accurate and complete as possible. However, there may be mistakes both typographical and in content. Therefore, this book should be used as a general guide and is not the ultimate source of information contained herein. The author and publisher shall not be liable or responsible to any person or entity with respect to any loss or damage caused or alleged to have been caused directly or indirectly by the information contained in this book.

Acknowledgements

Liz

I would like to give a special thanks to my wonderful supportive husband, Ed Hooper, who read multiple drafts of my story and for words of encouragement. Thank you to Jazzy and Austin for putting up with me telling you my childhood stories.

A big thanks to Helena for gathering the family files through freedom of information and painstakingly piecing the information in chronological order so we could make sense of it all. Also, thanks to Helena for initiating the writing of the Ban story many years ago on her own and then together with Paul and myself. Thank you to Paul for encouraging Helena to join your stories together and to Dorothy Scott for encouraging me to write my story. Also, thank you Dorothy for the many hours reading our stories and being so gracious and warm in your feedback, as well as asking Raimond Gaita to read them.

Thank you to my friends for your support and encouragement and to Clare Allridge for prompting me to expand on some sections of my story.

Finally, thank you Alison Arnold for your professional editing and making our story more coherent and suggesting we merge our parents stories with ours.

We can never know what life has in store for us, but we have to keep on trying and never give up. In the time since I started writing this book with my siblings, my husband, Ed, has been diagnosed with pancreatic cancer. His prognosis is poor. While it has been devastating news for us, I know that I will use my inner strength and resilience. And just as Offla did, in escaping during the war, I will take a leap of faith into the dark and unknown.

Helena

To the most patient, kind and loving husband I could have hoped for. Ray Wilson, you've been my rock during the many years of trying to make sense of my childhood, throughout tears and laughter. Always encouraging me to strive for my best work by reading and rereading each and every page. You understood twenty-eight years ago four pages wasn't enough for me to write about my childhood. A condensed sixteen pages was handed to the social worker during our adoption course. The girl we hoped for didn't eventuate so we continued on with life with our three beautiful sons. The spark was lit during that cathartic experience and I thank you from the bottom of my heart for supporting me in keeping it burning.

To my sons Ryan, Dane and Callum Wilson. Thank you for bringing pleasure into my life and joy into my heart. I'm so proud of the men you've become. I was relieved once each of you turned five years of age as I hoped you would be able to remember at least something of me should I die. I know you've found it difficult to read previous versions of my story as you haven't wanted to strip the 'nurturer' label that comes with being your mother. Follow your heart and strip the labels away. I hope you love what you find.

To one of my main supporters, my brother Paul. Thank you for encouraging me to persevere and continue writing our story even though I sometimes questioned my reasoning. It made sense when you wrote your story to combine the two making it a stronger and more powerful tribute.

A gratitude of thanks to my sister Liz. Without you my childhood would have been empty. Without the letters our mother wrote to our uncle in Europe you sent me for safekeeping, the void in my heart would have remained. How blessed we were to discover our mother within her own words. Thank you for agreeing to add your story and for your never wavering love.

I thank all the parent figures who helped raise me, especially Lesley Fleming who remains a constant in my life. I could never forget my extended family for sharing and surviving a unique childhood including Ken and Peter Marshall, my brothers from another mother.

Many friends have read various versions of my story over the years. Thank you to Shelley McCready who has never wavered in her ability to encourage me to get the story published, even while she battled with her cancer diagnosis. Without a doubt she is the most positive person I know.

Thank you to Dorothy Scott and Shurlee Swain for your professional and personal interest in our story. And to Raimond Gaita, who was so moved after reading it, recommended his own editor take us on.

Finally, thanks to Alison Arnold. Your fine editing and professional input is what was needed. I appreciate the respect you've given our father, the main character. It cemented a bond and friendship I never expected.

Our father's leap of faith is an inspiration to me. It has enabled me to have a never-give-up attitude and to keep on marching throughout life. Sometimes even skipping, as my sister would say. Offla's greatest trait was resilience. He managed to cope in spite of setbacks, barriers and limited resources. He knew how much he wanted something and how much he was willing, and able, to overcome obstacles to get it.

Paul

My wife Helen, my daughter Lauren and my grandson Leo are my inspiration for me to write about my father's life regarding what it was like for him to lose his family. They have and will appreciate, in the case of Leo, who is still a baby, the life my siblings and I experienced being raised in a children's home and having to make sense of not being in a family environment. Helen has been an excellent sounding board for my thoughts and has helped me shape them into a text that I feel happy with.

My long-term friends Jerry and Marla Meehl have been very loyal and helpful during my thoughts and drafts stages and have offered suggestions that I have readily taken up.

Chris, Helena and Liz have been on the journey with me through Silky Oaks and into the adult world. I'm grateful for their company, now in the later stages of adulthood.

Thanks to George Hook for being the first to read my individual section apart from Helen and for telling me it was very interesting and worth pursuing.

And finally thanks to Dorothy Scott and Shurlee Swain, long term friends and academics in social work and history who encouraged me to think that our story was worth telling and be of interest to a wide range of people.

The two anecdotes we wrote about in the epilogue have been inspirational to me in learning to cope with whatever situation life throws at you and to keep moving forward in a positive direction even though you don't know what lies ahead. My brother Chris's favourite saying, inspired by Offla, is 'Keep on marching'.

*In loving memory of our parents
Jean Trevaskis and Zoltan Ban (Offla)*

*You lived for your children and will live forever
through your children's children.*

'But where are the snows of yester-year?'

— François Villon

Introduction

During the war, fighting for the Hungarian army, our father was held in two Russian prisoner of war camps. At the end of the war he was arrested by the Americans for illegal border crossing and incarcerated again. In one of those camps, he was dragged from his cell and marched to a shed near the latrines. A soldier with a rifle was waiting for him. On the ground were bullet casings. He was given his last rites, handed a blindfold and told to line up on the opposite wall.

He did so and waited to hear his final gunshot. However, after the shot was fired he realised he was still standing. The soldier had fired a blank. His blindfold was taken off and he was told he was free to go. New soldiers would be there soon, and 'Lieutenant Ban, maybe they'll take better aim.'

Our father, Zoltan Ban, or Zoli for short, later to become known as Offla, fled Europe and ended up in Australia, one of many post-war migrants whose stories are so important to this country. He came at a time when only 2 per cent of Australians spoke a language other than English and he came at a time when the mental illness he was to develop was barely understood.

Meanwhile, our mother, Jean Trevaskis, was making her way to Australia and to Hobart, where she would meet Zoli. She did not live long enough to tell us her stories, and we know little of her early life, only the names of her parents, our grandparents – Annie Elizabeth Trevaskis (nee Entwistle) and George Albert Trevaskis – and that she was born at home at 9 Ellaline Road, North West Fulham, England, on 23 October 1923. But we still feel her steady loving presence, and through her letters to one of our uncles, we know just how brave she was. Our mother died when she was thirty-nine, when our father's illness was building, knowing she was leaving her four children to an uncertain future. We are glad that she could not know that we would be taken from our father sixteen months after she died and made wards of the state. That we would then grow up in a children's home, all the while vaguely aware that our father was trying to regain custody of us.

This is the story of our family: four children growing up in state care, each of us experiencing it differently; and an eccentric, brave, unpredictable yet steadfast man who spent years trying to have us returned to him. It is a story of post-war Australia in the grip of anti-communist fervour, a story of mental illness, of the good and bad of institutional care. It is the story of family disruption and, ultimately, of resilience.

It has been pieced together from our father's stories, our memories, and Helena's painstaking research through our family's files, held by the Commonwealth Department of Immigration and Queensland's Children's Services Department.

Our brother Chris did not want to be part of writing this book and we respect that. We can't tell his story for him, but, of course, he pops up in ours.

Helena Wilson, Liz Ban, Paul Ban

Authors note

The Brisbane Special Hospital, the Brisbane Mental Hospital, and Wolston Park Hospital are the same hospital, renamed at various points. The complex is now called The Park Centre for Mental Health. Jean refers to the hospital as Goodna Mental Hospital.

The State Children Department later became the Children's Services Department, and has had many name changes since. Child welfare officers were employed by this department.

The Department of Migration was a subset of the Department of Immigration.

PART 1

Taken

1964–1965

Paul

The Inala Civic Centre in south-west Brisbane was like any other cluster of shops in a low-income area – unremarkable and nondescript. There was a paved area outside where our father, Zoli, took us to rollerskate on the weekends, and a newly planted garden near the road. We were quite familiar with the unemployment bureau, the bank and the police station.

The police came on a Monday, sixteen months after our mother died.

It was 10 August 1964, another mild, blue-sky winter day. We'd been to the Commonwealth Bank with Daddy. He and the manager argued, their voices raised, and our father was agitated as we left.

On the way home, he stopped to make a call from the public phone box beyond the garden. We waited on the footpath, all four of us trying to ignore the anxiety in his voice.

He was still distressed when he stepped out of the phone box.

It didn't seem to take long before a police car arrived. The bank manager had called them.

'Zoltan Ban?' the grey-uniformed officer said. 'We're going to take you to the police station for a chat.'

'Run, kiddies!' said our father.

But we didn't get very far. We were no match for four Queensland coppers who meant business.

I can't remember Daddy being caught, but I knew he had been down this road with the police before. We hadn't. My brother and two sisters were put into the police car and out of the corner of my eye I saw Daddy being taken to another car that had just arrived.

'Where are we going?' I asked as I got in the car.

'To the police station.' The officer didn't elaborate.

When we arrived at the station, my brother and sisters were told to wait in a room with a policeman while I was asked some details.

'You're Paul, nine years old, is that correct?'

'Yes,' I replied.

'And your brother Chris is eight? You're very close in age, aren't you? I have here that your sister Helena is six and the toddler Elizabeth is three?'

'That's right.' I wanted to tell him that Chris was fourteen months younger than me but I thought he probably already knew that anyway.

After the questions were over we were fingerprinted and photographed before being told we were being 'charged with neglect'.

I wasn't quite sure what he meant by that. I knew our clothes were all second-hand, from the op shop. And maybe Daddy could have washed them occasionally. But I couldn't understand the connection with what was happening to us. It all seemed like an adventure, or a dream.

Somehow, though, I knew it meant that I wasn't going back to my normal life. While I had no idea what lay ahead, I told myself I wouldn't cry and upset the others.

'Would you like to look at the cells?' beamed the friendly officer who was minding Chris, Helena and Bessie. 'There's no one in them.'

For half a second I thought he was going to put us in there, before realising he was just trying to entertain us.

Time both stood still and was rushing along. Were we in a movie? Was it *Candid Camera*? Would someone appear to reassure us it was all a joke? I liked the reaction on people's faces on *Candid Camera* when they found out it was just a gag. The TV in our rundown house was an escape into a world where my sisters hadn't scribbled on the walls and the grass wasn't growing long outside. I could still remember being so excited when we'd moved in to our housing commission home three years earlier. It had more than two rooms, unlike our previous house, and it had a toilet that flushed and a laundry.

'Righto, then, all into the car, you're going to somewhere where you will be looked after for a while.'

My mind was racing. 'What about our stuff at home? Can we stop and collect things?'

'Sorry, we have orders to take you straight there. Maybe you can get them later.'

Our house was full of toys and clothes from what Daddy called the 'junk shop'. None of them meant as much to me as our pets. We had guinea pigs and white mice that needed feeding, as well as kittens whose mother had abandoned them.

We got into the car and were driven through the streets of Brisbane. The driver told us we were going to a place where 'rescued' children go to be 'assessed'. I didn't know what assessed meant, but I had a pretty good idea of what he meant by rescued.

I don't remember being scared. Confused, maybe, and uncertain as to what was going on. But somehow, I had known that something like this was going to happen.

'Pretend this is still an adventure,' I thought, 'and the others will think that everything is okay.'

Helena

The police car drove away leaving us with strangers. At the top of a steep staircase lay the entrance to the Diamantina Receiving Home, an interim assessment centre for children awaiting their fate. Its name had changed a couple of years earlier from the Diamantina Receiving Depot and Infants' Home although it remained shortened to 'the Depot'.

We were separated almost immediately. Bessie was taken to the infants section, which was lined with rows of cots. I was placed in the girls dormitory to one side of the dining room.

There seemed to be children everywhere munching on sweets from sample bags. I discovered they'd just returned from an outing to the Brisbane Exhibition. They whispered excitedly about their day while I was allocated a bed in the centre row: a set of crisp white sheets, an unfamiliar pillow and a grey blanket dressed the iron-framed bed. When the light was switched off that evening, I worried about whether Bessie had managed to settle down and get to sleep without me. We had always shared a bedroom. Where were my brothers? Were they together? None of the girls in the beds beside me asked who I was or why I was there. I had come to accept my mummy was never coming back from the place the van took her away to. I didn't know where my daddy was. Why hadn't he come to take us home? My heart ached for him. It ached for my mummy, for my baby sister and my brothers. I quietly sobbed myself to sleep.

The following morning we were reunited in the supply room and the boys told us they'd been put in a dormitory on the other side of the dining room. We were given a suitcase, several items of clothing and shoes. A list containing our supplies was taped inside the suitcase. The clothes we arrived in were taken from us. The excitement of receiving new clothes masked the wonderment and confusion of the previous day.

Two days later, the dress and tattered cardigan I'd been wearing when we arrived were laid out on my bed to wear. They hadn't been washed. I was told to wait at the front entrance where I met Bessie and the boys. They were dressed in their old clothes too. We didn't speak to each other as we got in the car.

At the children's court we were led into the courtroom. Our names were read out, followed by the charge: 'You are a Neglected Child in that you are under the guardianship of Zoltan Ban, a person unfit to have such guardianship.'

The evidence was read by the arresting officer who said he knew the defendant children before the court.

> The children were in a filthy condition with uncombed hair, generally untidy and dirty. I then had a conversation with Mr Zoltan Ban and as a result of this conversation I was of the opinion that he was mentally ill. The defendant children have no relatives in Australia as far as can be ascertained. The father is of Hungarian nationality. I maintain that the four defendant children are neglected children in that the father is mentally ill. They have no other guardian.

After hearing the statement and seeing us huddled together in dirty clothes, the magistrate was satisfied that we were neglected. No one asked us any questions.

And so it was that on 13 August 1964, a half-page statement sealed our fate. We were committed to the care of the State Children Department until we each turned eighteen.

Paul

The Depot was to be our home while we waited. But no one told us what we were waiting for and the longer we stayed there the more settled I became.

I was in Grade 5 and was sent to the local primary school the day after we arrived. Wooloowin State Primary School happened to share a fence with the Depot. That day all the students in the class I was to be in were away on an excursion and the only person in the classroom was the teacher, who was busy with marking. He eyed me up and down when I came in and spoke to me in a friendly manner. He must have been told I was one of the Depot kids and I think he felt sorry for me. After some small talk, he shifted into teacher mode and started firing multiplication questions at me. To his evident surprise and pleasure I answered every one correctly. But my cockiness was taken down a peg when he launched into a series of division problems – my previous rapid-fire responses turned to hesitant ones, before finally getting the answer right.

Chris and I slept in a long row of beds in the boys dormitory. Chris's bed was a couple down from mine, as there was someone between us in age. After the children's court, the staff took away the clothes we had arrived in and we received a different set of freshly laundered clothes every Tuesday and Saturday. As it was only a temporary place, the clothes we received were only roughly our size, and they were only ours for the duration of the wear. Once they went into the wash, there was a good chance the next time you saw your favourite shirt that someone else would be wearing it. I didn't mind that so much. It was just nice to have clean clothes. When we lived in Inala with our father, we had worn our clothes until they became so dirty it was a relief to part with them.

I was old enough to do jobs around the property. One was wheeling an empty wheelbarrow to the nursery to collect wet nappies in the mornings. The nursery was filled with rows of babies in cots. Their smelly nappies were piled in a room waiting for delivery to the industrial laundry. I had to hold my nose as I loaded them into the wheelbarrow – and because they were saturated, the wheelbarrow was pretty heavy on the long journey to the laundry.

As time went on, with no apparent end to the waiting period, this life began to be a new normal. We walked in pairs to the local picture theatre on a Saturday afternoon to see whatever film was playing at the time. It was a good routine and one that I looked forward to. I found myself becoming Nurse King's pet. She must have liked something about me because she was always talking to me and bringing me things the other children didn't get.

After a while, I started to notice the regular movement of children through the facility, as a series of different boys occupied the bed beside me. Sometimes I would lie awake at night and imagine my father climbing through the window to collect Chris and me, before getting the girls and returning to our old house. I imagined holding the guinea pigs and the white mice again and seeing how much the kittens had grown.

Then one day, when we'd been at the Depot for two months, the matron called us into her office to announce the good news.

We were soon to be leaving for our new home. I realised she definitely wasn't talking about our house in Inala. When I asked where this new place was, Matron replied, 'It's beside the sea and it begins with S.' That was all the information she gave us. 'Is it Southport?' I asked. I had some idea about the Gold Coast and knew there was a place there called Southport.

The Depot had a special area where children who were about to move to their designated children's home (mine began with S!) were outfitted with sets of new clothes that were meant to last until we grew out of them. Finally, I was getting my own new clothes – the first time I could remember such an event. The nurse in the fitting rooms measured me and Chris up for size before giving us our allocated shirts (with collars!), t-shirts, good white shirts, play shorts, walk shorts, good shorts, long white socks, singlets, underpants, a pair of good black shiny shoes, a tie, a suit jacket and suit shorts. The suit was made from a heavy grey woollen material and became known as the 'Statey-issue blanket suit'. The blanket suit was the outfit of choice for the transfer to our mystery destination beside the sea. I felt we were a bit overdressed – as well as our suits, Chris and I had on our white shirts and ties with our shiny black shoes, capped off with a heavy application of hair oil. I don't remember what the girls wore, but I was glad they missed out on the hair oil.

Helena

At the Depot I played with Bessie as often as I could and rarely caught a glimpse of my brothers. I started at Wooloowin State School, where I was in Grade 1. We collected little lunch on our way through the back gate and returned to the home for big lunch.

When I'd started school earlier in the year, it had been a year since my mummy died, and Bessie had cried as I walked with Paul and Chris to the Inala State School, full of excitement.

Daddy had been giving me a bottle of warm milk on some evenings and weekends to help me settle. I lay on my bed comforted by suckling the teat and the warmth of the milk as it filled my belly. My brothers often teased me, leaving me a little embarrassed by their taunts. But I wasn't prepared to sacrifice what was my only real comfort at the time. My mummy was taken away in a van and hadn't returned. Even though I'd turned five and was learning to read and write, I yearned for all things maternal. I wanted my mother. What first began as an innocent theft of my baby sister's bottle led to my father understanding his daughter's need. It was just as easy to warm two bottles of milk as it was one.

I missed that bottle at the Depot. I missed my father.

Just as I was getting used to this new life I was uprooted again. This time, at least, I could say goodbye to my new friends, a luxury not afforded earlier when forced to leave behind school friends, neighbours, pets and my daddy.

In October, a stranger collected us and placed our newly fitted-out suitcases in her car.

Our new home had a sign at its grand entrance: Silky Oaks Children's Haven. The driveway led us to the top of a hill where a majestic double-storey wooden house stood. It was the original home when the eight acres were purchased in 1946, and was now commonly referred to as the 'old building'. There, we were met by the superintendents of Silky Oaks, a married couple, Mr Zander and Aunty Jean. Max and Jean Alexander. For the benefit of the young children, their surname was shortened. At the home, adults were known as 'the workers', with the men called 'Mister' and the women 'Aunty'.

I was escorted around the premises by Aunty Jean's daughter, Roslyn, who was my age. She was the youngest of their three children. My brothers were escorted to their dormitory by their carer, Mr Smith.

In the 1950s, a main brick building was added. The ground floor contained a spacious commercial kitchen with serving benches easily accessible to the dining room. The corridor led to the main lounge room with its black and white television magically transporting each child to another world several hours per week. For those not easily transfixed, Mr Zander's office and his means of punishment – the dreaded strap – weren't too far away. Beyond the back door was the boys dormitory, two large prefabricated Army huts joined together. A huge playing field sat between the dormitory and the large commercial laundry with its never-ending clothesline full of towels, sheets and a constant array of dangling clothes. And beside the laundry was the fence line for the Manly West State School. At the rear of the playing field was a variety of swings, jungle gym, trampoline and a large concrete sandpit with a slippery slide leading into it.

My sister and I shared a small bedroom in the older building. It was connected by a walkway to the main brick building, and its bedrooms housed girls of various ages. I wasn't sure how long we would remain together but was grateful to share with my sister again. She jumped into my bed at night and we cried ourselves to sleep.

'When is Daddy coming to take us home?' she asked.

My reply was consistent. 'If you are very good and do everything I tell you, he will come.'

Aunty Alice was our new carer and mother figure. Her long grey hair was thin and tied back into a bun held by bobby pins. She was middle-aged, slightly plump and plainly dressed.

It wasn't long before two vacant beds became available in the 'Little End' of the brick building and my sister and I were separated. This area was set up with two bedrooms of four to five girls of similar age, with one bathroom and toilet.

I had much in common with my new roommates, Debbie, Margaret and Kim. We arrived at Silky Oaks within twelve months of each other, none of us had a mother alive and we had a little sister in the next bedroom. Debbie had Kerry. Margaret had two, Diane and Marie. Kim had Michelle and, of course, I had my sister. Bessie's name was changed immediately upon arrival to Elizabeth as Aunty Jean preferred it. However, the kids quickly decided that Lizzy was much easier to say. (My sister was already on her third name and she was only three!) Three of the little sisters were three years of age; Marie was the youngest at one.

Aunty Alice slept in a simply furnished bedroom across from the little sisters and next door to the medical/first aid room. It was a privilege to receive permission to enter her room, use her hairbrush, smell her clothes or cuddle her pillow. I sought this out – my memories of my mother were fading and this feminine space helped to keep them alive.

A simple system reigned in the bedrooms whereby the oldest child was declared the leader. That was now me. And it would be my duty to not only deal with problems within the confines of our bedroom but also on the outside. Before any newcomer's name was asked, it was important to first establish their age. And in a large family of up to seventy children there had to be a hierarchy in place.

I started my third school of the year, Manly West State Primary School. My roommate Margaret and Roslyn, the superintendents' daughter, were in my class, making the transition a little easier. My teacher, Miss Martin, gave me a list of school supplies which I took to the book room underneath the Old Building that evening. It was run by one of the older teenage girls for half an hour on school nights. I patiently waited in line, listening intently to the question asked of each kid: 'Statey or Private?'

The occasional answer was 'Private' but most were 'Statey'. When it was my turn I received the routine question. Not understanding what it meant, I simply handed over my list. I received a slightly more aggressive 'Statey or Private?' After what seemed an eternity somebody towards the end of the line yelled, 'I think she's a Statey.' The others all agreed so a new card was selected from the box marked 'State' with my name printed at the top. My supplies were noted on my personal record card. After receiving them I returned to the bedroom and neatly placed everything in my port (schoolbag). The question was niggling at me so I asked the girls to explain what Statey and Private meant.

Kim said, 'Well, I'm a Private because my father and grandma have to pay for everything Michelle and I use.' She went on to explain that her family lived in a small house near the Wynnum waterfront. As there wasn't enough room for Kim and Michelle they lived at Silky Oaks instead.

Debbie and Margaret admitted that they were both Stateys. It was a relief that they were the same as me.

'What does it mean?' I asked

'It means that you are now owned by the State and the State pays for everything for you,' said Debbie. 'The best thing is, you don't have to show your used pencils or books if you're a Statey because the State doesn't care how many you use.'

'Yeah,' Margaret said. 'The Private kids have to show them because their parents don't like spending money.'

And so I discovered that day that my father didn't own me anymore. Somebody or something called 'the State' did, and they would buy me as many pencils and books as I liked!

Manly West and my new home were next door to each other, but we remained at school for lunch. My teacher was the most beautiful woman I had ever seen, and I adored her. But one day she did something that killed my adoration stone dead. Margaret had done something not to her liking and she punished Margaret by making her stand on her chair during class. When urine began to trickle down Margaret's leg, and her anxious tears flowed, our teacher did nothing.

That night, a meeting was held in the confines of our bedroom. As we comforted Margaret, we cemented the bond between the four of us. We would always look out for each other.

Earlier that year, when my family was still together, I'd used a slate board and chalk at school to learn to write the letters of the alphabet. It was such a treat when I received my first set of crayons – I was eager to draw pictures and write my name as often as I could. Paper was expensive so I improvised by using the walls of my bedroom. It wasn't long before my bedroom was covered with the artistic talents of a five-year-old. My talent ventured out into the living room and, with help from Bessie, the inside of our house became a work of art. The boys were horrified. My daddy didn't mind at all!

One day at Silky Oaks, my inner graffiti artist came out again and I scribbled the words 'bum', 'dick', 'wee' and 'poo' on the wall above my bed. When Aunty Alice demanded to know who'd done it, I knew better than to own up. And Debbie, Margaret and Kim knew better than to dob me in. What would our punishment be? One of Aunty Alice's trademark punishments was belting your backside with a wire coathanger. It helped to lessen the impact if you began screaming before it actually made contact. It was a bad idea to protect your backside with your hand as the sting lingered in the tips of your fingers longer than your rear end. (You were praised as a hero if you managed to call Aunty Alice a big fat pig during this ordeal.) But she was also well known for washing mouths out with soap for swearing or blasphemous words. Good Christian girls should never swear – even 'shut-up' was considered a swear word. And, so, we were all marched to the bathroom sink. By the end of that session, God, Jesus Christ and the twelve disciples would have been impressed with the purification of the four little sinners.

Time passed with no word from or about our father. His friend, Mr Dabrowski, had visited us at the Depot, and he visited us at Silky Oaks too. Mr Dabrowski had round tortoiseshell glasses and a round pleasant face. And we enjoyed his visits, someone from the time before.

In those first few months, inmates of various ages and nationalities continued to arrive and depart. These included Russians, Germans and Indigenous Australians. Silky Oaks would be a haven for some, for others it would be the opposite. Two young Russian girls were slapped until they ceased to speak in their mother tongue, the language they spoke with their parents. Beatings were accepted as fair punishment for naughty girls.

We quickly learnt the rules.

But often those who came to Silky Oaks were leaving something far worse. Many had alcoholic or violent parents while others were victims of sexual abuse. A young boy and his older sister arrived one day. Their stepmother had tried to drown the boy in the bathtub, with their father looking on in silence. His sister reported the attempted murder to authorities, thereby rescuing them. Some shared their horror stories with the other inmates. Others would wait long into adulthood before they could deal with their memories and emotions. The reason for my institutionalisation was instilled in me early: Mother dead – Father mental.

Paul

I saw very little of my sisters after we got to Silky Oaks. Instead of living in a sibling group, I was raised in a world of boys, much as if I'd been sent to boarding school.

The boys dormitory was just across the way from the office and we arrived there in no time. Mr Smith was the man in charge, and he was quiet but friendly and showed us to our beds. The beds were in four rows with an aisle between the rows. Beside each bed was a locker for personal belongings, like we'd had at the Depot. But unlike the Depot, every boy in the dorm also had their own cupboard with drawers and hanging space. The cupboards were all in a line along one wall of the dorm.

The section where Chris and I would be sleeping was known as the 'Little End' due to the younger ages of the boys. The other end of the dorm was called the 'Big End'. This was where you moved to when you grew too old for the Little End, or if there was a sudden influx of younger kids and no room left in the Little End. Between the Big End and the Little End was a long hallway. On one side of the hallway was Mr Smith's flat, and on the other were bathrooms and toilets.

As Chris and I were getting settled in, a sea of faces appeared to check out the new kids. Before long, one of the boys began to push

Chris around. I quickly stepped in to protect my little brother and, after a minor scuffle, the instigator of the skirmish realised he would have to deal with two new kids instead of one, and a new order was established.

Altogether there were twenty-two boys in the dorm. The beds in the Little End were allocated according to age, starting with the youngest boy, a two-year-old, at one end, and snaking around the room until it got to me, the oldest of the littlies. The Big End had the same age-based arrangement, but we weren't allowed to venture into the older boys' territory, and would have been chased away if we'd tried to.

Given that I was almost ten, I could already see that my days at the Little End were numbered, and that it wouldn't be long before I made my way to the other, shadowy dorm. For the time being, though, I was happy to be sleeping in a bed beside my brother.

One of the things that had been missing from my life in the year our father looked after us was a sense of routine. In particular, with my mother's death, we had lost the routine of family mealtimes. Silky Oaks made up for this in spades. First bell – one long ring and one short ring – meant we had to go to the bathroom and wash our faces and hands. Second bell – one long ring followed by two short rings – was the signal to go straight to the dining room and take our seat.

In contrast to my father's approach to mealtimes, dining at Silky Oaks was highly regulated. The dining room contained seven tables of six children, with an older boy and girl at the ends of each table to supervise the four younger children on the sides. Before we could eat our breakfast in the morning, there was a long Bible reading followed by a prayer which seemed to go for just as long as the Bible reading. The Bible was read in bite-sized chunks from cover to cover, returning to Genesis when we finished Revelations. I can recall lots of 'somebody begat somebody and somebody else begat somebody else' when we got back to the Old Testament, but mostly I was too busy daydreaming about rugby league or cricket to notice.

The main source of regulation at Silky Oaks, however, was the jobs roster, which was pinned behind a glass case in the hallway between the little end and the big end of the dorm. We were given jobs almost as soon as we arrived. The roster started with 'before breakfast' jobs, then 'after breakfast' jobs and finally 'after school' jobs. I don't know how often the roster changed and I can't remember ever appealing to the carer in charge of the roster to let me swap for an easier job. But one change I negotiated on my own was from feeding the chooks before breakfast to feeding the ducks. Duck duty involved going to the kitchen to collect the slops bin of leftover food and practically anything that wasn't paper, glass or plastic. As it was too heavy for one boy to manage, the chook boy had to help the duck boy lug it the few hundred metres from the kitchen to the pens, which were situated near the mulberry trees. While the chook boy simply had to put his hand in dry chicken feed and throw it about in whatever fashion he liked, the duck boy would mix mash into the slop in a trough and then pour the mixture into containers for the expectant ducks to eat.

I always thought the ducks looked far happier than the chooks. They seemed to have permanent smiles and quacked pleasurably while waiting for their gruel. So I offered the duck boy a trade. I showed him how to use a bowling action to spread the chook feed around and demonstrated the fun you could have trying out different techniques. For some reason, he bought my sales pitch. In return, he taught me the finer points of mixing mash with leftover sloppy food.

It didn't take long for me to realise the mistake I'd made. No matter how much I washed my hands before breakfast I couldn't get rid of the smell of slops, and I nearly gagged eating my toast of a morning. When I tried to swap back, the newly appointed chook boy was so relieved to have traded a smelly job for a clean job, and was so enjoying working on his bowling technique, that I had no viable sales pitch left. The result of my poor trade was that I was duck boy for what seemed like years, until the roster was finally changed.

One job that no one wanted was backyard clean up duty after breakfast. It meant being supervised by Chook White, having to stay together in a group for what seemed a long time but was probably only twenty minutes, and having to pick up all the papers and rubbish that Chook pointed to. Front yard duty was an entirely different proposition. First of all, it covered an area including the vast space where we used to play football and cricket as well as a lawn area where no one really walked. All the rubbish action was in the back yard, between the dormitories. If you were on front yard duty after breakfast, it basically meant free time before school.

Allocation to front yard and back yard duties was a daily affair. After breakfast, we would file down the stairs from the dining room and line up against the brick wall. Chook stood out the front like a sergeant in the army, usually with the stick he used to point to the rubbish, and chose our morning fate. The convention was that you alternated between front and back yard duties, so that you only had to 'work' every second day. It was a lot of responsibility to place on Chook's memory, as he didn't particularly care who he had to supervise.

Chook would point to each boy in turn. 'Ban, front; Nagle, back; Johnson, front; Marshall, back' and so on, until we were in our respective teams. One morning Chook made a mistake.

He called out, 'Marshall, back', for the second day in a row. An aggrieved Kenny Marshall quickly replied, 'Gee whiz, Chook, I did the back yard yesterday.' The next morning, Chook pointed his stick at Kenny and said, 'Whizzer, front yard'. We fell about laughing and Kenny was stuck with the nickname.

One of my favourite jobs before breakfast was to get the little kids out of bed and dress them for the day. The little kids were extremely cute, although some were what we called 'the wet bed kids'. But most of them were dry and it was fun to play with them while helping them to get dressed and make their beds.

There were also some weekend jobs. One of our Saturday morning jobs was to wash the Silky Oaks bus in the backyard. You could pretend to be the driver and take the bus on imaginary journeys instead of cleaning it. The main use for the bus was to ferry us all to church. On Sunday evenings after the evening service we would pile into the bus and alight in the back yard of the Oaks before heading to our respective dormitories. Mr Zander would always ask for a volunteer to open the bus shed doors for him. The job seemed to be reserved for the boys. It basically involved both opening the shed doors and closing them again once the bus was safely parked inside. As a reward, the volunteer got to sit in the prized front seat of the bus with Mr Zander on the way home from church. The bus shed was next to the 'wet bed tree', named because the wet bed mattresses were aired there during the day over an iron frame.

If I had a special request for something that needed Mr Zander's approval, I always made sure to volunteer as bus shed assistant, so I could speak to him alone. Annoyingly, he would never give me an answer to my requests straight away. He would always say, 'I'll put it on the agenda.' While this wasn't what I wanted to hear, at least my request had been 'recorded' and the answer would eventually filter back to me.

None of us asked where our father was. I had some idea that he was in hospital 'to get better'.

Liz

My earliest memories of Silky Oaks were of a long driveway, silky oak trees on the right and date palms on the left. This memory was followed by being swallowed up in the arms of a strange lady, feeling smothered and trying to squirm away from her. I was three years old. My mother had died when I was twenty-two months old and after a precious year with my father, my three older siblings and I were taken away.

We were separated at the home. Paul and Chris were sent to the boys dorm, and because they were close in age they were kept together throughout their time at Silky Oaks. Helena was three years older than me, and always just ahead of me in the home. So when I was in the Little End, she was in the Big End with the older girls. But when we arrived, we both stayed in the Old Building with the toddlers and she comforted me as I cried.

'I want my Daddy and I want to go home.'

'Where's Paul and Chris?'

'I'm scared.'

'Shush, be quiet, or we'll get into trouble,' she said. 'Go to sleep, I'm here.'

I sucked my thumb for comfort, and rubbed my index and middle finger between the sheets to help soothe myself. Helena stayed with me until a bed became available for her in the Little End. One day she was with me, comforting me, and the next she was gone.

I was on my own with other little girls and I needed to show I was okay, but secretly at night I would suck my thumb for comfort as I drifted off to sleep. A big girl called Tricia used to look after me and would help get me dressed and bathed. She was nice to me and was one of the older kids whose job was to help look after the little kids. I think she was about nine when I was three. I wasn't very long in the Old Building before I moved to the Little End. There were two sections within the Little End, the small children were in one room and the older girls were in the next room. There were four little girls, of similar age to me. Helena was in the big girls room, with the older sisters. Aunty Alice was our carer. She was a plump woman with long thin grey hair, which she wore in a bun. She was tough love, no nonsense, but she liked to turn everything into a song. She had never married and loved young children. Yet, if you misbehaved you would get a whack with a coathanger on the legs, a cake of soap in your mouth, or mustard on the tongue. I tried to avoid the wrath of Alice Connell on many occasions. One time, I was angry and called her 'Fatty Connell'. That resulted in her putting mustard on the end of my tongue and I recall running to the drink fountain by the laundry to wash the burning sensation from my mouth.

Aunty Alice was so busy looking after the children in her section that she was not aware of who'd had a bath. I remember telling a white lie on a number of occasions, by saying I'd had one when I hadn't. I wasn't alone —there was just too much fun to be had running around with our friends at the home to take time out for a bath. I loved playing Red Rover with all the kids on the lawn between the Little End and the boys dorm. It was one of our rituals after dinner. There were lots of squeals of excitement as the kids lined up on one side of the lawn and the person in the middle tried to catch you as you ran to the other side of the lawn. 'Caught you.' 'No you didn't'. If they caught you, you had to join them in the middle and help catch the other kids. The idea was to see who would be left standing as the numbers grew in the middle. I loved it as the older kids played with us younger ones. My other favourite game was hide and seek. We had lots of places to hide as the buildings were surrounded by trees and small bushes. We had a base and you had to get 'home' before the person 'in' saw you. There were always arguments, as there was an out-of-bounds area, and some kids would hide there to avoid getting caught. I was guilty of that a few times.

Though there were three years between Helena and me, we had a bond that sleeping in different buildings did not weaken. Helena was wise beyond her years. I idolised her and she naturally took on the role of my mother. It was Helena I turned to when I was upset, sad or needing advice while growing up in the home. I never wanted to get close to any of the adults and I don't know whether it was the fear that they too would disappear as my mother and father had, or whether I felt so attached to Helena, Paul and Chris that I didn't need anyone else.

I used to seek Paul out for chats while he peeled the spuds for the evening supper and Chris while he cleaned out the grease traps. The girls were not allowed to go into the boys dorm or vice versa. There was no policy for family groups to sit together at meal times, so I never sat at the same table with my siblings. It never crossed my mind to ask why I couldn't sit with my brothers and sister. It was just done that way. It was the norm that all the other families sat apart from their siblings and I never thought to challenge it.

Helena told me from an early age that if I were a good little girl, our dad would come back and take us out of the home, so I did my best to be good and tried to avoid trouble.

I was never told why I was in the children's home, or what my mother died from. It was left up to my imagination. Helena told me our father was going to come and get us, but I couldn't understand why he was taking so long. One of my brothers must have told me that our mother had a funny eye before she died and I had convinced myself she went blind because she looked at the sun and then died. (I found out as an adult that the radiation she'd had for her cancer affected her eye.) For a long time, I would tell my friends not to look at the sun or they would go blind and die.

Zoli

'It's a terrible thing to see somebody you love getting all confused, suspicious and mixed up for no reason,' Jean, the children's mother, once wrote. 'He's got some queer ideas about electricity and thought there was someone, he didn't know who, why or where, controlling everything he did or said with an electronic brain. He thought he was being "switched on" and then "switched off". He would suddenly say in the middle of a conversation, "I'm switched on," and then I would have to wait until he was "switched off" before I could speak to him again. He would be quite normal in between.'

Zoli had been arrested under the Mental Health Act. He was taken to the general hospital, his arm twisted behind his back as he resisted entry into the casualty ward. After being examined by a young intern, he stood to stretch his legs, then made a run for the exit. He believed the doctor had taken the same oath as those before him: 'Doctors stick together.' He was pursued, struck with a blunt instrument on the neck, he later told his children, and fell to his knees. That evening, he was taken to the Brisbane Special Hospital, on the Brisbane River in Wacol. It had once been called the Goodna Hospital for the Insane. He spent the next few weeks there in a drugged daze.

From the hospital, he managed to write to his Polish friend, Mr Dabrowski, asking him to check on the children.

During the two months the children were at the Depot, the director of the State Children Department assessed their situation. Given the tragedy they'd already experienced he felt they should be kept together. In this way, their tragic situation turned out to be a blessing. Larger sibling groups were sometimes separated due to a lack of placement resources with no forward planning of a reunion.

Paul

I got a chance to properly meet the boys at the 'big end' of the dorm in the lead-up to Christmas. Those who had been at the home for Christmases-past explained that Santa would visit the dorm on Christmas Eve and leave presents at the end of the bed in a pillowcase. The presents were mainly given by members of the church that ran the home, and through donations to the *Courier-Mail* Christmas Appeal.

Although I was pretty sure by this time that there was no such person as Santa, most of the boys in the Little End still believed in him. The Big End boys were not only convinced there was no real Santa Claus, they were betting on which staff member would deliver the presents. In order to find the winner, they decided to take it in turns spending an hour on watch in the bed of one of the Little End boys. Apparently, Santa always came to the Little End first, so it was there that he would be exposed, and his earthliness revealed. The plan was to place a tray on top of the door into the Little End that would come crashing down when Santa entered.

As I was the oldest boy in the Little End, the bigger boys included me in their plan. My job was to host a series of kids from the Big End in my bed for an hour at a time after the lights went out, and to tickle their backs to stop them from falling asleep. I can't remember volunteering for the job, but I guess it was my initiation into the Big End way of life, which would commence in the New Year.

The tickling plan worked okay for the first few hours, but by midnight I was struggling to stay awake. At about 2 a.m. there was a loud crash as the tray fell to the floor. My tickling had well and truly ceased by then and my Big End buddy and I were fast asleep. By the time we worked out what had happened, Santa had disappeared and all the little kids were stirring. By the time we had settled them back to sleep, the Santa caper was over, and the Big End boy I was meant to have kept awake had to slink back to his bed empty-handed.

Fortunately for me, he took full responsibility for falling asleep on the job, after the other boys who had been tickled vouched for my skills in keeping them awake. On Christmas morning, we found a note pinned to the outside of the door. It read, 'As there were some naughty boys awake last night, Santa has put your presents in the lounge room.'

Four days later I turned ten, and it was time to take my place in the Big End of the dorm. We'd been at Silky Oaks for two months. It was around this time, at the beginning of 1965, that Mr Abraham and Aunty Rene arrived to replace Mr Smith as the caregivers for the boys. This change was to have a lasting impact on my life.

Mr Abraham had been a sole caregiver at Silky Oaks before leaving to marry Aunty Rene and returning with her. They were a mature-aged couple, beyond the age of having children of their own, and seemed more like grandparents than parent-figures.

Mr Abraham woke us up in the morning, ensured we had our Bible reading and prayer, and sent us off to our pre-breakfast jobs. (I was still duck boy.) He made sure we had a bath or shower in the evenings, that we went to bed on time – with different bedtimes depending on the age of the boy – and that we observed the 'lights out' rule.

He was a pleasant and uncomplicated person, who devoted much of his adult life to caring for the boys at Silky Oaks. But he also had another life as a salesman of Rawleigh products. Rawleigh made ointments and antiseptic salves and their sales model at the time was similar to the Amway system. Unfortunately, some of the ointments were especially pungent, and Mr Abraham often smelt as though he'd been sampling his products.

I warmed to Aunty Rene immediately. She was gentle and non-judgmental. She didn't try to force her love on any of the boys in her care; she just allowed us to come to her at our own pace – which suited me perfectly.

Aunty Rene liked to share her home-brewed ginger beer with the 'big boys'. Some of those batches of beer were so good I could taste them years later. But the routine I loved most took place of an evening, after dinner, when Aunty Rene would make us all a cup of tea with biscuits in her flat and encourage us to sit and tell her about our day.

The Abrahams' flat was in the long hallway between the Big End and the Little End of the dorm, and it was always open for us to visit. Over the years that I lived at Silky Oaks, it provided me with a sanctuary from the rows of dormitory beds, and, even after I left the dorm later, I would still drop by to visit her. Aunty Rene was always welcoming, and I still remember the joy of hanging out with her after school and telling her my stories, just as I had done with my mother.

Mr Abraham and Aunty Rene adopted two infants while they were living at the Home. The children, Valerie and Stephen, weren't from Silky Oaks and we boys had no idea where they'd come from.

But the arrival of the two babies a couple of years apart didn't seem to interfere with Aunty Rene's capacity to care for us. In fact, we all became 'uncles,' or older siblings, to them, and their presence only increased the family feel of the dorm while they were there.

Paul

In late February, our father suddenly appeared in the grounds one day. It had been six months since we'd seen him.

Had he come to take us back to our home in Inala? Where had he been?

He didn't tell us at the time that he had been in a psychiatric hospital. And he didn't tell us that he had escaped from the hospital by climbing down a ladder that had fortuitously been left propped against a wall. I don't know how he discovered where we were, but there he was, calling out to us with a sense of urgency.

'Come, kiddies, the taxi is waiting for you. I'm taking you home.'

Although this was the moment I'd fantasised about when I was at the Depot, I'd begun to adjust to life in the dorm and at Silky Oaks and was in two minds about what to do.

'Is this okay?' said one mind. 'He is my father, and we do have a home to go to,' said the other.

Chris, Helena and Lizzy obeyed his instructions without hesitation, and I decided to follow suit.

I didn't think about taking anything with me – there wasn't enough time for that. And I remembered all our belongings in our house, including the mice and the guinea pigs, and assumed we would just pick up our life where we had left off. We all piled into the taxi and my father gave the driver our address in Inala.

Our house looked just as it had when we'd left it half a year earlier. Our clothes and toys were all there, and the crayon artwork provided by my sisters was still all over the walls. However, the pets had gone – either someone had taken them or they had found a ladder beside the wall – and the grass in the yard had reached its maximum height.

We got comfortable and reclaimed our rooms. It felt strange sleeping in our old beds. It was as though our old life had come back again and the Depot and Silky Oaks were a dream.

But the next morning a police car turned into the driveway, and then there was a knock on the front door. Bessie hid behind the couch. The two officers looked like giants silhouetted in the doorway. My father seemed so small in comparison, pleading with them to leave us alone.

They told me to go and sit in the front seat of the police car, and for Chris, Helena and Lizzy to wait in the back. Watching from the car, we saw the officers trying to reason with our father while he explained that he'd rescued his children, who had been kidnapped by the government. He kept trying to reassure them that everything was fine now we were all back home together, and that he didn't need their intervention. I could see from his face that he couldn't understand what they were telling him – that it was he who had kidnapped us.

As I sat there, I spotted a two-shilling coin wedged down the side of the front seat, and slowly pulled it out. While the officers continued trying to reason with my father, I smugly pocketed the coin. 'I'll teach you coppers you can't control everything.'

Helena

Word spread among the kids that he was waiting at the front gate in a taxi. Of course we weren't privy to the fact our father had been hospitalised, hence the reason he hadn't visited. He greeted us in his usual European way – a kiss on both cheeks – and told us to hop in the taxi.

Lizzy and I ran through the house clapping and singing, pulling our favourite toys out of boxes. I thanked her for being such a good girl. Our daddy wouldn't have come if either of us had been naughty. But it wasn't visiting day and I worried he would get into trouble. It was comforting sleeping in our familiar beds, even if for one night. I automatically reverted to the little girl of six months earlier by asking my daddy for assistance with my toileting. I'd no choice but to learn this skill once I became institutionalised.

The next morning we went to Mr Dabrowski's house, and then our father took us to Newstead Wharf. We watched the ships for a couple of hours, before going home again. The police found us there.

We saw him again in May after waiting patiently at the top of the driveway. He chose an area under the shade of a frangipani tree beside the fence dividing the home and the school. At first I was hesitant for I had recently fallen from that tree and winded myself while playing hide and seek. I remember him occasionally glancing at his silver fob watch kept in his trouser pocket. Timing and recording of details were always of particular importance to him. At the time I didn't understand why. He bought along four chickens which we were allowed to keep in the main chook pen. My sister and I loved and cared for those chicks until one day they disappeared. I was horrified to learn they'd been served up for Sunday lunch! It would take many years for me to contemplate eating chicken after that.

Visiting day was the first Saturday of the month between 2 p.m. and 4 p.m. and all the children eagerly awaited a visit from anyone linked to their past. Those with no visitors often joined another family group. Exclusive rights were given to families under a shady palm tree or any chosen area during this period. It was a natural understanding between us and a show of mutual respect. At the end of the two hours we returned to our bedrooms to pool the lollies, chocolates, comics and toys gratefully received.

In June, he 'kidnapped' us again and took us back to the Newstead Wharf. Mr Zander rang the police, who found us there after a couple of hours. It had become a familiar pattern with an ending that traumatised all. As I kissed and hugged my father goodbye I wondered if we would ever board that ship we kept visiting. I didn't realise this emotional embrace would be the last for a long, long time.

At some point Mr Zander and Aunty Jean told me that my father had finally abandoned my siblings and me to live with communists in Hungary. We would never see him again. I had to forget him.

I was so confused. Why did he want to live with communists? Why not us? I didn't understand who or what a communist was.

But it was obviously something very evil as the anger in their voices was frightening.

Nevertheless, something deep down in my gut knew that he would someday return. I prayed it would be to take us home forever. And so for many a visiting day, I waited at the top of the driveway. Two hours later when the last of the families bid their farewells, I returned to my room.

Part 2

Jean and Zoli

1952-1964

Meeting

Zoli and Jean met at the Royale Ballroom on Liverpool Street, the most popular dance hall in Hobart. It was December 1952, seven years after the war, when there was so much movement of people around the world.

At the time, Zoli was concerned about his limited English, and wanted to improve it. A group of his friends had recently put him in charge of ordering much-needed white sand shoes, and they had ended up with white underpants instead, much to everyone's amusement. He had been in Australia for almost two years, and found that Australian women spoke far too quickly for him to understand, and that often they were boisterous. He was keen to not only dance with women but to communicate with them too.

On an earlier night at the Royale, a rather plump woman had grabbed him almost as soon as he arrived. She led him through a number of barn dances before he begged to stop for a drink. The only thing he managed to understand was her name. Rosalie spoke quickly and was far more interested in dancing than idle chitchat. She was heavy on her feet, which wasn't a problem during a barn dance, but Zoli preferred to waltz to classical music and became annoyed as she stomped on his toes. Later, he discovered her nickname around the dance halls was 'Thundering Rosalie'.

On this Saturday night in December, Zoli headed off to the Royale Ballroom with his friend Stephen Hassman, who he'd met at the Bonegilla Migrant Reception and Training Camp, in north-east Victoria, when he'd first arrived in Australia. Stephen was handsome, younger and more confident than Zoli, despite his lack of English. Within minutes of arriving he was surrounded by a group of giggling girls. Zoli was handsome too, but quieter. A fourteen-year age gap made no difference to their friendship and Zoli enjoyed watching Stephen take turns dancing with the ladies.

This Saturday night, he scanned the room, hoping to avoid the clutches of Thundering Rosalie, and noticed a woman across with room, with auburn hair, wearing a dark grey tweed suit. Her skin was pale. She was alone. He took a deep breath and approached her.

'Would you like to dance?'

He was pleasantly surprised to find she was even more attractive close up.

'Yes, I would love to,' she said with a clear and precise accent .

'You are not Australian?' he asked.

'No, I am British.'

It was the first time since arriving in Australia he had managed a reasonable conversation with a woman. If he concentrated enough, he could understand almost everything she said.

'That is a nice leflant you have,' he said, looking at her neck.

She glanced down at the charm attached to her necklace. 'You mean elephant?' She smiled warmly. 'I adore them. They are enormous creatures with such gentle natures.'

'My name is Zoltan Ban, but my friends call me Zoli.'

'I am very pleased to meet you, Zoli. My name is Jean Trevaskis.'

Jean had migrated from England with her family several months earlier. Her father, George, briefly remained in England pending a medical clearance. He wouldn't let his daughter, his de facto wife, Maude Hibberts, and her son, Michael, miss the sailing date. His first wife, Annie, Jean's mother, had died in a motorcycle accident when Jean was only eight years old. After her death, he'd struggled to run a bicycle shop and raise their daughter. Now he was about to begin a new life with his adult daughter and new family on the other side of the world. George arrived shortly after his family, but ten days later suffered a stroke. This left him partially paralysed, and resulted in the amputation of his leg. Jean kept busy at night helping Maude nurse her ailing father. By day she worked as a clerk typist with Trans Australian Airlines (TAA). The company had been impressed with her four years of service in the Signals division of the British Royal Air Force during the war.

The last dance was played. The evening came to an end. Zoli and Jean arranged to see each other again. On their way home, his friend Stephen said, 'You had eyes for only one lady tonight, Zoli.'

Jean and Zoli were very different.

Jean was British, an only child who had lost her mother at a young age. Zoli was Hungarian, the second of four boys to Ferenc and Ilona Ban: Ferenc, named after his father, Laszlo and Lajos.

Zoli was born in 1917, during World War I. The family rented a small apartment in Hajos utca, the street beside the magnificent Budapest Opera House which fronts Andrassy Avenue. The boys often snuck in to watch performances, occasionally appearing as extras in small plays. The period between the two wars was full of hardships – including food shortages and political instability – but the family of six was close-knit, with the four brothers playing together each day. They spoke six languages – Hungarian, German,

French, Italian, Russian and a little English. Zoli was particularly fond of his youngest brother Lajos, and often protected him from neighbourhood bullies.

He was studying an Economics degree at Ferenc Jozsef University in the country's third largest city, Szeged, near the Romanian border, when at nineteen, halfway through his degree, he was conscripted as a lieutenant in the army. He did twelve months military training while studying in his spare time.

Two years later, in 1939, World War II began and Hungary allied itself with Germany, hoping to reclaim land lost in the last war, and helping to invade Yugoslavia and the Soviet Union. Zoli was assigned Economic Advisor and Field Supplier of money, food, clothing and general stocks and sent to the Eastern Front in Ukraine, where Hitler was waging war against the Soviet Union. His title betrayed nothing of the horror of the Eastern Front, where he 'saw everything' regarding death and suffering. On one occasion, he was talking to someone and a shell fragment went through the man's head. Zoli picked up his brains and didn't know what to do with them. At times, he also fought, but as an officer he wasn't the cannon fodder that so many privates were.

Through all this, he continued with his studies part-time, one day setting off alone on a long march from the front to the university campus, which was now under Soviet occupation, to sit his final exam.

It was 4 February 1944 and he'd been granted two day's leave. When the exam was over, his papers were stamped and he found refuge for the night in the ruins of a nearby castle before returning to the frontline. That evening he felt an eerie presence – a sense that someone or something was watching him. He felt certain it wasn't a deserter or even the enemy. It wasn't until after the war ended that he discovered he had been the uninvited guest of a previous owner of the castle, Count Dracula himself!

While fighting against the Soviet Union, the Hungarian government began secret armistice negotiations with the United Kingdom and the United States. The betrayal was discovered, German forces occupied Hungary in March 1944, and the government was overthrown.

There was discord and mistrust everywhere. Zoli, along with many soldiers and civilians, was detained and questioned regarding his connections with the previous government.

His brother Ferenc was found lying outside in the snow with a bullet in his throat. German soldiers had been seen entering his house. Ferenc's wife, Maria, had been killed in an air raid attack a year earlier. Their infant daughter, Eva, had been staying with the boys' mother, Ilona.

Ilona Ban's losses were already many: her beloved husband, Ferenc Snr, had also died in an air raid. Now she identified her firstborn's body. She dragged it onto her sled and hauled it to the cemetery, where she dug her son's grave.

In the last year of the war, Soviet forces defeated the Hungarian and German armies in Hungary. Again, soldiers were interrogated, this time regarding their allegiance to Germany. Rumours spread far and wide of multiple executions.

Zoli was detained in a Russian camp in Uzhhorod, Czechoslovakia, not far from the border of Hungary. The prisoners were told they'd been fighting in the wrong army. Hungary should never have allied itself with the Germans. Zoli found this difficult to comprehend after seven years of such an alliance. Rumours surfaced they were to be transferred across the border into Russia for a more thorough interrogation. The fear of execution was rife. Zoli had no intention of joining this new ally, the Russian army to 'help liberate Hungary'. But he knew better than to vocalise his thoughts and remained in Uzhhorod.

Several months later he was released and, under the Russians' watchful eye, toiled as a labourer at an agricultural farm in Siroki, Trepcice, Czechoslovakia.

Zoli had lost his father and sister-in-law during an air raid. His brother had been murdered by German soldiers and his surviving siblings, Laszlo and Lajos, were now married. He was confident they would care for their mother who was raising Ferenc's infant daughter, Eva. He could see no other solution but to escape from the Russians and his beloved homeland.

Zoli made his way to Austria and crossed the border into Germany. He had no identification papers and was questioned by American soldiers. Once his fingerprints were recorded, he was charged with illegal frontier crossing and imprisoned for one month.

When released, he continued on to Munich, headquarters for the American military, where he found casual employment shovelling coal from railway carriages. He befriended a Romanian man who worked alongside him. He'd studied Chemistry prior to the war and, like Zoli, had fled his homeland after Soviet occupation. They saved enough cash to move on after a few weeks.

The Romanian was friendly with a woman who had a pass to cross the border daily into France. She knew many of the French and German coal miners who also passed through the border daily and could easily obtain a couple of their passes.

Money was exchanged and the pair each received overalls and boots to look the part as they crossed into France near Strassberg. They mingled briefly with the mineworkers and quickly set off for the train station bound for Paris.

It was agreed if they were detained and questioned the best outcome would be to offer to join the French Foreign Legion. Fortunately their offer wasn't required.

In Paris, they went their separate ways. Zoli found work with the railways department sorting parcels from carriages and after a couple of months was offered a job at the Citroen (Renault) auto factory pressing out the shapes of bonnets.

His French girlfriend at the time also worked at the factory and after several months she suggested they immigrate to Canada. She also suggested as it would be beneficial to their application, they should marry before applying. Marriage wasn't part of Zoli's plans. Neither was Canada. So with encouragement from friends he moved to Switzerland where he learned the art of glass blowing.

He kept in regular contact with his brothers, checking on his mother. Laszlo and Lajos encouraged him to settle down and choose a country to call home. Zoli preferred his motherland but feared execution as a deserter if he returned. There was another reason he chose not to return. After three years of coalition governments, the communists established a one-party dictatorship, under Hungarian-born Mátyás Rákosi, and transformed Hungary into a 'People's Democracy'. Forced collectivisation, industrialisation and a reign of terror followed. Thousands of displaced Hungarians were immigrating to new countries, with the Western world welcoming them with open arms. Zoli enquired with the Swiss authorities who suggested Venezuela might be a good opportunity. Documents were prepared and the date set for travel. But he missed the connecting train on the last day heading to Genoa Harbour. It may have had something to do with the previous evening's celebrations. Or it was simply not his destiny.

Sometime later, under the resettlement program through the

International Refugee Organisation, he applied to immigrate to Australia, a country he knew little about. He was aware it was on the other side of the world, away from painful reminders of war. Zoli was physically healthy for a 33-year-old. But with the traumatic events of the previous few years, it is probable the deterioration of his mental health had already begun.

His application was accepted on 30 May 1950 once he was proven medically fit. There was no evidence of active tuberculosis and having had scarlet fever as a child was not detrimental to his application. A Certificate of Identity was issued in place of a passport and he made his way to the Bremerhaven Wharf near Hamburg, Germany where he boarded the ship MV *Goya*. She was used by the Norwegians during the war. Her job was now to transport thousands of hopeful immigrants to a new country and the prospect of a brighter future. She sailed over Northern Europe past England. She continued through the English Channel past Gibraltar in the Mediterranean. It was two weeks before she arrived in the Suez Canal via the Red Sea. It was another six weeks before she docked in Melbourne.

Zoli and Jean's romance blossomed and she was welcomed into Zoli's group of friends. She was softly spoken and shy – content for Zoli to do most of the talking while she sat quietly in the background.

One day, the couple boarded the bus on their way to meet their friends for a picnic. Zoli climbed the steps behind Jean and she went ahead to find a seat as the bus pulled off. He found some loose change in his pocket and as he went to hand it to the driver the bus suddenly tilted to the side. The coins flew out of his hand and rolled down the aisle. He scrambled to retrieve the fare and as he stood up he saw Thundering Rosalie at the door.

She'd spotted him from a distance and hoped to catch him before he boarded the bus. Zoli paid the fare, giving her a nod as he hastily made his way to the back of the bus. Zoli saw Rosalie occasionally glimpsing at him and Jean. Then a couple of stops later Rosalie rang the bell. With a final wave, now certain of where Zoli's heart belonged, she hopped off the bus.

'I would like you to meet my family now that my father is feeling better,' Jean said.

'I'd like that,' Zoli replied. 'You should arrange it soon. I'm thinking of leaving for New Zealand.'

'You're what?'

'There is no work for me here other than labouring in mining camps,' he said. 'There may be better opportunities in New Zealand.'

'You can't leave now! We get on so well and I thought our relationship was leading to something more permanent.'

A relationship maybe, but a permanent relationship wasn't something Zoli had considered. He was frustrated at work as he should have been promoted to foreman by now. (He was labouring for the Zinc Company in nearby Risdon.) He had been coughing up blood, and had become convinced that someone – the new foreman, perhaps – was trying to poison him. Nothing his friends said could persuade him otherwise. A future there looked bleak. It would be simpler to move on.

'What do you mean by something more permanent?'

'Neither of us is getting any younger. You're almost thirty-six and I'm twenty-nine. Maybe it's time we settled down and got married.'

He listened as she continued. 'I want us to have children. I want them to feel safe and secure in our new country.'

He pondered for awhile about his future. A future that until now hadn't seemed possible. 'Okay, if that's what you want, we'll get married. And we'll have lots of Australian children!'

The Registry Office was booked for the next available date. Stephen would be the best man and Jean's work colleague Patricia Jones would be her bridesmaid.

Three weeks before the wedding Zoli received an urgent message to phone Jean. She was sobbing. Her father had suffered a massive heart attack. The doctors couldn't do anything for him. George Albert Trevaskis died a little more than five months after his arrival in Australia. Jean's stepmother, Maude, was heartbroken but remained in Tasmania with her son.

On 23 January 1953, Zoli and Jean married in a simple ceremony in the Registrar General's Office. The men managed to smile despite their throbbing heads. They'd had a pre-wedding dinner celebration the night before, with the groom and best man indulging in copious amounts of red wine. The bride and her bridesmaid decided to call it a night when the men's robust singing and dancing to their national songs became too boisterous.

It was just as well the Registrar paid attention as Stephen signed as witness on the marriage certificate. He mistakenly almost signed as the groom. The men roared with laughter while the bride was only slightly amused.

Almost every bride's dream was to buy a home to raise a family in as soon as possible. Jean was no exception. However, her husband preferred not to be indebted with a mortgage so he paid cash for a used caravan. He arranged for it to be towed to a vacant allotment on the outskirts of the Royal Botanical Gardens. Their nearest neighbour was Sir Ronald Hibbert Cross, the Governor of Tasmania. The historic Government House was a far cry from Jean's caravan. She was impressed with the immaculate gardens nearby but equally concerned at the apparent lack of a bathroom facility until Zoli pointed to the public amenities block nearby. It certainly wasn't ideal for the new bride but she agreed to live there on the condition it would be for twelve months only. They hoped to have saved enough to buy a house by then.

Within weeks Jean fell pregnant and her dream began to unfold. But then she suffered a dreadful miscarriage, and upon her doctor's advice was to wait at least twelve months before trying again. In time, her health improved, but Zoli's deteriorated. He was coughing up blood more regularly, but refused medical attention until his foreman ordered him to report for a full examination.

Zoli was furious and accused the doctor of fabricating the results when diagnosed as being unfit to work. After three years of exposure to mineral dusts and fumes, he was suspended until he could prove he was fit enough to return.

His wife and friends were concerned with his accusation that the foreman or the doctor was forcing his illness. Jean thought something wasn't quite right with his mind so he agreed to admit himself into the Lachlan Park Hospital, thirty or so kilometres north-east of Hobart. The hospital, run by the government, replaced the Mental Diseases Hospital in 1937. It was a secure mental asylum which, in addition to adults, held children and adolescents, including wards of the State.

The Commonwealth Migration Office, a unit within the Immigration Department, was notified by the hospital and a pro forma 'Particulars of an Immigrant who comes within the scope of Section 8A(1)C for Deportation' was forwarded to the Immigration Department in Canberra for consideration.

Zoli remained heavily medicated while under observation for four months. The doctor's theory was that his soul was deeply affected by the war and he was suffering with severe depression. Once released, he was permitted to return to work. The Immigration Department noted that no deportation action would be contemplated.

Jean received counselling from a social worker from the Migration Office during her husband's confinement, John Tarbath. They discussed the family's accommodation crisis and Jean's concerns for her husband's health. As a result, the caravan was sold and Zoli purchased a block of land in Moonah, in Hobart, and had a small kit home built on it. He returned to the zinc works and several months later Jean gave birth to a son, Paul Zoltan. With the stabilising effect of the house and the added interest of their child, John Tarbath could see no reason why Zoli should suffer a further breakdown and recommended his naturalisation (that he be granted citizenship). Zoli was stateless, and preoccupied by this. He first applied for naturalisation as an Australian citizen on 26 June 1952 after being in Australia for almost nineteen months. But he was still within the two-year exemption period under the Immigration Act and would not be eligible until after 8 November 1955. He applied to be released from the exemption period with no luck.

Fourteen months later, another son, Christopher Ferenc, was born.

After Chris's birth, Zoli's health deteriorated again, leaving Tarbath concerned he was suicidal. The Immigration Minister's office became interested.

Tarbath reported that

> discreet enquiries amongst Mr Ban's supervisors revealed his work record is satisfactory and he was regarded as a quiet and good citizen. Mr and Mrs Ban had nominated his sixteen year old niece, Eva to migrate to Australia. Mr Ban became

aggressive stating that the nomination of his niece was his own affair and the only thing he had done wrong was to take the least line of resistance and join the Communist Party when the Communists gained control of Hungary. He joined to obtain peace for his family. His desire to nominate his niece was to ascertain the true conditions appertaining in Hungary, with a view to reuniting the whole of his family. He claimed that he was being denied peace of mind by the Department refusing to naturalise him and the enforced separation from members of his family. He was informed that enquiries were being made to ensure the wellbeing of his niece and his application was receiving consideration. Mrs Ban wanted to do anything that would make her husband happy and was concerned that he had received no treatment for a nervous condition since his discharge from the hospital over two years ago. She claimed her husband was a worrier and worried himself into fits of depression. He was extremely concerned of the delay to his naturalisation. Mr Ban is emotionally very immature and does and says some rather silly things when under stress but the fact remains that he has been discharged from Lachlan Park Hospital for two years and has been employed in the one position for nearly five years. He may be regarded as an odd character but his behaviour gave me no reason to believe that there is a likelihood of his breaking down in the future under normal circumstances.

A Certificate of Identity was issued (with a re-entry permit valid for twelve months if Zoli wanted to travel outside Australia). Zoli wasn't satisfied and sought legal advice. A month later, he received a letter advising of the Immigration Minister, Harold Holt's, approval for his naturalisation. He would receive details of the ceremony at which he would be required to attend to take the Oath of Allegiance and receive his naturalisation certificate.

Zoli's brother Laszlo now had a son (also named Laszlo) and Lajos was estranged from his wife and children (Istvan and Ildiko). Their mother, Ilona, remained active and healthy at sixty-four and his orphaned niece, Eva, was growing up fast.

His homeland was still under Soviet control, but following the death of Stalin in 1953, Mátyás Rákosi's totalitarian regime began to liberalise. In 1955, however, the Soviet Union established the Warsaw Pact, which bound Hungary and other satellite states to its rule. In October 1956, police fired upon a crowd of university students protesting against the government and its Soviet-imposed policies, killing one student. This ignited the Hungarian Revolution, which spread across the country, brought the government to its knees and forced Soviet troops to withdraw.

A week later, the Soviets reasserted control and crossed the Hungarian border. Within a few weeks the revolution was liquidated. Hungary was in shambles, thousands had been killed and imprisoned and over two hundred thousand fled the country. Lajos was one of this number – making his way to Switzerland. Laszlo remained in Hungary with his wife and son, his mother Ilona and niece Eva.

On hearing of the collapse of the revolution, Zoli was referred to a psychiatrist who considered him to be somewhat depressed and schizoid, but fit for work. Zoli begged John Tarbath to stop the vibrations in his head and asked the social worker to accompany him to the Department of Mental Hygiene, but he refused to be treated as an outpatient or voluntary boarder at a mental hospital. His condition deteriorated and, in the New Year, 1957, he was admitted to the Royal Hobart Hospital where he was certified as insane. He was diagnosed with possible schizophrenia – an illness that disrupts the functioning of the human mind, and causes intense episodes of psychosis involving delusions and hallucinations and longer periods of reduced expression, motivation and functioning. He was transferred back to the Lachlan Park Mental Hospital, his employment was terminated on medical grounds, and his application for naturalisation was deferred. Jean had no choice but to seek financial assistance from the government.

Eight weeks later he was discharged on trial leave. He'd had a good recovery, though medical opinion was that he may be liable to further breakdowns. The question of his naturalisation awaited termination of the trial period and his records noted that it should be deferred for three years from the date of final discharge.

The house in Moonah was sold in November and the family moved north to Sydney with no accommodation or employment prospects. The good news was that prior to their departure Zoli received a letter from the minister inviting him to attend a ceremony at his local town hall. He would be asked to renounce allegiance to his former country and take an Oath of Allegiance to Her Majesty Queen Elizabeth the Second. He would be given a Certificate of Naturalisation showing his acceptance as a full member of the Australian community and a British subject. He would enjoy the same rights, privileges and responsibilities as native-born Australians.

When they arrived in Sydney, Zoli registered his address with the Migration Department of Immigration and enquired about the ceremony. He was told the approval had been withdrawn and would be re-examined in three years. Within weeks, the family moved further north to Queensland, where Jean hoped her husband's health would improve.

Brisbane

They boarded briefly at the People's Palace on Edward Street in the CBD, built by the Salvation Army as accommodation for the travelling working class, then they moved into a small flat in North Quay on the Brisbane River.

The search for the ideal suburb to raise their growing family led them to the bayside suburb of Wynnum Manly. The boys swam in the shallow tidal wading pool in Moreton Bay. They had picnics under the pine, bauhinia and fig trees lining the foreshore. They watched the calm waters ebb out to sea leaving mudflats and seaweed. One day, Jean spotted a vacancy sign on The Esplanade and before long they moved into a small flat opposite the wading pool.

Next door, was a fish and chip shop. The owner, Mrs Scott, lived above the shop. She befriended Jean and helped out with the boys in her spare time. It was late 1957. Jean was now pregnant with her third child.

Zoli, struggling to find employment, wanted to uproot the family and sail to England or Europe. He was granted a Certificate of Identity to leave Australia but the minister refused to grant him a re-entry visa.

Thursday 22nd May, 1958

Dear Lajos,

This is Jean writing, wife of your brother Zoltan. I don't know if you can understand much English, but perhaps you can find someone to translate for you. I don't understand Hungarian except for a few odd words.

Your card from Paris arrived yesterday and your letter today. The reason I am writing is that Zoli sailed for Europe the day before yesterday on Tuesday 20th May. I believe he wrote and told you that we were hoping to sail for England or Europe soon. I will explain what the position is.

I was able to obtain a British Passport as I am still a British subject and the children are included in my Passport. They have the choice of either being Australian or British subjects. Zoli unfortunately is still Stateless as his application for naturalisation as an Australian was differed until the end of 1960. That was because of that illness he had. I think that is most unfair because it is a thing he couldn't help. He would have been naturalised by now. Because of that he was unable to get a Passport, but was issued with a Certificate of Identity. Also he should have a re-entry permit to Australia in order to obtain visas. But that was refused. So he hasn't any visas. We had all booked our passages on the Italian ship 'Roma' which sailed from Brisbane on 20th May but because of Zoli not getting the visas, we cancelled our bookings.

Anyway Zoli said he was going to try to get a job on the Roma, so we all went to the wharf where the ship was. Zoli went on board and made enquiries and told them he hadn't any visas and asked for a job. He showed them the cheque returning the passage money, which the shipping office sent. That was to prove his story. He was told to wait and that they would telephone the shipping office about him. The children and I waited on the wharf. Later on he enquired again and was told he had to wait to see a certain person. The children and I went on board ship then to wait with him. The ship was sailing at 7.00pm. At 6.15pm Zoli helped us off and went back again. When it was near the sailing time, Zoli said he wouldn't ask again in case they said no and he would take a chance and stay on board. So that is what he did.

They have coloured streamers here when the ships leave. He had hold of one end and I had the other and when the ship pulled out it broke. So all I have now is half a pink streamer. I have his bankbook and some cheques he endorsed on the back. I hope the bank lets me draw the money out because Zoli won't be able to now. He wrote a note authorising me to close his account, so I hope it will be alright.

Of course I could have sailed too if I knew Zoli would have been able to but I didn't want to go before him in case he couldn't leave Australia. It is different with me being left because I have a Passport. I couldn't leave now because I am expecting a baby about 16th July and I don't want it born on a ship or in a country where I can't understand the language. Zoli said I should be able to leave at the end of August. There is a ship leaving Brisbane on 12th September, so that will probably be alright. It all depends on what happens to Zoli too. He hasn't come home yet, so he must still be on the ship. I am very worried about him, wondering if they have given him a job or locked him up. I shan't be happy until I hear from him.

This ship is the 'Roma', Flotta Lauro Line, and is due at

the following ports: – Djakarta, Indonesia 29th May (may stop or may not) – Singapore, Malaysia 31st May – Colombo, Ceylon, 4th June – Cochin, India, 5th June (may stop or may not) – Massaua, Eritrea, 11th June (may stop or may not) – Port Said, Egypt, 14th June – Malta, 17th June (may stop or may not) – Messina, Sicily, 18th June – Naples, Italy, 18th June – Genoa, Italy, 19th June. That is as far as the ship goes, Genoa.

I do hope you can help him; he is going to try to see you and hopes to settle in Switzerland or Hungary. Would you please tell him exactly what it is like in Hungary now and if it would be safe for him to go back. He is very anxious to see your mother again and I would like to meet her too, but I don't want Zoli to go anywhere dangerous. I hope it will be alright to go there.

I will keep your letter and card here until I hear from Zoli in case he shouldn't get them. He only has the clothes he was wearing and £4 with him. I can't send him anything yet, either. He said he is going to write to you. Are you at the same address? When I write to him I'll give him your address again. I wrote today and told him you must be in Paris.

Well here's wishing you the very best and I do hope you and Zoli will be able to meet each other again. You will have lots to talk over after all these years, won't you?

Yours sincerely,
Jean, Paul and Christopher

Zoli was discovered not long after the vessel left Brisbane. He was charged with being a stowaway and met by a police escort at Thursday Island, the very tip of Australia. He was admitted to hospital and kept under observation for several weeks, then discharged just prior to the birth of their third child, a daughter, on 30 July 1958.

The baby was two weeks overdue. No doubt Jean was relieved when she entered the world. Zoli wanted to name her after his mother, Ilona. It was finally decided her name would be a variant of the Greek Goddess Helen of Troy and Ilona. She was named Helena Carmen.

Social workers from Migration continued to monitor the family situation. Savings were dwindling as they were regularly drawn on for food. Over the Christmas period, Zoli was advised he couldn't remain on unemployment benefits indefinitely and should apply for sickness benefits. He refused to see a doctor and insisted he was fit. Jean offered to find work but soon realised there would be little financial gain as they would need to pay a babysitter to look after the children.

Zoli wrote a letter to the Minister for Justice asking for a job as a hangman and, in doing so, alarmed the authorities. T M Nulty, a Commonwealth Migration Officer with the Department of Immigration, discussed the letter with Dr J A Hede at the Brisbane Psychiatric Clinic on Mary Street, who became Zoli's doctor. The doctor agreed that the chance Zoli would voluntarily undergo medical treatment was slight, and advised Nulty that Zoli's condition would make itself known in some antisocial way. They could take action then.

Paul

The second time my father tried to stowaway, he decided to take me with him. It was February 1959. I was four.

Of course, I didn't know about his plan at the time. When Daddy took me to look at a big ship in the dock, the *Fair Sky*, and suggested we go on board to look around, I had no idea what lay ahead. I can't remember being aware that the ship was leaving, and it was only when I realised we were at sea that I knew I was in for an adventure. I had my father with me, so as far as I was concerned everything was okay. I didn't know that he hadn't told my mother about his plan, and that he hadn't brought any spare clothes or food with us.

We walked around the upper deck until we found some deck chairs, where we set up camp and I slept for a while. After I woke up, we went to look at the ship's swimming pool. It was round and had ladders going down into the water. I was keen to go for a swim. However, I didn't have any bathers with me. 'No problem,' Daddy said, and proceeded to take off my pants and underpants, leaving me naked from the waist down. He held me in his arms while he descended the ladder, and the water came up to my waist and wet the bottom of my shirt. I remember being embarrassed that I didn't have any pants on, and I felt that people were looking at me. Daddy reassured me they weren't watching and told me to enjoy myself. That was a big ask for a little boy who was conscious that he was the only one in the pool not wearing any bathers.

After the swim, we went back to our deck chairs so I could dry out in the sun, as we didn't have towels. We stayed on the deck until it was dark. We must have looked suspicious remaining in the one spot while others started heading to their cabins to prepare for the evening, because someone in a uniform approached us and asked us where our cabin was located. I can't remember what Daddy said, but it didn't take long for the man to realise we didn't have a cabin to go to, and for us to realise that this was going to be a problem. We were eventually given a room to sleep in for the night, which was more comfortable than trying to sleep on the deck chairs.

The next day we were told to be ready to leave the ship, as a police boat from Cairns was coming to collect us. By then word had spread among the passengers that there was a stowaway on board with his four-year-old son. I don't know what people were told, but a lot of the passengers gathered on the deck of the ship to watch us climb down the ladder into the police boat. Once we were on board, some began throwing money into the boat for us. I ran around the boat collecting the coins and notes wrapped around coins. I handed the money over to the police. I have no idea how much was collected or what happened to it.

When we arrived in Cairns I was taken to the Cairns Base Hospital, where I was checked over before spending the night in a hospital bed. I didn't know where my Daddy had been taken, but the nurses looked after me and made a fuss of me because I was a minor celebrity – the famous stowaway boy. The next day our story was spread across the front page of the Cairns Post, while I was reunited with my father and we were put on the train to Brisbane.

My mother had called the police when my father failed to come home. In a newspaper report:

Mrs Z. Ban said her husband had left home with Paul early Tuesday morning to try to get work in Brisbane. She said he always took Paul with him when he went in to the city. 'Recently, he's been thinking of trying to get back to his home in Hungary because he thinks he will get work and be happier there.

I've never known whether we were put off the *Fair Sky* in Cairns because my mother alerted the police or because we were discovered by the officer on the ship. I wasn't scared on the ship but, of course, I shouldn't have been there, and my mother must have been beside herself.

Jean's letters

The headlines for the famous stowaway boy ranged from the factual – 'Police take man, son, 4, from liner', 'Wynnum stowaway fined £20' – to the colourful – '(All over for Paul) STOWAWAY AT 4!' – and show Zoli and Paul arriving home – 'Stowaways back with family', accompanied by a photo of Jean holding baby Helena, Zoli holding Paul, and Paul holding a guinea pig.

Two weeks later, Zoli applied to renew his Certificate of Identity and re-entry visa. He still wanted to leave with his family, It was declined when he couldn't provide evidence of travel bookings. It didn't help that he wrote on the form that the purpose of his journey was 'remote control by ultrasonic waves at brain areas'.

The social services unit of the Immigration Department proposed to terminate Zoli's unemployment benefits because he was considered to be unemployable. Given he couldn't control his own affairs, and concerned as to what might happen when his funds ran out, the department wanted Zoli admitted to a mental institution. They asked the inspector at the Woolloongabba police station to take whatever steps were in his power to make this happen.

Jean was also not well. A social worker had noted that she 'was walking very badly, and . . . had been ill for some time with rheumatism.'

Soon after, on 9 July 1959, Zoli was arrested, charged with being mentally sick and committed to the Brisbane General Hospital. Apparently, he had approached a plain-clothes police officer requesting firearms. He wanted to shoot someone in the Immigration Department. He was certified and escorted to the Brisbane Mental Hospital – later to be named the Brisbane Special Hospital – on the Brisbane River in Wacol. There, he was diagnosed with paranoid schizophrenia. There was no likelihood he would be discharged in the near future.

Jean applied for a widow's pension. Her only other income was child endowment and some government relief. She had worked at the Northgate Cannery for a week but was forced to give it up when she became ill. She applied for monetary assistance through the State Children Department. Under the provisions of the State Children Act she had to formally admit her children to the State and sign a form requesting her children reside with her. This was the only way she could receive an allowance to maintain them.

The State Children Department opened a file on the Ban family, three weeks before Helena's first birthday in July 1959, and approved some financial assistance for the family for a six-month period.

Before Christmas, Jean wrote to Zoli's mother, Ilona.

21st December, 1959

Dear Mother

I do hope you can find someone to translate this letter into Hungarian for you. I have often felt I would like to write to you, but as I cannot write in Hungarian, and you do not understand English, I haven't done so.

Offla's Children

Zoli is in hospital, and when I visited him on Saturday, he gave me this letter (which I enclose) to forward on to you.

He wants very much to see you again, and he told me he has asked you to help him to go back to Hungary. I don't know if it is wise for him to go back or not. Do you think it will be safe for him, and for us (the children and I)? I want him to be happy and be able to settle down all right when he comes out of hospital.

I expect you must worry a lot about Zoli, wondering how he is, especially if you have heard about his being mentally sick. I don't know why he got sick, the Doctors told me they couldn't find a reason, said it may be the result of what he went through during the war.

He has been in the Goodna Mental Hospital for six months now, the longest time he has been in hospital. I went with the children to see him yesterday and the day before, but his Doctor wasn't there unfortunately. Zoli seemed to me to be very well, I hope the Doctor thinks the same. The first time Zoli was in hospital in Tasmania, he was there about four months, and the second time for six weeks. It is a tragedy isn't it; Zoli is so intelligent and clever and is such a good man. He is a wonderful husband and father. He really loves the children and will play with them for hours. When he tried to stow away in a ship going to Europe it wasn't that he wanted to leave us, he really thought we would be able to follow him. The first time I had the money as well as a Passport, but the second time I didn't have the money. When he gets sick he thinks nobody wants him in Australia and that everybody is against him and of course that is not true. People have been very kind and helpful to us and I have never met anyone who doesn't like Zoli.

We were living in a flat in Wynnum Central when Zoli went to hospital but also we had paid a small deposit on a block of land at Lindum, which is next to Wynnum. I knew I couldn't afford to pay off the land and the rent of the flat, so I bought a second hand marquee tent and have it on the land. I have had a kitchen built on the end of it and have it quite comfortable inside. I think it much better than paying rent to someone else. It takes nearly three years to pay for the land, £270, and seven months have gone already.

I am very disappointed Zoli cannot be home for Christmas, so are the children. I have bought them some toys and also a wading pool made of canvas. The wading pool was delivered on Friday and is a great success. They love it and there is plenty of room. We went to a party given by the 'Good Neighbour Club' and they had some plastic boats from 'Father Christmas', so they are just right for them to sail in the pool.

Paul is the eldest, he will be 5 on December 29th (Paul Zoltan) and he will be starting school on January 25th. I can't believe it. It doesn't seem long since he was a baby. I went up to see the Headmaster of the nearest school and had him enrolled. He will have to wear a grey shirt with maroon collar and cuffs and grey shorts. Christopher (Christopher Ferenc) will be 4 years next February. He is always telling me how much money he is going to get me when he is a big man and Helena (Helena Carmen) is 1 year 5 months. She is late walking but she managed three steps for Zoli to see yesterday. We were very pleased. She feeds herself quite well and is learning lots of words. She is very sweet. She can say 'egan' and 'nem' too.

Offla's Children

The children often talk about you. They would love to see you and so would I. I have no relations out here, the same as Zoli. My father died three weeks before we got married and my mother died when I was 8 years old.

I expect you will wonder how I manage for money. Well, while Zoli is in a Mental Hospital I get a widow's pension, which is £6 per week and also I have state aid for the children £3.15 per week, plus child endowment £5 per month. I think Australia is a good country because I am able to keep my children and also stay home with them. I was worried about that at first because I thought if I have to go out to work I should have to pay somebody to look after three children and that would probably take most of my wages.

If you are able to understand this letter, or can find somebody else who can understand it and would like me to write to you again giving you some news, I will be only too pleased. I don't know if Zoli tells you much when he writes.

Has your son Laszlo any more children? We know he has a little boy Laszlo, who I think must have been 5 years old in September. I was very sorry to hear about Lajos and his wife separating. I think it would be lovely for Zoli if Lajos came out to Australia. That is if Zoli can't go back to Europe. The trouble is he is stateless, and his naturalisation to an Australian citizen has been postponed because of his mental sickness. It doesn't seem fair, because people can't help it if they are sick, and unless he is naturalised he can't get a passport.

Well, I hope you have a happy Christmas and that all is well with you.

Have you any photographs of yourself and family that you could send out here? I will have to get some more photographs taken of the children to send to you. They have grown a lot since the last ones were taken.

Wishing you all the very best.
Love Jean, Paul, Christopher & Helena

Jean and the children spent Christmas day at the hospital.

On 3 January 1960, the *Sunday Truth* published a 'Happy New Year Story', alongside a photograph of Jean, Paul and Chris standing in front of a house in Hemmant while Helena sat on the ground. They had ended 1959 living in a tent on the block of land in Lindum, but started the new year in a house. The owner, a man named Mr Beck, had offered it to Jean free of rent until Zoli completed his treatment and was able to take charge of his affairs. Their old neighbour Mrs Scott continued to help Jean with the children.

26th January, 1960

Dear Lajos

I am enclosing a letter for you from Zoli. I have kept it for about a week because I wanted to see what the Immigration Office had to say about Zoli first, and I also had to search for your address.

I expect this will come as a shock to you, but Zoli has been in the Goodna Mental Hospital for six months. He gave me a letter for your mother a while ago and I wrote a letter to her telling her what happened. Since then I have changed my address, but any letters will be forwarded on, if she writes to me. She would have to get my letter translated though, wouldn't she?

Zoli is still anxious to return to Europe, but is unable to because he has no passport or visas and now no money. I do hope he will settle down when he comes home. He can't have a passport because he isn't a naturalised Australian and he can't be naturalised until the authorities consider he is fully recovered from his mental illness. He was supposed to apply again after October 1960 but now he has had to go into hospital again, it will be deferred again. It is a shame. He was very keen to be naturalised too. He can't get any visas as he is stateless and a re-entry visa to Australia was refused, probably on account of his mental illness. They didn't give the reason. I expect in his letter to you he asks you to help him get to Europe, but I don't see how he can go.

I had to go to the Immigration Office to find out what they had to say about Zoli as he was firmly convinced that they had made a charge against him and would make him stay in the hospital, even if the Doctor said he was well and able to go out.

There is no criminal charge made against him at all, the police took him to hospital, to the General Hospital in Brisbane and charged him with being 'a person deeming to be of unsound mind'. He was kept at the General Hospital for a few days and certified, then they sent him to the mental hospital. They sent him there without me knowing but said they had to so that he could get the necessary treatment. He has been having shock treatment but finished that some time ago and is having tablets now. I had a letter from the Medical Superintendent of the hospital last week and he said Zoli was progressing satisfactorily but was not well enough to be discharged yet.

Zoli's address if you would like to write to him is Ward 8, Brisbane Mental Hospital, Goodna, Queensland, Australia.

By the way, I received the letter you wrote to me before, thank you very much. I didn't answer it because Zoli was home then and he was writing to you. I asked him to thank you. I suppose he told you that he was put off the ship at Thursday Island. He tried again last year and took Paul. I thought he had changed his mind about trying to go and I expected him home for tea. Instead he took Paul and went on board the 'Fair Sky'. I was terribly worried because apart from the difficulties of no passport etc., he did have enough money to pay his fare, but only just, he was showing signs of mental illness and he had little Paul with him. Paul was only 4 years old then and they had no clothes or anything. So I went to the Police Station and they got through to the ship and had him and Paul put off at Cairns, where he was fined £20 for stowing away. I felt awful having to go to the police but because of Paul I had to. Zoli said he gave himself up, as soon as the ship sailed so they would have put him off anyway. Zoli was quite all right when he came home, you would have thought he had been on a bus ride. The worst of it was that the newspapers kept putting bits in about him and took photographs and put a big photograph of us all right in the middle of the front page.

Zoli tried to get work here but there wasn't much work about, then when he was getting worse, he wasn't able to work. Of course Zoli doesn't know what he was like; he doesn't think there was anything wrong with him. It is a terrible thing to see somebody you love getting all confused and suspicious and mixed up for no reason. He got some queer ideas about electricity, and thought that there was someone, he didn't know who, or why, or where, controlling everything he did and said with an electronic brain. He thought he was being 'switched on' and then 'switched off'. He would suddenly say, in the middle of a conversation, 'I'm switched on', then I would have to wait until he was 'switched off', before I could speak to him again. He would be quite normal in between. The police knew he was sick because Zoli had written some rather odd letters to different offices and they had been given to the police to investigate. They spoke to him about them, but couldn't put him in hospital just for that.

The day he was taken to hospital, he took Paul and Christopher out shopping with him. I didn't like him taking them out when he seemed bad, but couldn't very well stop him. He called in at the Employment Bureau and Police Station. They are next door to each other and apparently he said he wanted to shoot someone in the Immigration Office and said he wanted a gun. They knew he was sick anyway, so I suppose he said some peculiar things too, and they decided it was time they took him to hospital. They brought the children home and took Zoli off in their car. Poor Zoli, he looked so confused, he didn't know what was happening to him, and he tried to run away, but they caught him. It does seem terrible to have to be treated as if you have done something wrong, but he just won't go in hospital voluntarily. This is the third time this has happened, so that's why they are keeping him in a bit longer.

Wednesday 27th January

When Zoli was in the hospital a few weeks, he escaped. He was only out for about three hours before they found him. We were living in the flat at 145 Esplanade, Wynnum Central, when

Zoli went to hospital and also we had signed a contract to buy a block of land and had paid the deposit. I decided I couldn't stay in the flat and pay off for the land as well, so I bought a second hand marquee tent and had it erected on the land and moved in with the children. The 'Lions Club' came and built me a cooking place out of a large wooden box we had, and also gave me a toilet. At Christmas time we had lots of food and things given to us. People were very kind and helpful. Then the lady who is head of the 'Good Neighbour Club' in Wynnum wrote to the 'Truth' newspaper to ask if they could help us to get some better accommodation. They published a story about us living in a tent, and a photograph, and as well as receiving several small sums of money we were very lucky in having a little house offered to us. The man who owns it said I could live in it rent free until Zoli can go to work again. Wasn't that wonderful of him? It has just two rooms, kitchen and bedroom, laundry and toilet outside, and it has electricity. There was no electricity on the land, but I had a water tap. I am still able to pay off for the land, so I am very lucky, aren't I? It takes nearly three years to pay and I have paid off eight months.

I get the widow's pension, which is £6 per week because I have three children. So I had to apply for State aid for the children and I get £3.15 per week for the three of them. I also get child endowment, which is £5 per month for the three of them.

I hope Zoli can settle down when he comes home, and will be able to find a job he likes. The Immigration Office said there is a special section of the Employment Bureau to help handicapped people find jobs, and Zoli would come under them.

I hope we have some better luck this year, it started off well, we moved into this house on January 1st. I love Zoli very much, he is a wonderful husband and father, and he is devoted to the children. They say you get married for better or worse, and I hope our 'worse' period is over now.

Paul started school on Monday. He looks very nice in his school shirt and shorts. I wish Zoli could see him. Luckily, Paul really likes school and looks forward to going. Poor Christopher gets upset because he wants to go to school too. He will be 4 years old on February 28th. Helena is 1½ years and she is learning things fast. Only thing she really objects to is sitting on her pot.

I received the picture card you sent to Zoli at Christmas time and I took it to him at the hospital. They are beautiful views of Switzerland, aren't they? I have been to Luzern and to Tellskapelle, and along the Axenstrasse to Fluëlen, which were on the card. I'd love to go to Switzerland again. Well, I'll say cheerio for now. I'll let you know how Zoli gets on.

Best wishes from
Jean, Paul, Chris & Helena

P.S. Have you any idea at all why Zoli should get mentally sick? The Doctors can't find a cause. We can only think it must be a result of the war, or conditions he went through. Also I think you wrote very good English. You must certainly have a good memory, after 20 years.

At the end of the six months, Jean's financial assistance ended. More reports were ordered. There was no real change with Zoli's heath and no prospect of him being discharged. The department agreed to keep helping Jean financially.

8th April, 1960

Dear Lajos

I was very pleased to receive your letter and also a letter from your girlfriend in Finland. I am also very pleased that you have met someone else now and you are not on your own. It must have been awful for you to have to leave all your family behind in Hungary. Do you hear how your children are getting on?

Your girlfriend, is 'Taina' her Christian name (like Lajos) and 'Vaittinen' her surname or family name? I ask because in Europe you write your names back to front, or else we write them back to front, but I should think 'Taina' must be her Christian name. I asked Zoli, but he said he didn't know. I would like to write to her but think she must be still on vacation, so will write a little later on.

Thank you for telling us that Zoli had some money in Switzerland. Zoli said he remembered about the gold. When we first got married he told me about it, but later on he said he didn't have it any more there, then after that he said he couldn't remember if he had any or not. He didn't think he had a life insurance because he said he cancelled it a long time ago. Has his friend, Herr Florian Sutter kept the payments up himself and is very kindly saying Zoli could have it or is Zoli mistaken? Anyway we will wait to see what happens when Zoli comes home from hospital. I can just manage all right now with the pension and state aid.

It would be wonderful if we could go to Switzerland and it is very good of you to say we could go to you but the biggest difficulty is Zoli not having a passport or visas. Zoli said I should write to the address you have given in Geneva, but I don't think I should write while he is in the Mental Hospital. Zoli asked me to write to the Hungarian Legation in London and to say he was in the Mental Hospital and they wrote to say they couldn't do anything about it while he was in the Mental Hospital. If I write and don't say anything about that, they will wonder why Zoli hasn't written himself.

I think Switzerland is a lovely country. I only saw it for ten days and it seemed just like pictures in a child's fairy-story book. The houses, they are so beautiful, aren't they, with all the shutters and window boxes. I went with another girl and we stayed in Brunnen, on Lake Lucerne. Zoli said he had left there only a few days before we arrived. It is funny to think we didn't meet until we were in Tasmania, on the other side of the world. We, neither of us thought we would ever go to Australia. I came out here because my father was very keen to come here and I always wanted to travel. There were seven of us, but my father had to travel on another ship, by himself, as he didn't pass his medical to come with us. He left only ten days afterwards though. Unfortunately after being in Tasmania for just two days, he had a stroke, later had a heart attack and died six months later. Also he had to have his leg off, after the stroke. I had met Zoli at that time and he used to wait for me outside the hospital. He wouldn't go in as Dad was so ill and then it was too late. My stepmother and stepbrother are still in Tasmania. Michael (my stepbrother) got married there. My cousin and his wife and son, went back to England. They came to see us to say goodbye. Paul was just 1 year old.

We had a letter from the Australian Red Cross, saying that Zoli's cousin, a Mr Andras Toth, who left Hungary recently wanted to establish contact with his cousin. Zoli said he could have got his (Zoli's) address from you, but I said he may not know your address. If you would like Andras Toth's address, it is – Simmernerstr. 14/19, Koblenz/Rhein, Germany.

When I saw the Doctor at the hospital three weeks ago he said they may let Zoli come home for a weekend if he continues to improve. He said although to me he seems quite normal, he (the Doctor) thinks there is still something that needs clearing up, deep down. They are giving him some new drug. Zoli has a Hungarian friend there, and luckily they have both been moved to a different ward, moved together, I mean. They are able to walk outside but have a big wire fence around so they can't escape. It is terrible to see men and women having to stay behind fences. Poor Zoli thought he was in a concentration camp at first. Really you can't blame them for thinking like that. Sometimes he thinks that I want him to stay there because I haven't taken him home and he won't believe that I can't take him unless the Doctor says I can. All the patients I've spoken to, say they were put there when there was nothing wrong with them. Zoli too, he doesn't believe that there was anything wrong with him.

When you write again, could you tell us something about the rest of your family? Is Laszlo still in Budapest, and has he any more children? We know he has little Laszlo, aged 5, I suppose. And your mother is she living on her own, now Eva is married? And how is Eva getting on, who did she marry, and has she a family? Why doesn't Laszlo write to Zoli? I can't remember his having written. Probably he doesn't like writing letters. Can you tell us something about Hungary? Also Zoli wants to know what work you are doing, and have you your own house or flat?

Best wishes from
Jean, Paul, Christopher & Helena

P.S. Am enclosing letter from Zoli and a photo of family. Not sure how old Helena was then. I have just got some luggage out of store, including my camera, so I will take some photos of the children to send you. (I don't understand Zoli's camera)

P.P.S. Paul loves school remembers all the stories they tell him. Comes first in racing!

The episode that led to Zoli being committed was weighing on his and Jean's mind. Jean wrote to T M Nulty, at the Department of Immigration.

7th May, 1960

Dear Mr Nulty

My husband, Zoltan Ban, who is a patient in Ward 5 of the Brisbane Mental Hospital, is most anxious that I write to you. He said that you have written a letter to the Doctor to say that he threatened you with a gun. I told him I had been to the Immigration Office before, to see Mr Annand and that he had assured me the Immigration Office hadn't made any charge against him, and that my husband was only charged with being 'a person deeming to be of unsound mind'. But my husband says he has seen this letter and he is worrying about it as he says he would never want to shoot anyone. Actually he has never had a gun or had access to a gun since I have known him and I can't imagine him harming anyone at all. This is the third time he has been in hospital and each time when he was sick he has said all sorts of odd things but he never gets violent at all. He always had lots of patience with the children and had the two boys with him on the day the police took him to hospital.

He is worrying because of this gun business, and the fact that the police found a knife in his bag, that he won't ever be released from the hospital. He didn't do anything with the knife; he just carried it in his bag.

I have told him that when the doctor says he can come home he will be able to, but he still worries about what he says you have said to the doctor.

I wonder if you would be good enough to write to him, to reassure him that everything will be all right. It may help him a lot. He seems very well to me when I visit him and I am hoping he will be able to come home soon.

Thanking you very much,
Yours faithfully, J Ban (Mrs)

Nulty – who was to become very involved in the family's situation – wrote back, assuring Jean that no charge had been nor would be made against her husband. He wished Zoli a speedy recovery and hoped that they would be reunited soon.

9th May, 1960

Dear Lajos
I am enclosing a letter, which Zoli gave me yesterday to send on to you. Zoli seems very well to me, just like his old self. I wish they would let him come home. The Doctor has written

to say I will be notified when he can come home on leave. It is awful to have to leave him there. He has made friends with another Hungarian there and they are always together. His friend usually plays with the children, while I talk to Zoli.

I haven't made any more photos yet. I have my camera now, also a film, so I will take some snaps of the children to send to you. Helena is learning how to talk quite quickly now. She tells the boys off when they are naughty. It will be lovely when Zoli can be home with them again. I will write to Taina shortly. Will say cheerio for now.

Yours sincerely, Jean

13th July 1960

Dear Lajos

At last I am sending you some photos of the children. It is a pity Paul was screwing up his face in the sun.

Zoli is still in the hospital. He seems very well to me, and quite like his old self. Two weeks ago, the Doctor gave him permission to go to the pictures once a week, a concert once a week and to a dance they have once a fortnight. Zoli has been working outside in the vegetable garden of the hospital for several weeks now. They say they are gradually giving him more freedom and responsibility. I am waiting for a letter from the Doctor now and I wrote to ask if he can come home yet, or at least have a walking out pass. The children and I go to see him every Sunday afternoon, and we see his Hungarian friend too. We have to see them in the dining room of their ward.

I'll get copies of these photos to send to your mother, so you can keep these. I hope she didn't worry too much when she got my letter. Zoli said I shouldn't have told your mother about him, but he gave me a letter to send to her, as he hadn't any envelopes and I saw he had put the words 'Brisbane Mental Hospital' in English, so I thought I should write to explain what happened. I didn't know what he had put, and thought she would be sure to worry, only having his version, so I think I did the right thing.

I don't remember if I told you that Paul came 5th out of 39 in his school examinations. Had a very good report. Helena will be 2 years old on July 30th. Time flies doesn't it. She is not a baby any more. I am saving up to buy her a doll and doll's pram. She loves dolls and she sits and sings to them sometimes. I am so pleased she is a girl.

It is one year ago today that Zoli went to the Brisbane Mental Hospital. He was taken to the Brisbane General Hospital on July 9th. I hope he will be home soon. Well, will say cheerio for now.

Best wishes from Jean

Several weeks later Zoli was granted leave for three months with the prospect of a likely extension. In Dr Hede's opinion, Zoli was fit to resume full employment, and finding employment quickly would help him adjust. Zoli found some casual work as a labourer for a while and then was placed on unemployment benefits.

Around October 1960, Jean discovered she was pregnant. Zoli's leave from hospital was extended. The family celebrated Christmas that year together at home. Afterwards, during an examination,

Jean's doctor discovered a malignant lump in her breast. She was hospitalised, treated with radiation and ordered to remain in hospital until the birth of her new baby.

Mr Beck sold the house in Hemmant after a rent-free sixteen months. The Queensland Housing Commission offered the family a house in Serviceton Avenue, Inala for minimal rent. The area was full of disadvantaged families including many migrants.

With Jean convalescing in hospital, Zoli cared for his children, now aged six, five and three. He packed their belongings and moved the family into the Inala house with the assistance of neighbours. Jean ensured everything went to plan during her weekend leave.

24th June, 1961

Dear Lajos

Zoli came up to visit me in hospital yesterday and brought me your letter. I didn't write before because Zoli said he was going to write to you and I didn't want to write unless he said I could.

Thank you very much for sending the money, Zoli did receive it all right. That was a very good idea to send it 'Pay Bearer', because if it had been made out in Zoli's name, it might have had to go in Zoli's Bank Book, and he is not allowed to draw anything out of it until he is discharged from the hospital. The Public Curator has it I think, but anyway Zoli only has £4 in it. He was able to cash the cheque all right after having to wait a few days while they checked up on the signature.

Every time I saw Zoli I asked him if he had written to you, and he always said he was going to, but he did say that he has written to your mother, and told her about it.

Zoli has been looking after the children for nine weeks

while I have been in hospital and I think they are being naughty for him. He has always been too easy with them, so I shall be really glad when I can go home and see to things.

As you probably noticed, we have changed our address. The little house in Hemmant was sold and we were fortunate enough to get a State Housing Commission house to rent at Inala. The rent is reduced while Zoli is not working. Zoli is very well and seems quite happy in the new house. The Doctor let me go home for a weekend to help pack up at Hemmant, then the neighbours helped him to move. At Inala, the neighbours next door (Dutch people) helped him too, so he was very lucky. I was worrying about him, having to move on his own, but he managed very well and is much more contented now.

I have been going home to Inala for weekends (except one) and so have been able to do a few things, but two days go so quickly. I am in the hospital this weekend though. I wonder if Zoli told you, I am expecting a baby on June 27th. That is why I am here. I have had a months' radiation treatment on my breast for a lump and after that they put me in here. I am all right now, but the Doctor thought I should stay here. The children could have gone into a children's home for children whose mothers are in hospital, but Zoli didn't like the idea.

If he had been working, they would have had to go until I came home. We are much better off in the new house, it has three bedrooms, lounge, kitchen, bathroom and laundry, and is a white stucco house with a red tiled roof. The school is about seven minutes walk away, and there is quite a good shopping centre in walking distance. At the other end of our road there is a 'drive-in shopping centre' being built and at our end there is a roller skating rink and a swimming pool and wading pool.

The bus stops outside the house and goes to 'Darra' station and from there we catch a train to Brisbane. Inala is 11 miles from Brisbane according to the map.

Of course we didn't really want to have another baby, I think three is quite enough, but as we have to have it, we hope it will be all right, and that it will be a girl. We decided to call it either Elizabeth Jennifer (my mother's second name was Elizabeth) or Roland George (my father's name was George). We will have to let you know when it is born. It can be any time now. Zoli told your mother about it.

Zoli wants me to ask you if you are still thinking of coming out to Australia, and if you are, when do you think you will come? You would be able to stay with us now, we have a bigger place. It will be good for him if you can come and I should like to see you too.

Wishing you all the best.
Love from Jean & Zoli

P.S. Zoli says he appreciates what your father and mother had to put up with, when you boys were all small.

On 30 June 1961, a Friday, Elizabeth Jennifer was born. The family affectionately called her Bessie.

Jean continued to need medical help for the malignant lump in her breast. Zoli attended the clinic regularly and his condition remained stable with medication. Paul and Chris were going to the local primary school while Bessie and Helena were regularly looked after by the Dutch family next door.

3rd April, 1962

Dear Lajos & Loty,

Well, first of all I must apologise for not writing to you before now. I know Zoli has been writing. I was very pleased to hear of your marriage, and I wish you every happiness together. But I was very sorry to hear you both have been in hospital, not a very good start. I hope you are both home again now, and I also hope, Lajos, that you do not have to diet any more. I know how miserable it is to diet (when I have been slimming, and on a diet).

Zoli said he thanked you for the presents and I really intended to write myself, before now to thank you for them. I was really thrilled with the music box. It was like having a breath of Switzerland sent to me. When we play it, the whole family, (except the baby) dances around the table. It reminds me of when I went to Switzerland for a holiday. The children are very thrilled with their presents too. We took some photos with the children holding some of the toys, but they didn't come out properly. I am sending one of them which has the doll you sent Helena, named 'Marianne', the dump truck you sent Paul, and the doll you sent Elizabeth named 'Loty'. Christopher loves his Lego game, and one of his friends was very surprised when I told him that Christopher's uncle, who lives in Switzerland, sent it. He asked, very impressed that you live in Switzerland, 'and does he eat Swiss cheese too?'

I have just filled in some application forms for permission for your mother to come to Australia. It would be lovely if she could come here, and I wish you could both come here too.

Paul is going to write you a letter, which I shall enclose.

The photographs that you sent us were very good, and I liked the colour. I have just had another look at them. They are beautiful, aren't they? Lajos is not really like Zoli in the face, but his hair reminds me of him, and there is a family resemblance.

Can Loty read English? I hope you can read this letter all right. I will close now, and wish you both good health and good fortune.

Love from Jean

Dear Uncle Lajos,
I have seven guinea pigs. I have a special guinea pig named Jean after my mother's name. We have a white cat named Snowball. He is always having fights in the daytime. We always look at him and he always has lumps of fur out of him. We have another cat named Taxi and have not seen her for a long time. I also have white mice to sell for 1/- each and the guinea pigs are 2/- each and thank you very much for the nice toys.

Love from Paul

Though both Jean and Zoli needed medical help, the 'worse period' that Jean had written about to Lajos seemed finally to be over.

Helena

We were so happy then.

Our back yard housed a large cage of guinea pigs, a smaller one with mice, green frogs, a cat endlessly producing kittens, and Oscar the dog. There was often a frog or a mouse perched on our shoulders while our enthusiastic father filmed us. We dressed up in home-made space suits, cowboy outfits and whatever we could lay our hands on for home movie entertainment. The large tree in the back yard was popular for climbing. Our unassuming mother quietly stood to the side as we pranced and danced about entertaining the film director.

A variety of musical instruments entertained us in the evenings. Zoli played the harmonica while my brothers and I selected tambourines, whistles and drums made of wooden spoons and saucepans. We marched around the kitchen table led by the Pied Piper himself merrily playing his harmonica. Little Bessie sat on our mother's lap, laughing and clapping to the music. Sometimes she joined the marching band.

Then, in 1963, our mother discovered another lump in her breast. She was thirty-nine years old.

Much of her time was spent in hospital and during her short stints at home we had to remain as quiet as four young children could. Thank God for our neighbours. Zoli was too distraught to deal with us for long. He'd changed. Everything had changed. Musical instruments remained in the box. Our father had no energy or interest in filming or playing with us. Members from our mother's church visited briefly as did other strangers.

When there was nothing more that could be done for her, she came home from hospital to spend her last few weeks.

She was bedridden and in turn we were allowed to pop in for quick chats. My sister and I shared the bedroom next door with Bessie's cot at one end and my bed the other.

Our mother's vision diminished considerably towards the end. She no longer had the strength to write to uncle Lajos. On 20 April 1963, she died in her bed at home, six months shy of her fortieth birthday.

Over ten thousand miles separated the home she was born in and the home in which she took her last breath. Her parents were both dead, and as much as she was loved by and loved Zoli, she must have been frightened for us and for him.

Our father called us into her room. We had never seen him cry before. He gently put his arms around us and said, 'Mummy has to go. It's time to say goodbye.'

As difficult as it was at their age, Paul and Chris at least understood our mother was dead. Bessie and I were too young to comprehend it.

A sheet was placed over her body by strangers who carried her on a stretcher to a waiting van. We watched ever so quietly as it reversed out of the driveway. I believe it almost broke my father's heart when I yelled, 'Bye, Mummy, see you when you get home!' Bessie and I waved goodbye.

Our mother was cremated at Mt Thompson Crematorium. Zoli collected her ashes to cherish.

Helena Wilson / Liz Ban / Paul Ban

Paul was eight years old – the same age our mum was when she lost her mother – Chris had recently turned seven, I was four and a half, and Bessie twenty-two months old.

Paul

She must have died during the night. I remember my father crying in the morning. He asked us to go into the bedroom and kiss her goodbye. Then he told us to go and play next door under the watchful eye of our Dutch neighbour, and not to look at what was going on at our place. However, I peeked when the ambulance arrived and I saw my mother being carried out of the house on a stretcher covered by a sheet. I knew she had been sick but I had no concept of the finality of death.

Her funeral was held a few days later.

Our father cared for us on his own for the next sixteen months. I remember feeling we weren't quite a normal family after our mother died, and it wasn't just because we only had one parent.

Without my mother around, all the routines we'd known were suddenly gone, and for many hours of the day my brother and I were left to our own devices while our father concentrated on looking after our younger sisters.

Chris and I were seven and eight at the time, and we quickly made the most of the lack of parental supervision. One of our early enterprises was a flourishing business in illicit pet sales at the local shopping centre. Our pet guinea pigs and mice seemed to produce offspring at a rapid rate, so there was no shortage of stock for our business. And to supplement our profits, we wandered the neighbourhood collecting bottles and old newspapers to sell to the shop next to the swimming pool. Recycling was alive and well in 1963!

Together, our earnings provided us with enough cash to fund a good supply of mixed lollies, the main objective of our commercial enterprises. But our business plan wasn't enough to feed my habit, as I also recall shoplifting large Cadbury chocolate bars from the supermarket (hiding them under my jumper) and occasionally stealing coins from my father's wallet when our pet sale profits ran low.

I cannot claim that the stolen sweets were necessary for my survival because there was certainly enough food to eat in our house. But one of the things we lost when my mother died was the routine of regular sit-down family meals. My father specialised in cooking the kind of hearty European stews where anything that could be thrown into a pot found its way there. In his view, designated meal times were unnecessary, and he told Chris and I that we should just grab a spoon and eat from the pot whenever we were hungry. When the pot was empty, he would simply cook up another stew.

Another routine that went missing after our mother died was a regular bath. I remember my father bathing Helena and Bessie, and possibly Chris. I assume he must have expected me to wash myself as well, but he never forced the issue and he never checked to see if I was clean. I spent a lot of time at the local swimming pool with Chris, where there was plenty of water, and there must have been showers there, but I can't remember ever having one. I must have smelt like chlorine much of the time.

What I do remember clearly is turning up to school unwashed. Every few days the teacher would send me to the toilet block with a cake of soap and tell me not to come back to class until I was clean.

For some reason, I didn't feel embarrassed about this. The teacher knew that my mother had died and must have assumed that my father was struggling to care for four young children on his own. There was never any shame dished out with the soap, just sympathy.

In August, four months after my mother died, Chris and I went Brisbane Royal Exhibition, known as 'the Ekka'. We had saved enough money from our business ventures to buy what we thought would be a swag of sample bags, and we headed out early, catching the bus from outside our house to Darra Station and then jumping on a train to the showgrounds. On our arrival, we decided to maximise our sample bag funds by sneaking in through a gap in the old wire fence to avoid the entrance fee. However, we soon discovered that our plan had a flaw: we had budgeted on sample bags costing a penny, and couldn't believe it when we discovered they were at least a shilling each. Undaunted, we set about collecting empty soft-drink bottles and traded them for money so we could at least buy a few bags between us, with hopefully as many chocolates and lollies as we could eat.

We spent all day wandering the showground together taking in the sights. As evening drew on, I recall thinking, 'We're just little kids – we shouldn't be out this late.' I don't know what time we eventually arrived home, but it was well after dark. I thought Daddy would be angry with us for staying out so late. But he hadn't been worried about us, and there were no stern words or punishment waiting for us when we got home.

Years later, our father told us stories about his childhood in Budapest, which suggested he'd enjoyed a great deal of freedom in his inner-city world, living in the same street as the Opera House. Maybe he thought he could trust us to wander the streets of suburban Brisbane as he had done in cosmopolitan Budapest. Then again, my father had taken me with him to stow away on an ocean liner when I was only four years old, so he clearly didn't have the best grasp on the tenets of protective parenting.

Despite his somewhat bohemian child-rearing style, I have some fond memories of spending time with him in this period. He insisted on teaching me basic mathematics, and showed me how to print in capital letters instead of using the 'running writing' that I'd learned at school. Through his life, my father remained disdainful of cursive script, and would always print in capital letters.

One of the many anomalies about my father was his lack of interest in teaching us how to speak in his native tongue. Like many European migrants, he was fluent in six languages. But he never shared his knowledge of Hungarian with me, or any other language for that matter. I discovered later that this had a lot to do with his beliefs about government conspiracies. There was no point in trying to learn a language when you could simply have it 'filmed in' if you had the right connections.

One thing he did instil in me, however, was an enduring love of reading. Although my reading material at the time was mainly comics, my father introduced me to my first 'literature' by buying me 'Classic Comics'. Much later, this style of literature came to be known as graphic novels. In Inala, I read *Twenty Thousand Leagues Under the Sea by* Jules Verne and *A Tale of Two* Cities by Charles Dickens – not bad for an eight-year-old who didn't bathe! For good measure, my father also taught me how to draw Mickey Mouse, just in case I might ever need to use that skill. It was the original 'Steamboat Willie' Mickey Mouse and not the later fleshier one who hung out with Minnie, Goofy and Pluto.

But other memories from this time are more troubling. It was clear to me that my father was really missing my mother, and it didn't take long for him to start sharing his grief with me and taking me into his confidence in a way that was well beyond my capacity to understand. He also began to share his anxieties with me, especially his fear that his family was not safe. He would have been well aware of the child welfare file that had been opened after the stowaway incident, and he suspected that the 'state' would take us away from him. I wasn't aware at the time that we were being monitored, but we were. My father had no family in Australia, and my mother had been an only child. So there were no relatives to support him in his newfound primary caregiver role. While my father reached out to friends and neighbours, he also sought help from the media and pleaded with the Immigration Department. And he was making a lot of waves that were registered by the relevant agencies.

The week after my mother died, my father asked me to write a letter to our old neighbours in Hobart, Mr and Mrs Meilands, telling them about her death. Many years later, their daughter, Margaret, tracked down my address in Melbourne and returned the letter to me. It arrived in the original envelope, which still contained the dried flower from my mother's funeral that I had sent them.

> I got 80% for an exam in school. Christopher doesn't know what he got. Daddy is at home alone with Oscar our black dog. I will send you a piece of flower from Mummy's funeral, if you like to keep it as a souvenir.

I told the Meilands that my mother had 'died of cancer,' and:

> Daddy keeps worrying about maybe they take us to the State Children's Home because we haven't a Mummy now.

Reading it now, it is obvious that much of it was dictated by my father, and that it was a plea for help. He – and I – were already aware of the possibility that we might be sent to a children's home.

At the same time, he was battling his recurring health issues, hearing the voices in his head and being 'switched on and off'. I was aware of my father's struggles with the voices, and was beginning to become confused by the sudden changes in his behaviour, especially when he shared his strange beliefs with me.

He was convinced that the Queensland police commissioner had been responsible for my mother's death, and he kept asking me to phone him to tell him to leave our family alone. I somehow knew that this wasn't the right thing to do, and I managed to avoid his requests. Chris, who was fourteen months younger than me, later told me that he called the police commissioner on our father's behalf.

He told me that we could communicate with our mother, and bring her back to life, if we all stood on hills with mirrors and reflected the sun through the mirrors in a relay fashion. I knew that wasn't true, but I would hear him out.

My dear Zoli and children

My dear Zoli and Children! Lajos wrote:

3rd May, 1963

The sad news of the death of Jean left both of us devastated. May God give you enough power to bear this terrible blow. Jean, who was delivered from her terrible suffering by death, cannot be replaced by anyone or anything for you, yet, one must resign oneself to the will of fate (or God). For you, Jean was the best wife, for the children, the best mother. Unfortunately, fate did not allow me to meet Jean in this lifetime. I lost her before I could see her. I'm haunted by qualms about having missed writing her a letter in amidst events of the recent months (new town, new job, new accommodation, moving house), before receiving the short and devastating news from you.

Zoli, be strong to bear the heavy blow. Do not lose your self-confidence. After the death of their mother, the children need double the amount of fatherly love. Do not lose your patience with them. I know it is a superhuman challenge for a man to raise four children – yet, I ask you not to lose confidence.

What are you going to do now? Once permanent residency shall be granted to me by the City of Basel in a few weeks, I shall try making arrangements for you and the children to be brought here. In the meantime, please let me know about your plans should the Australian authorities not grant you permission to enter the country. Would it be possible to send our mother to you? What if she sold the house and migrated to live with you?

The best solution would be if both you and the children and our mother could come here to us. Shouldn't we be able to provide assurance for you by the Australian authorities in order for you to travel and settle here? Tomorrow I shall write a letter to the local secretary of the 'Christian Peace Mission' to ask for advice how we could help you settle here.

Zoli, please accept our sincere sympathy, Loty and I both send our many hugs and kisses to you all until we see each other again.

Lajos and Loty

Zoli informed the State Children Department of his wife's death. He told them he was capable of caring for his children, as he had when Jean was in hospital. A year earlier, he reminded them, he had applied for his mother to immigrate to Australia. In light of his wife's death, he intended pressing forward with it. Ilona would be able to help with the children.

The department approved some monetary assistance for six weeks. But in view of the ages of the girls, it began surveillance on the family, with several authorities reporting regularly to T M Nulty at the Department of Immigration, the officer Jean had written to regarding Zoli's threat to shoot someone.

These authorities included the local branch of the Queensland Housing Commission (who found there was no cause for immediate concern), a social worker at the Brisbane Psychiatric Clinic on Mary Street where Zoli was being treated, a Sister Nelson at the same clinic (who said he often brought the younger children to the clinic and that there was a mutual fondness), the local police (who were satisfied he was making out all right with local help).

His psychiatrist, Dr Hede, confirmed Zoli's two severe bouts of paranoid schizophrenia, but considered him to be in a relatively satisfactory condition when he'd seen him a week earlier. He stressed that Zoli had a great affection for his children and didn't consider his health was such that it would mitigate against him caring for them. It would not help to propose to make alternative arrangements for the children.

He wrote:

29th April, 1963

Dear Mr Nulty

I know that Mr Ban and his family are well known to you but feel that it is in the interests of justice and fair treatment to Mr Ban that you be acquainted of recent developments.

...

The State Children Department have now indicated that, in view of the tender age of his four dependent children, unless a foster mother or some other suitable person be available for their care, the only alternative would be to have them placed in a State Home.

This would necessitate the family leaving their home and Mr Ban being left, without employment, to find alternative single accommodation. All of these factors have contributed to impose an added strain despite which Mr Ban is maintaining a very satisfactory adjustment. However it is my opinion that some efforts should be made to preserve the integrity of the family and if possible to arrange for Mr Ban's mother, who lives with a married son in Hungary, to be granted permission to enter Australia. Despite his mother's age of approximately 70 years, she is stated to be in good health and leading an active life and should be a suitable person to care for the children during Mr Ban's absence when he is able to be placed in employment.

An application was made to this effect by the late Mrs Ban in about April 1962, and it would be appreciated if you would investigate the possibility of special assistance in this matter.

Yours faithfully
Dr J A Hede (Psychiatrist)

Dear Dr Hede, Nulty replied

This is a distressing case and it is realised that Mr Ban's family problem has been aggravated by the loss of his wife. However, having carefully considered all aspects, it is considered that the admission to Australia of Mrs Ban would not be a practical step towards the solution of this problem.

In arriving at this decision I would mention in passing some of the factors prompting this decision. Mrs Ban is 71 years old and would be at least 72 years on arrival in Australia. It has been Departmental experience over many years that aged people who migrate late in life seldom readjust satisfactorily in their new environment and in a reasonable strong percentage of cases press their claims within a short time after arrival for return to their homeland. This readjustment is of course all the more difficult if the aged person cannot speak English. We are led to believe that this applies to Mrs Ban's case which leads to a further point. Mr Ban's four children are Australian born of an English mother and probably would be unable to converse with their grandmother.

Again, Mr Ban has no material reserves to draw upon nor is he likely to build up any reserve, and it is probable that Mrs Ban would immediately on arrival require assistance from the Department of Social Services. Moreover, having regard to the ages of the four children, the age of Mrs Ban and her probable life expectancy, it would seem that Mrs Ban's admission would be, at best, a temporary solution. There are also such other factors as to whether indeed Mrs Ban could meet our normal Immigration selection criteria, who would arrange and pay for her journey etc.

In all it is felt that even if the admission of Mrs Ban could be arranged, this would create rather than resolve a problem. Mr Ban has been advised accordingly. In conclusion our Senior Social Worker, Mr Tarbath, is aware of all the circumstances of this case and you may care to discuss with him any other aspects which you consider would help alleviate this distressing problem.

Yours sincerely
T M Nulty

A child welfare officer from the State Children Department paid the family a surprise home visit. Zoli had taken the three older children to the city leaving their neighbour to look after little Bessie at her house. Mrs Born invited him into her kitchen when she heard him knocking next door. She explained that she had migrated from Holland and did domestic work. Cleanliness was her fetish, and the officer noted that Bessie was 'well turned out'. Mrs Born said Zoli was being good to the children. 'Their manners are perfect. They are obedient, eat well and are never slapped. No child has the slightest blemish on their body.' She was a little concerned that Zoli was in the habit of bathing them and putting them into clean clothes only once per week. She suspected they often slept in their clothes as well. Paul had told her his father said that he would change the children and bathe them when he thought fit, not when she did. Bessie had arrived unwashed that morning and in an unsuitable outfit. But she felt for Zoli and the children.

'Have no fear for the children of the Ban family,' she said. 'I am willing to take care of them.'

Mr Tarbath, Zoli's social worker in the Immigration Department in Hobart, was transferred to Brisbane, and reacquainted himself with Zoli.

> Mr Ban is caught in a vicious circle. If we place him in employment, who will care for the children? If we don't place him in employment, he has inadequate finances to care for them. If he loses the children, he loses the house, and if we place him in employment, he will probably lose the children.

Zoli felt he was being persecuted by the department because his application to bring his mother to Australia had been pending for over a year. It was difficult, Mr Tarbath explained, because she was behind the Iron Curtain. Zoli thought the problem could be overcome by a simple phone call from one government to another.

He approached the *Sunday Truth* newspaper. On 9 June 1963, two months after Jean's death, the headline read: 'Wife dead, 4 children to care for, but Government refused plea for mother.'

> A heartbroken migrant father whose wife died a few weeks ago is making a desperate bid to bring his mother out from Hungary to help care for his four little children. But the Australian Immigration Department so far has not treated his plea very sympathetically.
>
> Ban said, 'I have no relatives out here and it is difficult to find work and look after the kiddies. Neighbours help, but if my mother were here my troubles would be over.'
>
> But the Immigration Department has thrown him into complete confusion. First he received a flat 'No' to his application that his mother be admitted to Australia from Hungary. Then he was told a decision would be made after the department made inquiries overseas.

The child welfare officer told Zoli that as he wasn't naturalised, his mother also wouldn't be. Therefore she wouldn't be entitled to a pension.

'My mother could live on a bowl of soup and wear my late wife's clothing,' Zoli replied.

On another surprise home visit, the child welfare officer saw that Bessie was wearing three adult pullovers. The children all had dirty legs, although Zoli explained they had been playing in the dirt that morning. He noted:

The children are properly fed and have good skin. The father is a man endeavouring to be a 'good mother' to his children. Under the circumstances the father is doing a satisfactory job at present. His need for light work, the fact that he is not naturalised and is an ex mental patient makes it hard for him to obtain employment. Dr Hede should be taken up on his suggestion and propose this man for an Invalid Pension forthwith.

But given that Zoli wasn't naturalised, the magistrate rejected the claim to transfer Zoli's unemployment benefits to an invalid pension. The employment office still believed he was capable of carrying out light work, so they persisted in sending him out to various jobs, always with the same negative outcome. Finally he was granted special benefits due to special hardships.

A bureaucratic mix-up doubled Zoli's rent. Mr Tarbath helped sort it out. The Housing Commission threatened to evict the family due to the untidy state of the yard. Zoli was beside himself with worry. When Mr Tarbath contacted them they admitted it was only bluff. Tarbath noticed evidence of petty persecution, in that hostile neighbours were dumping rubbish in the family's yard.

During his next home visit he noted the family was in need of clothing and blankets as they were living below the subsistence level.

Mrs Born reported she still wasn't happy that the children weren't bathed more than once weekly. 'The laundry is not on a par with that of a woman and occasionally when the father is absent the younger children are left in the custody of an older child.'

Zoli was just holding his own, but he wasn't well.

Zoli approached the United Nations High Commissioner for Refugees for assistance to return to Switzerland. The UNHCR sent a list of questions to Immigration. Zoli was presently of sound mind, Dr Hede told Immigration, but due to the UNHCR's involvement it was felt the application for naturalisation should be deferred.

Things were building.

The Housing Commission told the child welfare officer that the property was depreciating due to lack of care. Should the family be evicted, the officer replied, his department would undoubtedly assume custody of the children. Mr Tarbath then met with the Housing Commission – he had taken steps with Zoli to ensure that the exterior, at least, was presentable. The Housing Commission disagreed that much improvement had taken place. They wished to avoid evicting the family, but said they may be forced to.

A couple of weeks later, Zoli demanded a Certificate of Identity and re-entry visa from Immigration. He said he would leave, in any case, for Switzerland. He'd sell a small block of land if need be. He advised the State Children Department that he was returning to Switzerland with his children to reside with his brother, possibly as early as the following weekend.

Nearly sixteen months had passed since Jean died.

Two days later, Zoli argued with the manager of the Commonwealth Bank and the children were taken.

Part 3

Years of Change

1965–1969

Zoli

Within a month of the children being taken into care, Zoli was granted leave from the Brisbane Special hospital. His leave of absence was extended until 21 December as his condition had improved considerably. He remained on special benefits, regularly attending Dr Whyte, a local GP at Darra and was permitted to visit the children weekly with his friend Mr Dabrowski. Then the children were transferred from the Depot to the other side of the city.

As soon as he was able to, Zoli requested that the State Children Department discharge the children from Silky Oaks, and he applied to the Immigration Department for his brother Lajos and his wife Loty to reside in Australia to assist in their upbringing.

A child welfare officer at the State Children Department noted on file:

> I spoke to Dr G Whyte of Darra regarding Mr Z Ban's recent request for discharge of the children. Dr Whyte informed me that this man is "highly suspicious, perceptive and is not to be trusted". Owing to this, Doctor has referred Mr Ban on to Dr Charles at Psychiatric Clinic.

Even so, Dr Whyte suggested to Ivo Charles at the Mary Street clinic that the children be allowed home with Zoli for the Christmas holidays. He did not advise full custody until Zoli was in permanent employment, but he felt that the Christmas period would be a good trial period for both children and father. Mrs Born was again prepared to help with the children if need be.

Ivo Charles disagreed. Zoli was not capable of caring for the children at that moment, he said, and he felt that the department might have difficulty in getting the children back owing to Zoli's present unreliable behaviour.

The United Nations High Commissioner for Refugees, who Zoli had earlier approached for help to move to Switzerland, requested a report on his physical and mental state from the Immigration Department. The UNHCR had declined his first application, but advised that the Swiss Aliens' Police would be prepared to re-examine Zoli's case within a current scheme for handicapped refugees.

'The above-named,' the requested report read, 'was deluded and troublesome. His diagnosis is paranoid schizophrenia. His physical state is good. Since being on Largactil 100 mg t.d.s. and Stelazine 5 mg bd. he has improved. His short-term prognosis is good though a relapse is of course possible.'

Zoli couldn't understand or accept being told he could see his children for only two hours per month during the official visiting time at Silky Oaks. So he began visiting them on irregular days and at irregular times. In response, Charles Clark, director of the State Children Department, wrote to him to request he visit the home at the appointed times as it would be more convenient to all concerned.

In another letter in December, Clark informed Zoli that the children couldn't be discharged to him at present. The following morning, Zoli telephoned the department demanding his children be delivered to him at the Town Hall by midday. When this was refused, he demanded an appointment with the director himself. It was arranged on the basis that he popped in to see a doctor at the Welfare and Guidance Clinic beforehand. He agreed, hoping the doctor could help him. As he entered the clinic, two policemen arrested him. He was charged with being of unsound mind again and returned to the Brisbane Special Hospital. They found a toy revolver in his possession.

The year turned. It was now 1965.

Zoli absconded during a two-day leave pass in late February, taking the children from Silky Oaks. The police and Charles Clark were notified of their absence. Dr Gordon Urquhart, the Deputy Director of Psychiatric Services in Queensland, was notified in case any untoward incident occurred. They were seen in the vicinity of the Newstead wharves the next day, and the police sent. Zoli was returned to hospital in one vehicle and the children were returned to the home in another.

'I can remember us being at Newstead wharf,' Paul said, 'and think our father was trying to see if he could stow away with four children, like he did when I was four.'

The State Children and Immigration departments continued corresponding with the UNHCR with the real possibility existing of admission to Switzerland. Zoli's brother Lajos had told the Swiss authorities that he was willing to accept and care for the entire family. However, there still remained some confusion as to who was going to finance the repatriation costs if it went ahead.

Zoli's friend, and best man at Zoli and Jean's wedding, arrived in Brisbane. Stephen Hassman, his wife Pat, and their children were on holiday from Tasmania. Communication between the two friends had broken down and Stephen had no idea of the tragedy that had befallen Zoli. A surprise visit to the abandoned house in Inala left them bewildered, and they approached the local police, who were well able to fill them in. The Hassman family returned to Tasmania shocked and deeply saddened.

Mr Dabrowski continued to visit the children monthly, reporting to his friend in hospital.

The Brisbane Special Hospital informed the UNHCR that:

> Zoltan Ban, a male patient at this hospital is at present considered to be not sufficiently well to assume the responsibility of caring for his children on a journey overseas. His mental malady is of recurring type, relapses are unpredictable and no definite date or time can be assumed for remission of his present state.

In May, the Swiss authorities finally declined to accept the family for resettlement. Lajos, who had assured the authorities he would care for his brother's family, had changed his mind. His flat was now too small for everyone. His financial situation was not enough to contribute to his brother's upkeep and he was concerned the situation in Switzerland would not be any better than the one in Australia.

Zoli's mind turned to his application to Hungary for re-entry and admission.

He told John Tarbath at Immigration that he had received a Document of Identity from the Hungarian Embassy in Jakarta. He urgently wanted custody of his children to leave for Switzerland or Hungary, whichever was quicker. He admitted trying to obtain an appointment with the governor of Queensland through the governor's private secretary. He'd read that Sir Henry Abel Smith had visited a hospital and taken a deep interest in the welfare of the patients. He hoped that the governor might help him too.

'The patient is presently well enough to go out on leave for Saturday and Sunday 22nd and 23rd May,' the medical superintendent advised. 'He is well enough to visit the children on these days.'

The arrangement was made although Zoli had no intention of returning to hospital on Monday. Rather, he tried to obtain a doctor's recommendation for an extension of leave and for a discharge as being of sound mind and being capable of handling his own affairs. He did receive an extension until 19 June and applied to the Mental Health Authority for a discharge. He was requested to appear before the Mental Health Review Tribunal on 8 June.

On the first of June, he went to the State Children Department's offices, demanding his children. 'I had a most stormy discussion with this man,' the officer who saw Zoli noted on file. 'He was demanding that he be given his children in order to go to Hungary to his mother on the 8th June and in his broken English made mention of a High Court and the fact that he had made a booking on a boat for that date.'

With the assistance of a Hungarian priest, Zoli had applied to the Hungarian Embassy in Jakarta for permission to return to Hungary. He intended to transit to Switzerland and leave the children with Lajos in Basil while he investigated his mother's ability to care for them. Immigration received several telephone calls from shipping and airline companies requesting payment of bookings. But they had never agreed to pay for the family's travel expenses.

During this time, the Housing Commission took over the Inala house again, and the public curator's office, who were managing Zoli's financial affairs, auctioned off many of his personal possessions for twenty pounds. Mr Dabrowski offered him a room in Rosemary Street, a few minutes walk from Zoli's house in Serviceton Avenue.

Zoli had appointed two firms of solicitors to act on his behalf and said he could produce a medical certificate stating he was now mentally and physically well. The department quickly advised the solicitors of the situation. Zoli had approached the Federal Member for Salisbury, Doug Sherrington, who told Immigration that he would be grateful if they could do anything to expedite their decision regarding his repatriation.

When he did not turn up at the Mental Health Review Tribunal on 8 June, his application for discharge was refused. The Immigration Department was concerned that the position was quite untenable and that Zoli might even turn violent.

On Saturday 12 June, Zoli took the children from Silky Oaks again. Again the police were called and the children were picked up after a couple of hours.

On the Monday he went back to the State Children Department's offices, again demanding the children.

A week later, on a visit to a social worker, Mr Roesler, at Immigration, Roesler reported that Zoli was particularly delusional, requesting a Certificate of Identity and five hundred pounds which he thought the UNHCR had sent for travel expenses. He accused Mr Roesler of collaborating in the kidnapping of his children and 'swore in his mother tongue'. When Roesler threatened to call the police, he promptly disappeared.

The medical superintendent of the Brisbane Special Hospital revoked Zoli's leave. From 24 June, he was considered absent without leave and plans were in place between the hospital, the police and the State Children Department for him to be taken into custody and returned to hospital. However, Zoli had already made his way to Sydney and to the office of the UNHCR. He presented a Document of Identity bearing an official stamp from the Hungarian Embassy in Jakarta and a letter offering to reinstate his nationality. There was no re-entry permit to Hungary and until it was obtained they told him they were not able to proceed with his repatriation. The documents looked suspicious.

In July, his repatriation to Hungary at the expense of the Commonwealth was denied so Zoli applied for a travel document and re-entry permit for himself and the children. He reapplied for naturalisation. As back-up he applied for a rental house through the New South Wales Housing Commission.

When word filtered through to Queensland, the director of the State Children Department, Charles Clark, advised the Queensland Housing Commission to inform their New South Wales counterpart that Mr Ban was not considered to be a good tenant. The department advised Immigration that under no circumstances would the children be released to their father's custody in his present mental state. Dr Urquhart, Director of Psychiatric Services, confirmed that Mr Ban was still a patient and was absent without leave.

Zoli was now residing at the Salvation Army Hostel in Albion Street, Surry Hills. He approached the head of the Australian Council of Churches for assistance to return to Brisbane to see his children, though he suspected he would be taken into custody as soon as he returned. He was severely frustrated with the government and its reasons for not granting custody: 'You have no job. You have no home for the children to live in. The children have no mother to care for them.'

His children needed a mother figure who would also love them and he had applied to bring his mother to Australia through legal channels. At seventy-three years of age, he knew she was still agile enough to care for her grandchildren while he worked. He saw no alternative but to return to Budapest and bring her back. The

Offla's Children

problem was he had no passport, no money and no ticket to travel abroad.

On 27 September 1965, a call was received at Immigration and followed up by a letter from McIlwraith McEacharn Limited, Shipowners, Agents and Coal Contractors. They had detained a stowaway aboard their vessel R.H.M.S. *Australis*. They intended to deliver Zoltan Ban to the British Authorities in Southampton.

Two days later, a postcard was received by the public curator's office. It had been posted in Suva, Fiji.

PLEASE SEND MY FOUR CHILDREN —
PAUL — CHRIS — HELENA — ELIZABETH — IMMEDIATELY
AFTER ME. I AM ON 'AUSTRALIS'. ON THE WAY
BACK TO EUROPE. ORDER BY AIR FROM THE
GHOST BRIGADE. ERIC WINSLOW WOODWARD
GOVERNOR OF NSW WILL SEND YOU THE RAZOR.
ALCOHOLIC ANONYMOUS — RAZOR GANG -
BY ORDER
Z. BAN
WITH THE COMPLIMENTS OF THE CHIEF
OF THE PUBLIC INFORMATION SERVICES.
THIS PUBLICATION IS FREE OF CHARGE.

The ship departed from Sydney on 17 September and sailed to New Zealand before arriving in Fiji. Zoli avoided capture until the ship sailed from Fijian waters. Then he was discovered and locked in a storeroom. Within hours a second stowaway, a Fijian, joined him in the makeshift cell.

The *Australis* sailed on through the Panama Canal and to Miami, Florida, where two FBI agents interviewed the stowaways only to discover that neither of them was seeking asylum in the United States. The Fijian planned to sail on to England to be with family. Zoli was bound for Hungary via England. They remained on board to be dealt with by the British authorities. The ship continued to sail north-east before finally docking at Southampton.

The Fijian chose his time wisely and picked the lock the day they arrived. He escaped onto the wharf and to freedom while the 53-year-old was easily captured. The British authorities had planned on returning Zoli to Australia, but the International Refugee Organization had heard of his plight and arranged his onward journey to Hungary.

Zoli arrived in Budapest on 23 October 1965. Within days, he attempted to smuggle his elderly mother across the border into Austria. He was detained and questioned at length. His brother Laszlo was notified to collect his bewildered mother. Zoli was charged with attempted illegal border crossing and imprisoned for several weeks. When Laszlo contacted Lajos in Switzerland, they were both furious at Zoli's attempt to kidnap their mother.

As soon as Zoli was released he wrote to the State Children Department.

> I have arranged accommodation to my children by my mother in Budapest. My mother will look after my children. Please send my children immediately because I can't stand any longer. I feel lonely without my children. Please send your message to my address. Thank you.

Paul

As children outnumbered adults about six to one, settling into Silky Oaks meant adjusting to a world of interaction with peers. For me, that meant boys more than girls. Not that we were officially segregated – it was just that I was at a stage where girls were a mystery to me while boys wanted to do the same things as me, like play cricket and football in the front yard.

For some reason I find difficult to identify I can't recall spending much time with my brother. If my mother had not died and we'd stayed together as a family, surely Chris and I would still be roaming the streets of Brisbane after dark. But the routines and regulations of the children's home meant that I ended up with a new group of siblings. And the arrival of two of them, the Marshall boys, Kenny and Peter, heralded the beginning of life-long friendships with them both. Kenny occupied the bed beside mine throughout my entire time at the Home, both in the dorm and beyond, and we went on to rent a house together after we left. Although Peter was younger and a few beds further along, he and I bonded over a love of sport.

Having boys around my age always on hand for cricket and football matches dominated my life in the dorm. As I was the second oldest after Kenny Marshall in our row of beds, I would often nominate myself to be captain, and I always chose Peter Marshall to be in my team as he excelled at most sports.

The front yard of Silky Oaks was as big as a football oval, and this was where we spent most of our time. The yard was bordered by the local primary school to the west, and by Jackie Singer's house to the east. Looking back now, it's obvious that Jackie must have been affected by poor mental health. But all we knew as kids was that he lived with his mother in a ramshackle house surrounded by overgrown grass, and that he would speak loudly to himself as he policed the grounds of his home. Jackie was an adult of indeterminate age, who sported large holes in the seat of his pants and no underwear. His pants were kept in place with a cord instead of a belt, and they were always threatening to fall down.

Our world and Jackie's world met whenever someone hit a four or a six and the cricket ball ended up in Jackie's jungle. No one wanted to retrieve it, but we couldn't keep playing without it. After someone was eventually nominated, the unlucky scavenger not only had to retrieve the ball, but also had to find it among Jackie's piles of junk and long grass. The clock was ticking, as Jackie didn't like us going into his yard and would appear out of nowhere talking loudly either to one of us or himself while hitching up his trousers.

The front yard also became a riding paddock for a time during the period we had Donny the horse. Someone must have donated Donny to Silky Oaks thinking he would be a good pet for home kids. As he was near the end of his days – he was at least fifteen – he had a sway back like a hammock. He spent most of his time eating grass in the back yard near the chook pens. However, on Saturday afternoons, we would take turns riding him around the front yard, often with two of us on board the hammock and sometimes more.

Poor Donny. He'd probably expected to have a relaxing

retirement giving children some pleasure by letting them pat him and watch him eat grass peacefully while he sunned himself in the yard. But we had other ideas. We thought we could return him to his former glory by getting him to race from the bottom corner of the yard up to where the 'good lawn' began in front of the girls dormitory. Donny would manage a canter for us, but a gallop was way beyond him.

Not surprisingly, Donny didn't enjoy a long retirement. After his death, he was cremated in the corner of the back yard where he'd enjoyed his meals and some respite from his Saturday afternoon ordeal. The cremation took the form of a huge bonfire, with wood piled up around his dead body, and the site became a landmark for many years afterwards. It also offered us a way to tease the girls, by threatening to throw them into Donny's cold and long-lasting ashes.

Apart from cricket and football and our short period of illicit horseriding, the boys in the dorm went through various fads. I don't know who started the silkworm craze, but it seemed to make sense given the host of mulberry trees near the chook pens. There must have been some original silkworms to start things off, and it wasn't long before we all had our personal silkworm collection.

The worm stage was the most interesting because they were like little pets and you could see them eating the leaves. When they reached the chrysalis stage they produced silk, which we were only marginally interested in. The moth stage was short-lived, with eggs being laid on the mulberry leaves and baby silkworms being born. At this point, things became interesting again, with baby silkworms being traded if someone's collection met with misfortune.

We kept our collections in shoeboxes lined with mulberry leaves in a room under the dorm. At some point, however, we noticed that the silkworms were disappearing. We developed a roster, taking turns to guard the shoeboxes as best we could, to try and uncover where the silkworms were going. The mystery was solved when one of the younger boys was caught sneaking in to snack on the silkworms. He obviously thought they were a delicacy!

Monopoly was another game we played regularly. In fact, it became something of an addiction for a time. I used to dream about which streets were best to collect rent from once they had hotels on them. There were always willing players, with someone ready to take over another boy's properties if he had to leave the game to do his rostered chores.

As I got older, a more challenging hobby emerged in the form of chess. I don't know where the chess sets came from, but they were in constant use. The game required more brainpower than Monopoly, and my dreams of real estate were soon replaced with nights of planning strategic chess moves in my sleep.

Another boys dorm hobby that seems a little strange looking back on it was knitting. At one stage, practically all of the boys on the little side of the Big End were knitting something. Though, most of our projects were never finished – due to boredom with the process.

Donated books were housed at the end of the row of cupboards in the dorm. They were in no danger of being overused, as practically all of the boys preferred comic books. But over time I worked my way through the complete set of Enid Blyton's *Secret Seven*, graduated to *The Famous Five* and then moved on to *The Bobbsey Twins*. I didn't think about why I liked these books so much at the time. But I was reading about adventures shared by a group of peers – of course they resonated with me. My life in the boys dorm was one long adventure, with Aunty Rene providing the 'lashings of ginger beer'.

My life had changed completely, but I was happy at Silky Oaks.

Paul

My father left for Europe the year I moved to the Big End of the dorm, and at some point after that I noticed a pile of clothes, crockery and toys stacked along the inside wall of the bus shed. I recognised them from our house in Inala. They must have been collected when it was clear that no one was returning. Nobody told me that they belonged to my family, and I wasn't sure if I was allowed to take any of my toys. I don't know where all these things ended up, but I never did see them again.

A jar containing my mother's ashes had been sitting on a shelf in the kitchen when we left the house. What had happened to them?

My connection to my father and sisters was fading. I was forgetting that I was part of the Ban family. My identity as a Silky Oaks kid was taking over. And, like so many children who grow up in care – especially those removed from their parents as infants – I was grappling with the question of who I was.

Among my school friends, I was known as one of the 'home kids'. Within this, I was a member of a very large family with many, many 'sort of' siblings and a shared history that dated back to 1940 when 'The Children's Haven' opened. Like in any large family, there was an established hierarchy among the Silky Oaks kids, which operated according to a combination of age and seniority – in this case the length of time you had been in the home. The longer you stayed, the greater your status.

Being a home kid came with a number of benefits. I had always loved sport, and as Silky Oaks kids we got to compete in inter-home athletics carnivals with teams from other children's homes throughout Brisbane. First place was a blue triangular pennant, second place a red one, and third place a green one. My favourite sport was running, a love I shared with Peter Marshall. The carnivals were a source of great pleasure to me. I especially liked cheering on the younger Silky Oaks kids in their events. While I seemed to be a perennial red pennant recipient, Peter – the star athlete of Silky Oaks – usually collected the blue pennant.

I enjoyed the annual picnic organised by the Bus and Tram Driver's Association. It was usually held at Sandgate or Redcliffe, beachside suburbs on the other side of town. This meant a trip in a convoy of buses. Although the picnics were meant to be a fun day out, we were somewhat embarrassed by the large signs on the side of the buses, which read 'Crippled Children and Orphans'. I was also confused the first year, as I knew that most of the Silky Oaks kids weren't orphans or crippled. When our bus stopped to collect children from the nearby Pamela Rolls Convalescent Home for Crippled Children I figured it out. I'd never met a crippled person before I met these kids, although the Silky Oaks kids would sometimes call each other 'spastic' in our games. After we met these kids, we stopped using the word. We were lucky to just be 'orphans'.

The downside of being a home kid, of course, whether or not you were orphaned, was the absence of a 'normal' parent-child relationship. I knew I had been lucky to have my wonderful mother for the first eight years of my life. And I had been doubly blessed when

Aunty Rene came along to care for the boys in the dorm. She had the same gentle style of caregiving as my mother.

Despite having twenty-two boys to look after, Aunty Rene somehow managed to make each of us feel special. She knew that I loved to read the newspaper, so she would keep aside her copy of the *Courier-Mail* each day so that I could read it of an evening with my cup of tea. I still have the copy she kept for me on the day of the moon landing. Across the top of the front page, in Aunty Rene's bold handwriting, is 'THIS PAGE IS TO BE KEPT FOR PAUL BAN' – just in case any of the other boys happened to think it was as good a souvenir as I did.

I lived with the Abrahams for five years, until I was fifteen – a crucial period for figuring out who I was. Although my connection to my own family had faded a little, I never felt compelled to abandon this part of my identity, and I never had to engage in any battles with the Abrahams to assert my individuality. I credit Aunty Rene with giving me this freedom. I don't know whether it was simply her gentle style or the fact that she had so many children to care for that she had no time for intense over-parenting, but she always made me feel cherished and secure while respecting my independence.

But as far as a father went, Mr Abraham was more of a grandfather figure. And what I badly needed was a male role model to help guide me into adulthood.

My actual father was still alive, but he was in Europe, and I'm not sure he would have fit the bill in any event, given his troubled relationship with societal conventions. So I took my inspiration from some of my male teachers, who went beyond their role and took an interest in me, from some of the older boys at school, and especially from the bigger boys in the dorm, who were like older brothers.

Alan 'Chook' White and Teddy Green, who were in Year 12 when I began high school, both played in the A-grade rugby league team for the school, and were house captains and prefects. Teddy was also school vice-captain, and an all-round athlete – he could run middle distance as well as throw the discus. Chook was school captain and threw the shot put. With their achievements as my guide, I went on in turn to become a house captain, prefect, middle distance runner and an A-grade rugby league player, culminating in the award of a 'Full Pocket' for rugby league when I reached Year 12.

It's not that I forgot I had a father. It's just that he was on the other side of the world, and life in the Oaks went along, its rules designed to ensure the smooth management of sixty to seventy children, providing the boundaries I'd yearned for when we'd lived with my father.

I knew my father hadn't wanted us to be taken from him, and I had some idea that he was on a quest to get the International Red Cross to intervene on his behalf with the Australian Government to recover his children. We received the occasional postcard from him with messages like 'Help is on the way'. But no one ever explained to me exactly where he was, or what he was doing – assuming that they knew.

Despite what I felt was a frustratingly minimal amount of correspondence from my father, Mr Zander was not thrilled about his inflammatory messages. After one such postcard arrived, he called me into his office and asked me to explain why my father seemed to believe we were being held against our will.

What was I supposed to say?

Helena

For reasons unknown Mr Dabrowski stopped visiting us once Zoli left for Europe. He was replaced by our elderly neighbour, Mrs Hall from Hemmant. She was a regular visitor from October 1966 to February 1968 arriving on the set monthly visiting days for the 2 hour duration. Unlike our father who had broken all the rules.

Mrs Hall remembered our birthdays for some time after she ceased to visit by sending a card with a handkerchief and a coin enclosed. I have no idea what happened to her. She just stopped coming.

Nineteen sixty-six was a year of change. I was in Grade 3 and had just grasped the concept of pounds, shillings and pence when it was replaced with decimal currency. My roommates, Debbie, Margaret and Kim, and I transferred to the Big End of the dormitory, leaving the little sisters behind and bidding farewell to Aunty Alice. We settled into Brenda Marshall's (sister of Kenny and Peter) vacated bedroom – she had transferred down the hallway. It felt like we'd spread our wings and flown the coop. The reality was our new coop was down the hallway and around the corner into the wing of another dormitory.

The superintendents transferred to the newly built Grey Cottage to supervise young teenagers. They were replaced by newcomers, a married couple with two sons. I could barely remember a time when I had both a father and mother figure in my life. Mr Melville was a tall handsome man with a bushy moustache that tickled your nose when he kissed you goodnight. In private, he allowed us to call him Uncle Bruce. Aunty Joan wore her bleached blonde hair tied back. Her eyes were the colour of the sky on a perfect day. Her smile was so warm it could melt my heart.

Roslyn transferred buildings with her parents, Aunty Jean and Mr Zander. I could never bond with her as closely as with other home kids. We were from two different worlds. She lived with her parents. I didn't. But Brenda and I alternated as Roslyn's guest on occasional sleepovers. We watched television in her family's private lounge while Aunty Jean knitted and Mr Zander read the paper dressed in pyjamas. The room was barely large enough to seat them all comfortably. We bathed just before being tucked into bed, unlike the chaotic afternoon sessions in the dormitories. A glass of milk and biscuit were delivered with a kiss goodnight. I thought luxuries like this only existed on family television shows. I knew it was beneficial to remain firm friends with Roslyn if I wanted to continue this experience.

The bond between my little sister and me began to subside just as Brenda Marshall and I grew closer. So close, that we decided to become blood sisters and stole a knife from the kitchen to perform the ritual. The cuts on the tips of our fingers was ever so slight but they drew enough blood. We swore that nothing or nobody could ever separate us ... except at bedtime when we returned to our respective rooms.

We became the daughters Aunty Joan yearned for. We giggled as she poured smelly solution onto rollers in our hair. We were thrilled with the resulting Shirley Temple lookalike curls. We experimented with her perfumes and lipsticks. We were grateful to receive individual attention, a privilege denied to the others.

The back yard was the centre of most activities, and one day I glanced through the window of the bus shed. A stack of boxes caught my eye. I strained for a better glimpse and realised my doll was dangling from one of them. Other toys and oddments from our home were inside. My brothers already knew of their existence. In fact, Chris had broken the lock on the door to retrieve his orange monkey. He hid it under his bed in fear of repercussions. We kept vigil on our belongings for a while, if only to remind us of a life that once existed.

Occasionally my siblings and I were summoned to the office and presented with a parcel of toys, often with no letter or card enclosed. We were informed it must be from our father as it came from 'that place over there'. Scrutinising each toy, one of the superintendents commented that our father must have forgotten our ages. The toys weren't really suitable for us. 'He still thinks you are babies!'

I was just happy to know he was still alive.

Another time, a postcard arrived addressed to Bessie (now known as Lizzy at the home) with a picture of Queen Elizabeth II on the front. This was definitely from our father as he signed off with his name. It was also from Bessie's godmother. We didn't know she had one until now. Our father said the picture on the front was our Aunty Bessie and Bessie's fairy godmother. She would protect her and was ordering transport for us to go to our grandmother in Hungary. Bessie's godmother had four children and was the head of the British Empire. He hoped Bessie was happy with his choice of a fairy godmother. He sent his love, said to keep smiling, to cheer up and he would see her soon.

Aunty Jean was often caring, but at times she had a somewhat negative and sarcastic manner. And she was in this mode as she read aloud the postcard addressed to my five-year-old sister.

We stood silently while our father was belittled. All the workers at Silky Oaks were devout members of the religious order the Open Brethren, who operated the home along with the Council of Silky Oaks. The frenzy of anti-communist feeling during the 1950s had left everyone reeling. And we were the offspring of a man whose homeland was occupied by communists. The challenge to save us from damnation would be great.

I retreated from the office full of hatred for the superintendents and yet I had a glimmer of hope. Queen Elizabeth II was our aunt! She was Lizzy's fairy godmother! If anybody in the world had the power to reunite our family, it would be her.

The next year, the little sisters commenced school. Lizzy desperately wanted to spend time with me at school but I preferred the company of my peers who had become sisters to me. I was slowly losing the blood connection with my real sister. It had almost ceased to exist with my brothers. The thread that once united us as a family was broken. We had become integrated into institutional living.

Each morning, we awoke to a passage read from the Bible followed by a short prayer. Chores had to be done before breakfast, including its preparation. Food was purchased in bulk and stored in large bins. The commercial toaster cooked a dozen slices at a time with bread crusts supposed to be kept to feed the chooks down the back. Melted butter on warm crust was far too tempting for those in the production line and the large family of chooks often missed out.

The making of school lunches was a well-disciplined process. Some of the team were 'bread butterers' while others slapped on fillings. A cooked breakfast was prepared by the workers and a paid cook from the outside world prepared the evening meal. Communication between the workers relied heavily on an internal phone system between each building. There was a set number of rings for each worker. You couldn't help but count every time the phone rang to see who it was for. I suppose in many ways we were a larger version of the Von Trapp family from *The Sound of Music* with all our bells and whistles!

Mealtime was often the only time I saw my brothers. An acknowledgement or smile from across the room reminded us who we were. It never crossed their minds to allow siblings to dine together. And we never thought to ask.

When we were quietly seated, Mr Zander read a lengthy passage from the Bible followed by an even lengthier prayer. He thanked God for almost everything and prayed for the safety of Brethren missionaries overseas and at Aboriginal missions in Doomadgee in Queensland, Umeewarra in South Australia and Kurrawang in Western Australia. This repetitive prayer lasted up to ten minutes leaving most of us fidgeting with one eye open. It didn't end when he said 'Amen' as a boy was then chosen to say grace. It was said at speed for two reasons: firstly the boys were embarrassed and secondly we were all starving! 'Our dear Heavenly Father, we thank you for this food. Please bless it to strengthen our bodies for use in thy service for Jesus sake. Amen.' If it wasn't loud enough or clear enough it had to be repeated. Finally the chatter of children replaced the difficult silence. The workers ate breakfast in a separate dining room leaving Mr Zander with his large stick to supervise troublemakers.

Tables lined up in turn at the servery bench for a choice of cereals. It was repeated for the cooked breakfast. Girls teams washed the dishes and cutlery while the boys scrubbed the pots and pans. We were pushed for time with the school bell looming, but still mucked about and flicked each other with the edge of the tea-towel. Ouch! That hurt! When finally dressed in our school uniform, we collected lunch from a basket and headed to the connecting gate. Those from the slapped-up-sandwich production line automatically threw their lunch in the bin conveniently located nearby. A slice of cake or piece of fruit would suffice until a friend from the outside world shared their lunch with you.

Women volunteers from church groups were rostered to bake cakes and slices and attend to laundry duties. Bed-wetters of various ages were regularly marched to the laundry with their smelly sheets and pyjamas. Emotional problems lay deep within these kids who also struggled academically and attended a special school nearby.

The volunteers formed part of the Women's Auxiliary and provided an ironing and mending service. At the end of the day, neatly folded clothes were placed in baskets ready for collection by a representative from each dormitory. If an item was accidentally placed in your cupboard you just wore it regardless of the label.

Rainy days must have been a nightmare for the volunteers, as a bed-wetter doesn't wait for the sun to shine. It was well received when a large commercial dryer was donated to the home. This modern contraption fascinated the kids and one weekend, while the laundry was empty, Kim dared my sister Lizzy to jump inside the dryer. Once inside, the door was slammed shut and the knob turned on. My sister ended up with a few bruises and so did Kim when she received a beating with Mr Zander's strap. She was ordered to sit on the mat outside his office for the remainder of the day.

The dreaded mat was in full view of a busy walkway and even busier back yard. Depending on the crime, punishment varied from time sitting on the mat to a beating with the leather strap. The physical pain disappeared quickly but the humility of sitting on the mat lingered. Physical punishment was Mr Zander's domain as superintendent. There were always sympathetic enquiries from passersby: 'How long you got?' 'One hour.' 'Okay, meet you for Red Rover later.'

My rebellious streak was strong. I had my fair quota of sitting on the bristly mat. I remember being told at a young age by Aunty Jean that my naughtiness was due to my nasty communist streak. I assumed I'd inherited it from my father as it was obvious to me she didn't like him. I wasn't sure if they even liked me. My list of enemies was growing. It included both Aunty Jean and Mr Zander, who also occasionally called me a communist and didn't like my father. It included our Grade 2 teacher, who had been odd, with a nervous habit of shuffling around the classroom with his finger held up against his closed lips telling us to shush. We often mimicked him and one day he caught Kim in the act. To our horror, Mr Foreman dragged her to the front of the class, lifted her dress and pulled down her knickers. He slapped her hard several times on the backside with his hand. That evening the event was discussed in the sanctity of our bedroom. As the leader of the dorm, I desperately needed to create spells like Samantha on *Bewitched*. She only had to wriggle her nose. No matter how often I bent and cracked my double-jointed fingers I couldn't stop the evil from entering our lives. I vowed that one day I would seek revenge and return us to a time when we lived with our families. A time before fate stepped in. A time before my nasty communist streak became apparent. I didn't mind being punished for not doing my chores but somehow I couldn't control that bloody streak. I was often accused of being a communist. I just didn't know what it was. When I found out, years later – that it was a theory or system of social organisation in which all property is owned by the community and each person contributes and receives according to their ability and needs – it sounded suspiciously like my life in Silky Oaks.

There were after school chores with Red Rover squeezed somewhere between. The television was turned on at 4 p.m. for the younger ones; the older kids joined them when chores were done. First warning bell rang followed by second bell at 5.30 p.m. for the evening meal. Again, there were designated tables without thought for sibling interaction. Washing up teams alternated weekly and I had a big crush on my team leader. I rinsed the dishes after Teddy Green washed them. Once I challenged him to a game of table tennis mistaking his feelings for me when he announced the score as one–love. I thought he loved me. He was a teenager, I was nine.

A while later, the boys beckoned me over to the sandpit. Teddy was sitting buried up to his waist. 'Teddy's lost his worm and wants you to find it,' they said. It wasn't unusual for kids to be losing worms as many of us kept silkworms in shoeboxes underneath the boys dormitory. They were pale in colour, soft to touch and grew rapidly due to a bountiful supply of mulberry leaves. I dug in the area his worm was last seen. I found something soft and yelled, 'I've got it!' I pulled hard. Teddy yelled in excruciating pain leaving the other boys screaming with laughter. It took a few seconds for me to realise that it wasn't a worm at all. I was so embarrassed. My heart broke, leaving me wary of boys after that.

The relationship between Aunty Joan, Brenda and I had grown so strong that when Aunty Joan confided she was leaving the home we naturally thought she would take us with her. 'Things aren't as simple as that,' she said.

I begged her to stay. I not only needed her, I needed what she could give me – she *saw* me, as myself not one of group. And she dealt with me with a feminine touch.

Liz

I started school in 1967, when we'd been at Silky Oaks for two and half years.

I was five and a half and I couldn't wait. Kindy or pre-school were not compulsory then, so I'd spent my time playing on the swing set or in the large sand pit with the other children my age. Under the Old Building there was a toy room and two wooden rocking horses I used to love riding. The room was often locked and we could only go there under supervision. I would hang off the wire cyclone fence in the grounds of Silky Oaks and look longingly at the children at school playing on the swings during recess, wishing I were there.

My first day at school I met Carol Weeks, who became my best friend. Carol was a cute little blonde-haired girl, with blue eyes. She was confident and bright. Each morning before school started I would wait at the front gate for her to arrive and she would give me one of her calcium tablets from home. I thought they were lollies. Some days she gave me her tuckshop money and I would give her my pumpkin scones.

A few months after Grade 1 started, Carol invited me and Michelle, another home kid, to her place for a play after school. Michelle and I looked at each other, knowing full well that we would not be allowed to go if we asked the adults. So we decided not to ask. Carol lived across the main road and about three hundred metres from Silky Oaks. We had a great time playing with her at her house and meeting her two brothers. I thought Carol was rich, as she had a big house and a housekeeper like the Brady Bunch family on television. While her parents worked, Mrs Farr looked after the children, made afternoon tea and cooked the evening meal. We drank the milk, ate the cookies and fruit Mrs Farr gave us, and tried to enjoy the moment, knowing that we would get into trouble when we got home.

After a couple of hours, we said goodbye and headed home. We looked at the cars and waited for a gap before running across the road and down the street to Silky Oaks. I was nervous. It was getting late and Aunty Alice would be wondering where we were.

The belting Aunty Alice gave us with a coat hanger when we got home was worth it, just to see where Carol lived and to do what other kids did – play at their friends' houses after school.

I had a favourite outfit then – a cute little pleated white skirt and a grey short-sleeved jumper with a woollen koala stitched on the front, a grey woollen hat and shiny pointed black shoes which I wore with long white lace-trimmed socks. I loved that outfit and was upset when it no longer fit me and I had to hand it down to another little kid.

Some days I would swing on the swing set and look out over Moreton Bay at Moreton Island – Silky Oaks was set on eight acres on a hill overlooking the bay – and think the white sand dunes I could see in the distance were the snow-capped mountains of Europe. I believed my father was there across the waters and would one day come back and take us home. I struggled to remember him and what he looked like.

Hungary and Queen Elizabeth

Behind the scenes, Zoli continued trying to have the children repatriated to Hungary. In 1965 and 1966, there were many letters: from Charles Clark, director of the State Children Department, to Miss Kelso, director of the International Social Services in Melbourne. To and from the Geneva offices of the International Red Cross. The United Nations High Commissioner for Refugees. From doctors, psychiatrists, from the Hungarian Red Cross, the Immigration Department, the New Settlers' Federation of Australia, the Department of External Affairs in Australia, its counterpart in Hungary, which agreed to the repatriation of the children, and said that the Hungarian State was prepared to take responsibility for the children until they reached the age of twenty-one.

In all these letters, the following questions were debated: Was Zoli well enough to look after Paul, Chris, Helena and Elizabeth if they were sent to him in Hungary? What would happen to the children if he became unwell again?

The Hungarian Red Cross informed Mr Clark:

> Since Mr Ban is back in Hungary he is doing well, he had neither to be hospitalised nor to be given medical care. He has found a job and during the daytime he is working at home and in the garden. His mother too is in good health and she is taking care herself of the household. She as well as her son is looking forward with impatience to the arrival of the children of who she will take care. Besides Mr Zoltan Ban she has two more sons, one living in Switzerland and the other is living with his wife and his son not far from his mother's place. In case Mr Ban would have to be hospitalised the married brother and the grandmother would take care of the children.

These concerns might have been resolvable, but there was another question at play, one which the Australian authorities considered to trump all others: Was it, in fact, in the best interests of the children?

The State Children Department had several child welfare officers working the case.

One, Miss McDonald, interviewed the children at the home, asking them if they were happy there. They were unaware of the consequences of the questions.

> I have talked with Paul, Christopher and Helena concerning their father's request. Elizabeth, I feel is too young and I did not wish to risk confusing her. She has improved tremendously since she has been at Silky Oaks and has become very attached to Mr Alexander. Paul told me that he does not want to go to his father. He is happy at Silky Oaks and does well at school. He understands that his father has been mentally sick and has memories of his actions that have made him feel very uncomfortable. Paul was very attached to his mother. He added

that when he had finished his schooling he might think about going to Hungary.

Christopher told me that he did not wish to leave Silky Oaks before he had finished at High School. He may then like to go to his father.

Helena is very much 'daddy's girl'. Her eyes sparkled when I told her that he had asked about the children going to live with him in Hungary. 'I want to go very much,' she said. 'I am not very happy here.' Helena is not interested in being with her brothers but she would like her little sister to be with her.

The Ban children do well at school. Their behaviour is good and they are quite attractive in appearance. The boys in particular give the impression that they have found security at Silky Oaks. The little girls also have improved very much in themselves.

At another time, only the boys were visited.

The boys definitely want to remain in Australia. They are old enough to have their own say in this and I feel they have a right to make their own decision. It is stated that the children have positive feelings but I would wonder how strong this is, as far as Paul and Chris are concerned. They have never verbalised any negative feelings about their father nor have shown any strong positive feelings either. The children, particularly the boys, were showing evident signs of fear. They became disturbed after seeing their father, to the extent of looking over their shoulders to see if they were being followed. The boys have improved markedly since contact with their father has ceased and their schoolwork is well above average. I personally feel that the children should remain together in Australia. They are settled at Silky Oaks and are taking part in all activities.

Another officer noted with regards to the girls . . .

They apparently did not fully appreciate the situation or what going back to Hungary would involve and their intentions were not particularly clear although their statements, if taken at face value, on that occasion would have indicated their willingness to return.

Mr Clark wrote to Miss Kelso:

It is appreciated that through the whole of this episode Mr Ban has shown strong emotional ties with his children but because of his sickness the children have not reacted in the same manner. Their attitude is rather one of fear of him. The problem of their going to a foreign country is great enough without having to contend with a father who may still be suffering from a mental disorder. The father's rights are appreciated but on the other hand it is my responsibility under the law of Queensland to protect the interests of the children. I would therefore need to have positive evidence from the Hungarian authorities that Mr Ban had improved mentally to such an extent that he could care for his children and also that he had adequate accommodation for them and was capable to carry out their assimilation into the Hungarian community.

The letter Zoli wrote to Her Majesty Queen Elizabeth II seeking her assistance would not have assuaged the concerns of the Australian authorities. Zoli asked her to grant him British or Australian citizenship and to arrange a gratis passage by air to Sydney for him, his niece Eva, her husband and their son. He asked for her personal protection to restore his family life. He believed in resurrection and asked the Queen to bring back his wife. He sent a copy of this letter to Immigration. Attached with it was a completed Application for Naturalisation as an Australian Citizen containing a fictitious Royal Seal of approval. Words to the effect that citizenship was granted was completed in his own handwriting.

When the Czechoslovakian embassy in Sydney intervened on behalf of the Hungarian Government in support of Zoli's case for his children, it triggered an international dispute as to the nationality of the children. The Hungarian Government considered them Hungarian citizens by descent. The Hungarian Red Cross felt that 'the Australian authorities' apprehension with respect to the children are somewhat exaggerated.' Had Zoli not been Hungarian, would the response of the Australian authorities have been different? What if Hungary had not been behind the iron curtain?

According to External Affairs in Australia:

The children may be regarded as Hungarian citizens under Hungarian Law, but as they were born in Australia we regard them as Australian citizens and they are therefore subject to Australian law and entitled to its protection.

As did Charles Clark:

Whilst appreciating the feelings of Mr Ban, I consider that the Hungarian Authorities are also overlooking the fundamental principle – the welfare of the children. They were born in

Australia and are regarded primarily as Australian citizens. They know only the Australian way of life and in addition to having the problem of their father, would need considerable adjustment to live in a foreign country without any knowledge of the language. The Hungarian authorities are furthermore overlooking the fact that Mr Ban has been under prolonged specialist psychiatric care whilst in Queensland and that his health condition is very well known, being regarded as chronic. A much more intensive evaluation of the situation would be needed, strongly inclined towards the welfare of the children rather than the rights of the father.

A report on the children's progress was forwarded to Miss Kelso.

The children all are in good health and are developing well. Paul (aged 11) spent a short time in hospital in February this year but has been his usual vigorous self. He is of about average height for his age and is wiry and athletic in build. Christopher (aged 10) is very similar in physical features to Paul and both are quite capable little sportsmen. They were both selected to represent their school at Soccer during the football season and show a keen interest in other sports as well. Both boys now feel secure and settled at Silky Oaks and no longer cast furtive glances all around as they used to. Paul has come closest to verbalising the change that has occurred by stating that he no longer feels that people are constantly watching and following him. Both boys are quite emphatic that they do not wish to even consider going to Hungary until they have completed their formal education. The girls, Helena (aged 8) and Elizabeth (5) are both strongly built for their years and are also of about average height although Elizabeth is growing quickly at the present time. They are friendly, responsive little people now, as opposed to their earlier fearfulness. Helena is clever at school and is regularly placed in the first five in a relatively large class. Elizabeth has not yet commenced school but is looking forward to starting next year. Arrangements are being made for a photograph to be obtained of the four children and this will be forwarded to you for transmission to Mr Ban as soon as it comes to hand. I trust this information will be of some help to Mr Ban who is undoubtedly feeling the separation from his children very acutely.

Charles Clark promised to make further enquiries with Max Alexander, Mr Zander, regarding photographs of the children that could be sent to Zoli. His department and Immigration began to discuss grounds to refuse admission to Australia, should Zoli reapply for entry.

If Zoli did return, T M Nulty asked Clark, would it be of any benefit to the children or would such a step have the opposite effect on them? Would Mr Clark be prepared to release the children to their father should he come back?

'There was no simple answer,' Mr Clark replied:

It is the policy of this Department to make every reasonable effort to achieve restoration of family groups when such a goal is in the best interests of the children, and in this particular instance there is no doubt as to Mr Ban's concern for, and interest in, his children. However any decision regarding their return to his care would be subject to a number of considerations.

Offla's Children

He was sure of one thing, however: that the children be 'properly prepared for a renewal of contact with him' should Zoli try to come back.

As adults, none of the siblings recall being scared of their father. In reading the file later, Helena found this idea particularly difficult.

'I was once told the State knew everything about me,' she said.

> Did the State know when they snatched my siblings and me from our father's care and placed us in an institution, that the 'furtive glances' and 'fearful looks' may have been the result of being forced to leave the only family life we knew? We were raised by strangers without a kind word said about the person we loved most, our father. There was no counselling for the years of grief that followed the death of our mother.
>
> Was it a convenience to think we were scared of our father?

Zoli kept in touch with Mrs Scott, owner of the fish and chip shop, friend and neighbour from the Wynnum waterfront. She contacted the authorities over one letter she received from him. She was concerned Zoli may attempt to re-enter Australia.

> I received your letter August 12th and thank you very much that you visiting my children. I am very pleased too that Paul came top of his class. What's about the girls, my two little daughter, are they well too? Did you told them that I am now by my mother, by their granny in Hungary and I try everything to reunite them with the rest of my family? Please ask them

next what they think about to see me soon. Did they have any complain against the manager or it is prohibited lamentation. The manager receive a month about $200 subsidise for my children and he never let them go because this sum is a very nice income and he never send me a report from my children. It seem he is annoys. He is covered by authority. Kidnapping business. I hope you and your family are all in good health. Please write me soon. My best regards.

That year, the public curator auctioned off the block of land Jean had bought, for $760, with barely a profit made. She'd purchased it six years earlier for £270 ($600). She had struggled to keep up payments yet owned it within three years. Her estate was finalised a year later, after payment of arrears of rates and other incidental costs were deducted. An amount of $172.20 was held in trust for Zoli and a one-sixth share, $89.68, was sent to the home in the form of a cheque for each of the children.

In 1967, Miss Kelso asked that Dr Urquhart, now the Director of Psychiatric Services in Queensland, put together a report and questionnaire that may be forwarded to the authorities in Budapest, in order to glean more information as to Zoli's health. Dr Urquhart was prepared to do this, he said, but would not be able to provide it for some time.

The letters continued.

Zoli contacted the public curator. He asked for a passport or a Certificate of Identity, now turning his thoughts to coming back to Australia. 'I am shipwrecked,' he wrote. 'I am sinking.'

The public curator made enquiries and the Department of Immigration confirmed they held the Certificate of Identity at their office. But after this, a memo was written that the certificate should *not* be made available to Zoli.

Zoli wrote to the Governor of Queensland, Sir Alan Mansfield.

> I apologise for the liberty but some friends of mine told me to see if you could do anything for me in my trouble . . . Please give me a reasonable opportunity to live properly in Brisbane with my four children. I have the honour to be Sir, Your Excellency's most humble and obedient servant.

A detailed memorandum was prepared for The Honourable B M Snedden, Minister for Immigration. '. . . It is a serious thing to keep a father apart from his own children,' it noted. However, the resulting letter to Zoli read:

> While your desire to be re-united with your children is fully understood and appreciated, consideration for your re-entry to Australia can only be given if you are able to demonstrate to the satisfaction of the Director, Department of Children's Services, Queensland, that your health has improved to the stage where you will be able to provide a proper home and parental care for your children.

More than fourteen months passed since Miss Kelso had requested the report and questionnaire from Dr Urquhart, and it had not yet been done.

The International Red Cross wrote:

> The Hungarian Red Cross states that Mr Ban who is very attached to his children is greatly suffering from this separation

but his state of health does not require any medical treatment. The competent Hungarian authorities therefore showed understanding and gave him an emigration passport.

We do not know what will be the attitude of the Australian authorities in this case; would they still be opposed to this reunion, even in this new light when it is now the father who would like to join his children whom he had abandoned at the time leaving Australia illegally? We have not been informed whether the visa request has already been submitted, perhaps even refused, but in any case we are writing by the same mail to the Australian Red Cross, asking for their collaboration so that Mr Ban obtains a return permit and we ask you to be kind enough to support us, through your Australian Branch, in this case in which the Secretary General of the Hungarian Red Cross has personally asked for our intervention.

If Zoli could not have the children sent to him, would the Australian authorities now not allow him to return to them?

The children had now been at Silky Oaks for three years.

Paul

In the 1950s, Australia was a nation of churchgoers. When Billy Graham – a mega-popular American evangelist – came to town in 1959 with his 'crusade', more than three million Australians (out of a population of ten million) came to hear him speak, and millions more listened on the radio. But by 1968, when he made a return visit, there had been a fundamental shift in attitudes, and church attendance was in rapid decline. At Silky Oaks, however, the forces of liberal change were yet to be felt, and it was still pretty much the 1950s as far as churchgoing was concerned.

We spent practically all of Sunday in church-related activities. First off, right after breakfast, was Sunday School at the Wynnum Gospel Hall. After a quick return to Silky Oaks for morning tea, it was back to the hall.

Morning service was a mysterious and mind-numbingly boring affair. It went for an hour and a half and involved a constant rhythm of alternating prayers and hymns sung without any musical accompaniment. In between, a member of the congregation would suddenly stand up to speak on a Bible-related topic that he (it was always a he) thought relevant to the meeting. The seemingly unplanned nature of the interjection was a function of the speaker having been 'led by God' to share a lesson with the congregation. However, there were occasions when two men would jump up to speak at the same time, and one was forced to back down, like roosters in a pen. This was mildly entertaining. Maybe God had led both of them to speak at the same time to see who would win?

After the morning service, we went home for Sunday lunch. The afternoons were meant to be a rest period, though we had to keep our good shoes and long white socks on, and read a Bible passage along with our Scripture Union notes beforehand. Then we were meant to have 'quiet reflective time' lying on our beds. But that coincided with the 3 p.m. kick-off for Brisbane rugby league matches. My quiet reflection involved listening to Wynnum-Manly playing the Valleys or Brothers through an earpiece with a crystal set hidden under my pillow. Later, I graduated to a transistor radio.

The Sunday evening meal was simple and informal – bread and jam. Then we were bundled off to the Gospel Hall yet again for the evening service: livelier hymns, accompanied by an organ and sometimes a guitar, followed by someone giving their testimony regarding how they became a Christian. As women were not allowed to speak in church – it wasn't called Brethren for nothing – they had to sing their testimony.

The testimonies were followed by an gospel sermon, which inevitably led to a call for people to come forward to 'accept Jesus as their own personal saviour'. The hymns accompanying this plea were dramatic in tone, and people tended to make the journey to the speaker's stage in tears. As the gospel service was made up of church regulars, you would have thought there would be no one left to accept Jesus as their saviour. But there was a category called 'backsliders' – those who had committed themselves at some stage but had fallen by the wayside. There were apparently enough of them to keep the Sunday night aisle traffic flowing in a lively fashion. After all, who hadn't experienced a bit of backsliding?

We had supper before going to bed. And, in case we'd missed the message of the day, we were made to listen to Billy Graham's Gospel Hour over crackly speakers while we lay on our sheets heading towards slumber.

Helena

Those Sundays.

Silky Oaks had a duty to the church and to the committee that oversaw it, and we filled the pews, all of us kids. It was the fashionable day of the week. The girls wore a variety of hats with their best dress, shoes and socks while the boys wore crisp white shirts, thin black ties and black shorts with polished shoes and socks. If we didn't nod off during the service, we amused each other by writing silly notes, pulling faces or smuggling in a novel to read. The subject of the service was beyond a child's comprehension, the length of it beyond our ability to sit still. It was such a relief when the final Amen came. You got a clip over the ears as you entered the bus if you'd been caught sleeping or misbehaving, and you'd find yourself an unwilling member of the washing-up team after lunch.

Those of us who were rostered on to prepare the midday meal were excused from morning service and supervised by two adults. We cooked for the usual inmates and elders or deacons from church. Sunday lunch was a huge feat. A hot roast meal during the cooler months and cold meat and salads in the warmer months. Dessert always followed the main meal.

In the rest period, we jumped from bed to bed pretending the floor was the sea filled with sharks. Hide and seek was nearly as popular as sliding races down the hallways in socks. Socks were to remain on – the logic being that if our feet were clean then we weren't required to bathe. It didn't bother us not bathing on a Sunday, although I did wonder what God's thoughts were on the matter.

The evening service was more family orientated, with singing. There was the occasional testimony, but the best source of entertainment for us kids were the baptisms. The floor of the stage opened to reveal a pool of water large enough for two people to enter. We liked to place bets on whether the victim would swallow water while submerged and arise coughing and spluttering!

During the week, there were daily morning and evening prayers in our bedroom, and a Bible reading and prayer before breakfast. There were Girls and Boys Rally Clubs held in the old church hall on Tuesday and Thursday evenings respectively and Friday evening activities for teenagers were followed by a religious message and prayer. And, of course, we went to the Brisbane Exhibition grounds to witness the Reverend Billy Graham preach the gospel to thousands. If only we were there for the fireworks, the speedway, or the annual Ekka Show Day instead of an evening with the reverend!

Liz

Breakfast was in the dining room. Before we could eat, we were read a piece from the Bible, followed by prayer and grace. Once I timed it – it had taken twenty minutes. Can you imagine seventy hungry children having to sit and listen to someone drone on for that long before they could eat?

There was so much religion being taught to us that I started to switch off and distract myself by daydreaming. I recall being bored in Sunday school and was tired of hearing about the stories the Sunday school teacher was teaching us, so I would play up as a way of getting kicked out of the class thereby avoiding anymore stories.

When I was about eight, I wanted a red scooter with white pump-up tyres for Christmas and I thought I would test God by asking him for it. After all, I had been a good girl most of the time. My suspicions about the existence of God were confirmed on Christmas morning when the scooter didn't come.

When I was eleven and the Kerrs were my caregivers, I challenged their beliefs about religion. What proof was there that there was an afterlife? What if I spent my whole life being good and missing out on having fun, only to find out there was no heaven? Mrs Kerr said I was blasphemous for even thinking such a thing!

Paul

As in most Australian households of the 1960s, the job of meting out punishment to naughty children at Silky Oaks was a masculine preserve. Mr Zander's office was where you went for a reprimand and, occasionally, to get the strap or a smack with a small cane.

The parade of children going into his office could be seen from the TV room. Over the noise of the TV, and with the glass doors closed, we couldn't hear what transpired. But then the 'offender' would emerge crying and rubbing his legs. It was like seeing a silent movie in the background while watching regular TV at the same time.

Mr Zander's office had two entrances, the one that could be observed from the TV room and a second outer door that led onto a walkway between the boys dorm and the scullery. On the floor outside this door was 'the Mat', where some of the offenders had to sit. Because it was public, we would usually chat to the temporary resident and it became something of a social activity for repeat offenders. One particular boy was on the Mat so often we called it his second home. He didn't seem to mind it, and if we walked past and he wasn't there, we wondered if he was okay.

I never had to sit on the Mat while I was at Silky Oaks, and I was punished only once by Mr Zander – a couple of smacks with the small cane. A group of us had let off firecrackers in the disused chook pen and started an impromptu bonfire. The punishment felt like it fit the crime.

While churchgoing and discipline were standard parts of family life in the 1960s, school holidays took on a unique flavour for home kids. We were 'on call' for families who wanted to take us for the holidays and give us a taste of 'normal family life'. We called them the 'holiday people' and, usually, they were associated with the Brethren church.

The holiday people would nominate the age and gender of the child they would like to 'rescue'. The most sought-after were girls under ten. Seeing that I was an older boy, I had few experiences of being taken away by holiday people. But when I was eleven, Chris and I spent six weeks over the Christmas holidays with a family who lived half an hour away in Sunnybank. We played backyard cricket and the older boys in the family taught us how to bat. For the two weeks after Christmas Day we went to Rainbow Bay on the Gold Coast, where we stayed right on the beach and our backyard cricket turned into beach cricket.

When I was twelve, and waiting for secondary school to start, my holiday people were a family with one young child who lived on a farm outside Brisbane. The couple had decided to take a set of twins from Silky Oaks who were the same age as their son, but they also wanted to take two older boys and Kenny Marshall and I got the gig. When they came to collect us, I suddenly overstepped the mark of politeness and asked them whether they could manage two additional boys from the home. Paul and Mick Davis were a little younger than Kenny and me, and they had never been taken on holidays by anyone. To my surprise, they agreed to take us all!

Then Uncle John and Aunty Rose – as they asked us to call them – had another surprise in store for us. Due to their religious beliefs, they didn't believe in giving presents at Christmas! Usually, holiday people went overboard with presents in an attempt to compensate for the unfortunate backgrounds of the 'rescued' children. However, all was not lost. After a few days of feeling sorry for ourselves, we discovered that Uncle John and Aunty Rose believed in giving presents for New Year's, and the boxing gloves that Kenny and I received got a good working out by us all.

At the end of Year 9, when I was thirteen and too old to be selected by well-meaning holiday people, Mr Abraham and Aunty Rene decided to take Chris and me with them on their Christmas vacation. They were meant to be having their annual break from caring for us boys, but they realised we wouldn't be going anywhere and invited us to join them – which, of course, we jumped at. We had a great time swimming in the surf and a nearby lagoon on the Sunshine Coast and returned to Silky Oaks at the end of the holidays as brown as berries.

The next year, when I was waiting for my school results over the summer holidays, I went with Kenny to his grandparents, who lived at Noosaville on the Sunshine Coast, for a few weeks. Like my father, Kenny's mother also suffered from paranoid schizophrenia, and he hadn't had much contact with his grandparents. Kenny's grandfather was eccentric, gruff and barely spoke to us. He insisted on turning the sound off during the ads when we were watching TV, creating sudden vacuums of silence in the room. We didn't mind him being a little weird, as long as he left us alone. There was a great deal to enjoy for two adolescent boys with a lack of surveillance and Silky Oaks routines. The teenage girl next door occasionally mowed the lawn in her black bikini. She was older than us, and Kenny and

I were too intimidated to talk to her. But we were always glad when the summer grass began to grow.

Unfortunately, the holiday didn't end well. Bored one afternoon, I mindlessly drew symbols on a dusty mirror in the house – some stars and swastikas. That night, after Kenny's grandfather had seen them, he accused me of being a member of the Hitler Youth and launched into a long tirade about exposing sleeper cells in Australia, with me as his first catch. He told me to pack my bags and leave first thing the next morning. Kenny decided to come with me, as he was pretty sure I wasn't hiding my true identity as a spy.

Dr Laszlo Boldog

In the middle of 1968, Zoli wrote to Immigration and to the Children's Services Department (the renamed State Children Department). He reiterated the reason he had gone abroad to Hungary, added a fragmented argument regarding the constitution, and provided a medical update:

> I have been examined by Specialist in Hungary, Budapest, Dr Sai Halasz Majusluti Rendelo. Diagnosis: Composmentis. The Hungarian Red Cross forwarded this certificate to Australia Red Cross.

Immigration replied:

> Your letter of the 10th ultimo has been received and in reply, I desire to inform you that we are still awaiting a Certificate from a fully qualified Doctor of Medicine and until this comes to hand, further consideration of your case must remain in abeyance.

The Australian Government wasn't satisfied with the medical report the Hungarian Red Cross had forwarded to the International Social

Services Headquarters in Geneva. So Zoli provided, from Budapest, a general medical report on his physical health:

> This is to certify that I have examined Mr Z Ban and found him to be in good mental health and he is able to manage his own affairs. Since years suffers from rheumatism, rheumatoid arthritis chronic discop lumbago. His disablement 67% and degree of disablement is certified by advisory committee on the health and welfare of handicapped persons.

It ended with a recommendation for immigration to Australia and was signed by a Doctor Laszlo Boldog, Budapest.

Doctor Laszlo Boldog's handwriting was suspiciously similar to Zoli's own.

Helena

We always looked forward to school holidays.

I was a cute, blonde-haired, blue-green-eyed little girl. A popular choice for the holiday people. I remember being taken out by several families over the years and that none ever offered to include my siblings. A young married couple from near the Gold Coast invited me to spend several holidays with them; some kids returned to the same families for years. I grew to love Beth and Derry Hall and wanted so much to be part of their family. But when they had their first child, I never heard from them again.

Fred and Norma Mattress invited me for the Christmas holidays of 1967 when I was nine. Fred managed the Musgrave Park Swimming Pool in South Brisbane and taught me to dive and swim. The three swimming pools reminded me of the complex opposite our home in Inala where we spent most weekends. Fred and Norma's house overlooked the complex and I liked to watch people from the balcony. They invited me again the following year for the August school holidays. Norma was heavily pregnant and I suspected my days were numbered.

*

We were looked after in other ways too.

Each year, the *Courier-Mail* sought donations of gifts for underprivileged children at Christmas time. Those of us not invited away by holiday people received these gifts on Christmas morning.

There was a yearly RACQ (Royal Automobile Club of Queensland) picnic, where members of the club collected kids from children's homes and piled us into their vehicles decorated with streamers and balloons. Seatbelts weren't compulsory in those days, so the more the merrier! We drove through the streets screaming and waving to passersby until we arrived at a park where we ate lunch and played games.

The Trammies picnic (though there were few trams left), at Sutton Beach in Redcliffe, started with the kindness of the drivers who collected kids from homes all over Brisbane. The bus arrived at Silky Oaks with a large banner on the front headed 'Orphans and Crippled Children'. When we were seated the driver drove about a mile down the road to collect a group of crippled children. In those days they were commonly referred to as 'spastics' – nowadays, of course, we know they have cerebal palsy. There was bewilderment but mostly amusement at the banner advertising the contents of the bus. So we did what kids do best, and hung out the windows mimicking the 'spastic' kids we'd just collected. The reaction from the public as we drove down the main streets of Brisbane was priceless. It was easy pretending to be a 'spastic'. But how do you pretend to be an orphan? Off to the amenities block to change into swimming togs as soon as we arrived. The calm waters of Moreton Bay made it easier for adults to keep an eye on all the kids. We entertained each other by impersonating a drowning spastic – more a reaction to how we kids were labelled, I hope, than cruelty.

The annual Trammies picnic enabled kids to reconnect with those who had been transferred from one home to another. It was a reunion of friendships, and young romance blossomed. Entertainment was also on hand – the highlight being the talent quest on centre stage. We supported all acts regardless of whether they were blessed with talent or not. And I danced along to Nancy Sinatra's 'These boots are made for walking'. Up till then, music was hymns in church services and songs from Sunday school. I loved this modern music. I loved Nancy Sinatra and desperately wanted a pair of boots!

Our own Bedford bus, driven by Mr Zander, was used for many outings. Singalongs kept boredom at bay. 'He's got the whole world in His hands' was a simple song and to ensure it lasted much of the trip we included the names of everyone on the bus. Another favourite was 'Ten Green Bottles'. By the time we reached 'one hundred green bottles hanging on the wall', you can imagine Mr Zander's desire to accelerate the pedal.

The Silky Oaks kids had their own anthem, which was apparently pinched and adapted from the Margaret Marr Boys Home at Wynnum North.

> The Silky Oaks boys are we, The Silky Oaks boys are we,
> We're always up to mischief, No matter where we be.
> The teacher thinks we're lazy, But he makes a great mistake,
> For whenever you see the Silky Oaks boys, they're always wide awake!
> One morning in the playground, a copper said to me
> 'If you are one of those Silky Oaks boys, just come along with me!'
> He grabbed me by the collar, and tried to run me in,
> But I got me fist and knocked him stiff, and we all began to sing –
> Never an egg for breakfast, never an egg for tea,

But a hunk of bread as big as your head, And as hard as hard can be;
And if you do not like it, a hunk of bread and jam,
Which will land you up at Roma Street, in the Black Maria van.

The girls, of course, preferred to sing the line as 'The Silky Oaks boys are weak.'

We were invited to previews at Her Majesty's Theatre and special screenings of new movies. *Mary Poppins. The Sound of Music.* We saw the fireworks at the Brisbane Exhibition grounds. We went to City Hall for the annual Lord Mayor's Christmas Pantomime.

I should have been content with this, with three decent meals a day, regular outings, clean bed linen and decent clothes to wear. But I wasn't. My life lacked the most basic and fundamental need of a child – the love and nurturing from a parent. If I thought it possible, I would have traded these privileges for a life not thought to be ideal by some. Even as a child I was familiar with the phrase 'Blood is thicker than water' and I feared my Hungarian blood was diluting the longer I stayed at Silky Oaks. I was prepared to live with communists if it meant being with my father. I was even prepared to serve time sitting on the mat if the superintendents or any of the workers discovered my thoughts.

When I was ten, in 1968, I dreamed my father was coming to take me home soon.

My carer, Aunty Em, became concerned when word filtered through. She thought it best handled formally. I was summoned to the office where I found Aunty Jean.

'It was only a dream, Helena. Your father is never coming back. He abandoned you a long time ago.'

Offla's Children

I sometimes still waited at the top of the drive on visiting day. My father had been gone for more than 3 years.

I was wrong about Fred and Norma Mattress.

Before Christmas that year, I was summoned to the office. I thought: If one of those kids has dobbed on me again for talking about my dream I'll kill 'em!

But—

'Mr and Mrs Mattress would like you to spend the Christmas holidays with them.'

I was surprised they were still interested in me. I knew they'd had a baby girl, Janine, and I didn't understand why they would still want me.

I began calling them Uncle Fred and Aunty Norma instead of Mr and Mrs Mattress. I immediately loved Janine, who was four months old. My swimming strokes improved and I finally mastered diving. I was having a wonderful time when Aunty Norma said, 'We heard you had a dream that your father is coming to take you home.'

'It's true,' I replied. 'I know it was a dream but it was so real!'

'Mr and Mrs Alexander asked us to talk to you about this, Helena. Your father abandoned you a long time ago and you have to accept that he is never coming back.'

I burst into tears. Why would they lie to me? I knew they loved me because they told me so. Uncle Fred and Aunty Norma lovingly embraced me until the tears dried up.

'How would you feel if we asked you to live with us permanently?'

'What do you mean by permanently?' I asked.

'It means you would pack up all your belongings at Silky Oaks and live with us not just for the school holidays but forever. Janine will become your sister and we will become your mum and dad.'

'Janine will be my sister and you will be my mum and dad?'

'Yes, and if you aren't comfortable calling us Mum and Dad you can keep calling us Uncle Fred and Aunty Norma.'

'But where will I go to school?' I asked. 'And my last name isn't the same as yours.'

'There are plenty of good schools in our neighbourhood and we can legally change your surname from Ban to Mattress.'

I wasn't sure whether I liked the sound of Helena Mattress. But the idea of starting afresh with a mother, a father and another little sister appealed to me greatly. To live in a normal-sized house with only three bedrooms rather than a group of buildings with dormitories. Faded memories of Inala rushed back: living close to a swimming pool complex! We talked for hours about the future – my future. Uncle Fred said how proud he would be to one day escort me down the aisle on my wedding day. It was an exciting end to my holiday, but there was something that had been niggling at me from the moment the conversation began. There were only three bedrooms. Uncle Fred and Aunty Norma slept in one. Baby Janine slept in the other.

'I know Lizzy can share my bedroom, but where will Paul and Chris sleep?'

They glanced at each other before replying, 'It's only you that we want. Your brothers and sister will have to stay at Silky Oaks. Maybe one day a nice family will want them too.'

It was after dusk and I ran outside. I crept underneath the bench in the corner of the patio. Uncle Fred and Aunty Norma understood I needed time alone and let me be. I cried a swimming pool of tears thinking about what they'd offered. I'd lost my biological mother when I was four and a half. I'd lost several substitute mothers since. The idea of a permanent mother and father appealed to me greatly, but the sacrifice I would have to make weighed heavily on my conscience. It was difficult enough to comprehend that my father may never come back. Imagining having to exchange my siblings for this loving new family was beyond me.

The night before my return to Silky Oaks, as we sat around the television, I told them my decision: 'If Paul, Chris and Lizzy can't come to live with you then I can't either. Our father is coming back to take us home so we have to stay together.'

The drive back to Silky Oaks the next day was long and quiet. When they hugged and kissed me goodbye I knew I would never see them again.

Liz

I'd spent a holiday with the Brennan family, on their farm. Aunty Em was a lovely, warm lady, and she and Mr Brennan had three children still living at home. I remember sitting around in the evenings in the lounge room listening to stories on the radio as they didn't have a television. One of their sons played the banjo and I thought he was so talented. I wished I could have learnt to play a musical instrument.

There'd been no talk of them moving to Silky Oaks, so when they later arrived as the new house parents, when I was in the Little End, I was surprised to see them. Even though I had spent a holiday with them, they never showed me any more affection or interest than the other girls.

The workers came and went.

As with children, they were easily replaced. If they were sent by the Lord then that was good enough. No experiences or references required! Mr Brennan had a frightful scar along his arm, the result of being caught in machinery. He was extremely strict and religious, and he idolised Mr Zander. He believed in the old adage, 'Children should be seen and not heard'. At times Silky Oaks housed up to seventy children. How on earth we could have remained silent was beyond me.

I remember 'back-chatting' Mr B once, and running to my room and shoving my school exercise book down inside my underpants before he found me. He then gave me a good smack on the behind, only to find the book. I quickly learnt that was a mistake and got a bigger smack.

I wasn't close to any of the adult carers, the nurturing 'Aunties' and disciplinarian 'Misters'. I would see some girls holding the carers' hands or sitting on their laps, but I kept my distance, noticing the closeness came naturally to the other girls, but not to me. I didn't know why I didn't want to be cuddled. Some of the girls would hang out in the carers' flats, seeking attention, whereas I preferred to be playing outside.

I loved the outdoors, the swing-set and playing games. There was a never-ending supply of children to play with. Life felt like one big play date in Silky Oaks. We didn't need to ask our friends home after school as there was always someone available from the home. There was a garden bed full of plants, just outside the boys dorm and when it rained the frogs croaked so loud, it made it easy to collect them. I would keep them as pets in a shoe box and then release them after a few days, or trade them along with the frilly lizards I'd collected from climbing trees. There were mulberry trees, which were out of bounds as the berries stained our clothes purple and was hard to wash out. Nonetheless, we'd sneak to the trees, wrap the mulberries in the leaves and eat them. Just near the Grey Cottage and the New Building there was a stand of old fig trees. I regularly climbed them, especially when the fruit ripened, and would sit gorging myself.

I remember sitting in the bath when I was in the Little End and scooping the same amount of water from a small bucket on each breast so that I wouldn't grow up to have lopsided breasts.

I don't recall celebrating my birthday or having a birthday party as a child in Silky Oaks, and as an adult I have never really made a fuss about my birthday. But once Aunty Joan gave a birthday party for Helena. Helena was given a lot of pretty coloured plastic bangles that covered the length of her arm, and I was upset as I wanted one.

'You have so many bangles, can I have one, Helena?' I asked.

'No, you can't, it's not your birthday.'

I cried and made a fuss about not getting a bangle, so Aunty Joan told Helena she had to give me one. I remember feeling sheepish as Helena reluctantly handed me one.

I grew up with other girls of similar age to me and we moved to the Big End together. It was 1969 and we were eight. For a short time, I lived with my sister again.

When I first arrived in the Big End, the Brennans were the house parents. A couple of years later they were replaced by the Flemings, Bruce and Les. Helena and her friend Brenda were very close with the Flemings and spent a lot of time in their flat. I liked them too; they were young compared to the other house parents, and were friendly and fair with the kids. I can't remember how long the Flemings looked after me in the Big End, but it didn't seem long before they moved to the Grey Cottage.

I used to hang out under the boys dorm, near Aunty Rene and Mr Abraham's flat, where the water pipes were exposed. There, I would attach the clip from my small crystal radio set. The transistor worked by clipping the peg onto a metal object which served as an additional antenna to improve reception. I would often see Peter Edgar who was always sick hanging over a chair and another boy, whose job it was to hit Peter repeatedly on the back to loosen the mucous from his chest. The reception on my little green crystal radio was not very good and it was hard to hear. The cockatoos who lived in a bird cage beside the Abraham's flat continually squawked, and kids passing by interrupted, wanting to have a turn listening to the radio. But it was here where I would disappear into another world outside of Silky Oaks listening to music and stories on the radio.

Helena

The year Lizzy moved to the Big End was the most memorable of my childhood.

In March we were summoned to the office. Mr Zander held an envelope addressed to my siblings and me. He opened it to reveal a typed letter dated 13 March 1969 from Queen Elizabeth's Lady-in-Waiting, Margaret Hay. Aunty Jean pointed to the words BUCKINGHAM PALACE embossed in red and centred underneath the Royal Coat of Arms of the United Kingdom. I listened intently as she read the letter.

> I am commanded by The Queen to thank you for the little car which you have sent to Prince Edward on the occasion of his fifth birthday.
>
> Her Majesty thought it most kind of you to send him this lovely toy and wishes me to tell you what fun he is having playing with it. I am to send to you all The Queen's sincere thanks.

Confusion soon turned to elation. 'Is it really from the Queen?' I asked.

'Yes,' replied Aunty Jean. 'It's actually from her Lady-In-Waiting, who is like her secretary. Your father must have sent the little car from Europe and printed your names as the sender.'

'As this is a special letter,' Mr Zander said, 'I will keep it in the office for safekeeping.'

We agreed it should remain in the office and I returned to the dormitory to an astounded audience when I revealed the Queen had written to our family for the second time! The girls were still in awe of the first postcard even though Aunty Jean said that it was from our father and not the Queen. She tried in vain to convince me that the Queen was not my aunt or my sister's godmother. Yet she now admitted this second letter was actually from the Queen. I knew the Queen was busy travelling the world and holding parties at Buckingham Palace for her loyal subjects and I was convinced she would have signed the letter 'with love from your Aunty Bessie' if she had the time. As Queen Elizabeth II symbolised the head of the ultimate family, she was my only hope to restore our family unit.

The next day at school I excitedly relayed the news to my Grade 6 teacher and classmates. My classmates were impressed although Miss Hickey eyed me with suspicion asking me to produce it for show and tell.

'Mr Zander and Aunty Jean said that as it was such a special letter they would keep it in the office' I said. 'I'll ask them this afternoon if I can bring it tomorrow.'

'That would be nice, dear,' she said.

I raced home after school and headed to the office. Mr Zander was sitting at his desk fiddling with some papers. I explained about my promise to bring the letter to class the next day.

'I'm sorry, Helena, you've been told how special that letter is,' he said. 'It's not to leave this office.'

'But they won't believe me if I don't take it to school tomorrow,' I pleaded.

'It's safer here,' he said.

So that was that. After explaining why I couldn't produce the letter to Miss Hickey and the class, she replied, 'That's nice, dear.'

I couldn't believe it several weeks later when the school principal announced that Queen Elizabeth II would be visiting Australia the following year to meet all the schoolchildren of Brisbane. The classroom filled with chatter, and my heart skipped a beat. She was coming to Brisbane! And, I assumed, to my classroom. What an honour it would be to stand before her to recite poetry as I had with the principal. He often marked me ten out of ten. When she entered the room, I'd introduce her to Miss Hickey and the whole class! They'd have to believe she was my aunty then!

One day Aunty Em handed me two small leather cases. Both were semicircle in shape and fastened with a zip. The smaller one was grey and the larger one red.

'They were your mother's,' she said.

The larger one contained a sewing kit with a variety of coloured cotton reels, a thimble and various sized sewing needles neatly placed in holders. The smaller case was a manicure set.

'Where did they come from?'

'The bus shed was cleaned out and Aunty Jean thought you might like to keep them,' she said.

'But where are all our other things from Inala?' I asked.

'I'm sorry, Helena, Aunty Jean said it was all junk and taken to the rubbish dump.'

With much angst I thought about my Swiss doll sent from

Uncle Lajos. I thought about my books and my crayons lying in a pile of rubbish. If only I was asked to assist the cleaning up team I would have explained our possessions weren't junk at all. They were precious memories. And now all I had was my mother's manicure set and sewing kit. At the time I would have preferred my toys. I grew up to regret that my mother's possessions weren't kept safely in the office with the letter from the Queen. During that naïve and pre-pubescent period of my childhood I wasn't aware of their importance. I fear I may have swapped them during one of our regular swap meets. I dread to think what I received in exchange.

By this stage I'd progressed down the hallway to the final bedroom in the dormitory to share with Brenda. This was the final stage before the major transition to the Grey Cottage with Aunty Jean, Mr Zander, and their daughter Roslyn. Vacant beds were always filled as kids transferred from bed to bed and room to room. We christened each other with nicknames that sometimes persisted into adulthood. There were the twins, Twinkle Toes and Cannon Ball, Strawberry, Neddy Coyote, Slops, Monkey, Wallace B Shepherd and Juberella. Two sisters whose surname was Liddlelow, were called Big O and Little O but somehow was changed to Big Toad and Little Toad. My sister was Frilly Lizzy or Lizard and I was known as Hyena, hopefully due to the similarity of my name, but then later 'Funny' and 'Ox'.

We continued to tell each other our stories. Many a night, in the confines of our bedroom, we talked about family life before Silky Oaks. Some tragic, some filled with horror and a few happy memories. Those who couldn't remember their past invented one. When I discovered another girl was from Inala, we made up a story that we lived in the same street and played together in the park. We grasped onto anything that might connect us to the outside world, outside our present existence. We couldn't afford for our memories to disappear into darkness. They were already fading. We consoled, counselled and cuddled each other, sharing stories, including one of sexual abuse by a father whose daughters had to appear in court to testify against him. Stories of sexual exploits with older brothers and their mates on ironing boards and in other odd places left innocent little girls with eyes opened wide and mouths agape. Many had alcoholic or drug-addicted parents. And there were those kids whose parents didn't have room for them in their home or didn't want them at all. Destiny brought us together and united we would protect each other from further abuse.

I had a mother who died from cancer. I had a father who was mental and abandoned me to live with communists in that place over there. At least, this is what they told me. I was turning eleven soon and growing up.

Within the confines of the dormitory there were plenty of arguments between the girls. The first and only real fight Brenda and I had with Roslyn left her devastated. We didn't particularly care until Aunty Em was ordered to separate us as we made a nasty team. I packed my belongings and moved across the hallway. The demotion to share with Deborah, and Kim's little sister Michelle was humiliating at first due to the age difference. However, it did have its advantages with the two girls alternating each evening with one singing me to sleep while the other gently caressed my back! I was pampered like royalty in exile on one side while my blood sister and best friend pined for me on the other side. We were determined we wouldn't let a damn hallway come between us.

The following weekend, members from a sister Brethren church held a Sunday school picnic within the grounds of our home. We were instructed to be on our best behaviour and to mix with the children during the activities. Brenda and I, still fuming over our forced separation, were determined not to co-operate. So, we ganged up with Jenny, a teenager who was ostracised from almost everyone due to her lack of personal hygiene. She was the youngest of three siblings and lagged behind her peers emotionally and academically. She slept in her own small bedroom in the Big End as she wasn't welcome in the Grey Cottage.

After carefully checking behind us, we exited through the school gate and headed down the hill. Daringly, we stepped outside the confines of the school grounds and turned right towards a new housing subdivision. Much of the dense scrub had been cleared, and a handful of homes were mid-construction. At the end of the fresh bitumen road we sat on a log and grumbled about everything. After a while we needed to pee so we crouched down beside a shrub, baring our backsides to the world. We giggled at what Aunty Jean's reaction might be if she'd caught us in the act! When we got back, the picnic was over and no one had even noticed we weren't there.

Soon after, our old neighbour Mrs Scott, who owned the fish and chip shop next door in Inala, visited us for Bessie's eighth birthday. She was a loyal family support, encouraging my brothers to write letters to our father, which she forwarded to 'that place over there'. That day, she delivered a gift for Bessie that she'd bought on behalf of our father. It was mid-year and a peculiar feeling came over me. I couldn't put my finger on it, but something wonderful was about to happen.

On 21 July, children who lived near the school were permitted to go home. We were to witness Apollo 11's lunar module 'Eagle' land on the moon at the Sea of Tranquility. Astronaut Neil Armstrong was about to become the first man to set foot on the moon. I would have preferred to play a few games of red rover, but we were made to watch the live telecast. Yet, as the Eagle touched down on the moon's surface, and Neil Armstrong climbed down the ladder, I became instantly completely enthralled.

In the following days at school, we discussed the new space age. Miss Hickey said that by the year 2000 we might be flying around in spaceships rather than driving cars. She told us to imagine we were in the year 2000. One of my favourite afternoon cartoons was *The Jetsons*. Judy, the teenage daughter, had long blonde hair and I saw myself as her, with my hair blowing in the wind while manoeuvring a small spacecraft from building to building. Placing a small package into a machine and pressing a button would produce an instant meal. I'd have a robot maid called Rosie, who would attend to my chores before and after school and on weekends. Yes, I thought, I would enjoy this new space age.

'Have you thought about how old you will be in the year 2000?' Miss Hickey asked.

I grabbed my pen and paper and did the calculations. Unlike the youthful Judy Jetson, I would be forty-two! I'd probably be a wrinkly wheelchair-bound grandmother!

'That's right, class, most of you will be forty-two.'

What lay ahead for me at forty-two? Would fate continue to pound on my door? Was I destined for something positive? Was I destined for something memorable?

And was the moon landing the *something wonderful* that I'd felt was about to happen?

Liz

I remember when man walked on the moon and looking up on a bright full moon and wondering why I couldn't see the men walking on the moon as it was so bright and I was sure I would be able to see a silhouette of them walking around.

Ferenc Jnr, Laszlo, Ilona, Ferenc Snr, Lajos & Zoli – Budapest circa 1927

Nagymama Ilona & Nagypapa Ferenc – Budapest 1944

Uncle Lajos & Aunty Loty – Switzerland circa late 1960's

Uncle Lajos, Nagymama Ilona & Uncle Laszlo – Budapest circa early 1970's

Uncle Lajos, Nagymama Ilona & Uncle Laszlo in Nagymama's garden mid 1970's

Laszlo and Zoli – Budapest circa 1947

Zoli the Lieutenant – WWII

Laszlo, Ilona, Eva, Lajos – Budapest 1949

Young Ilona

Nagymama Ilona – aged in her 80's

Zoli, Laszlo, Ferenc, Lajos – 1940

Right: Zoli – Tasmania 1952

Jean with Zoli's Hungarian friends (Stephen Hassman on right) in Hobart, Tasmania 1952

Paul & Chris – potty training
Tasmania 1958

Chris, Paul & Jean Tasmania 1958

Left: Chris, Helena, Jean, Zoli & Paul – Living in a tent in Lindum 1958

Jean, Chris, Paul & Zoli - Hobart Tasmania – 1958

Zoli, Chris, Paul – Tasmania 1958

Family in Inala – 1962

Family in Inala – 1961

Chris, Paul, Bessie (Liz), Helena on Ferry - Brisbane 1963

Helena, Jean, Chris, Paul, Liz – Brisbane September 1962

Family – Brisbane 1962

Left: Chris, Jean, Helena, Paul - Inala September 1962

Right: Helena holding Bessie (Liz) 1962

3 in a tub Hemmant 1961

Aunty Alice's girls – Helena back left, Liz front row 2nd from left – early 1960's

Helena – Hemmant 1961

Helena, Paul, Chris – Hemmant 1961

Left: Liz, Helena, Chris, Paul – Silky Oaks mid 1960's

Back stairs to Main Building at Silky Oaks leading to kitchen and dining (girl's dormitory upstairs)

Left: Boy's dormitory.

Brenda, Peter & Kenny Marshall – mid 1960's

Paul, Liz, Helena & Chris – late 1960's

Helena on left on see-saw in backyard late 1960's

Above: Liz, Kerry, Debbie, Kim & Michelle – circa 1965

Right: Liz on right sharing her guinea pigs – late 1960's

Liz & Helena – circa 1966

Setting tram on concrete blocks – late 1960's

Old building on right – new building on left with girl's dormitory upstairs and living & dining downstairs

Silky Oaks family photo – mid 1960's. Chris, Paul – 3rd & 4th in 3rd row from front standing, Liz front row 4th from right, Helena 3rd row standing, 2nd from right.

Left: Aunty Alice waving off kids to Sunday School in our brown bus – 1960's

Right: Paul (on right) 1966

Left: Stowaways back with family 1958

Bottom Left: Happy New Year Story – 1960

Bottom Right: Stow away at 4 – 1958

Left: German translation – Bureaucracy makes 4 children orphans – 1969

Right: Tragic Bid for Family – 1969

Brenda & Helena – Grey Cottage Silky Oaks 1973

Ban family tram – circa 1972

Offla and family at tram – 1972

Paul, Helena, Chris & Offla – tram 1971

Brenda, Ann, Helena & Petra – Grey Cottage 1971

Grey Cottage – dining table – Chris on left, Paul 2nd on right, Kenny 1st on right

Grey Cottage – rear view

Grey Cottage – front view

Helena & Liz – 1971

Helena & Paul – 1970

Jean & Max Alexander – Silky Oaks superintendents

Helena, Offla, Liz near mulberry trees – 1971

Paul, Liz & Helena - 1973

Right: Offla walks Helena down the aisle – 6th November 1976

Helen & Paul with Lauren as baby 1980

Offla's clothes in readiness for when he gets out of bed

Loty, Liz & Lajos in Switzerland 1983

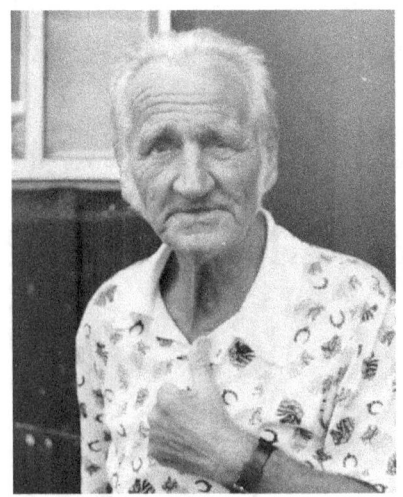

Left: Offla

Offla on bike in Cairns – 1983

Family Christmas get together 1986 – Brisbane

Family get together 1988 – Brisbane

Family get together 1993 – Brisbane

Happy 74th birthday Grandpa!

Happy 80th Birthday Offla – 1997

Happy 82nd Birthday Offla – 1999

Happy 88th birthday Grandpa!

Son-in-laws Ray & Ed with Offla on his 88th birthday

Chris, Offla, Liz, Helena & Paul – Brisbane 1988

Chris, Helena, Offla, Liz & Paul – Brisbane early 1990's

Helena's family moved to Papua New Guinea 1993

Chris, Offla & Paul – 1995

Left: Helena's 40th birthday 1998 (aka Sandy & Danny from movie Grease)

Below: Helena's 40th birthday Grease theme. 21 years later Paul's 1st grandchild would be part of ONJ's family!

Liz & family in Budapest January 1998

Helena, Offla & Liz poolside Sunshine Coast 2000

Laszlo & Paul in Budapest – 2001

Lauren with Grandpa Offla

Offla with Austin

A proud grandfather at Melissa's wedding

Right: Catching lizards with Callum

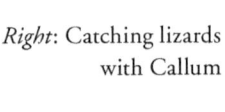

A proud grandfather with Ryan

Offla with grandkids

Offla with grandkids Christmas

Above: Sunshine Coast – Liz pregnant with Austin

Left: Offla loved the beach

Below: Offla setting the Richard Burton hairstyle trend

Left: Laszlo, Liz & Laszlo Jnr - Budapest 1983

Right: Laszlo visited Zoli in Brisbane 2001

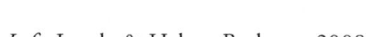

Left: Laszlo & Helena Budapest 2008

Right: Laszlo & Helena Budapest 2013

Liz, Austin, Ed & Jazzy Egypt 2007

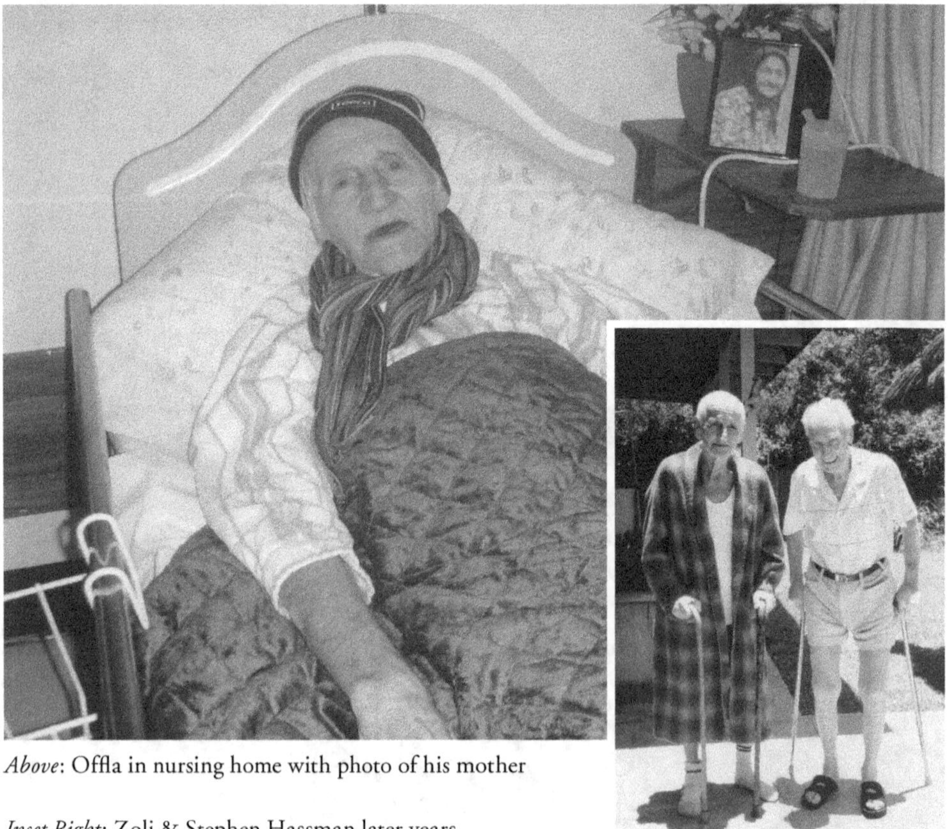

Above: Offla in nursing home with photo of his mother

Inset Right: Zoli & Stephen Hassman later years

4 delicate parcels – 6th September 2010

8 grandchildren (Ryan deployed) & 4 great grandchildren at the Wake 6th September 2010

At the Wake 6th September 2010

Boys with Aunty Rene Abraham in nursing home

Helena & Liz with Aunty Jean in nursing home

Helena and Lesley Fleming

Paul & Lauren - Marathon du Medoc, France 2014

Paul & Lauren – The Colour Run, Melbourne 2015

Helena & Liz supporting Paul after stem cell transplant 2016

Above: Liz & family skiing in Italy 2016

Left: Peter, Chris, Paul, Helena, Kenny & Liz

Below: Chris, Peter, Helena, Kenny & Paul

Left: Paul with grandson Leo 2019

Right: Helen & Paul in Budapest – 2019

Left: Laszlo & Paul – Budapest 2019

Jazz, Liz, Ed & Austin, April 2018 1 month before Ed's diagnosis

Callum, Helena, Ray, Dane & Ryan – Christmas 2019

Part 4

The return

1969 and on

Liz

I was eight years old when my father finally returned. He'd sent a couple of postcards from Hungary, but apart from that he was absent for four years. I was unaware at the time that he'd gone to bring his mother to Australia to look after us. I did not know he was imprisoned in Budapest for trying to escape with his mother. I knew I had relatives in Europe, wherever that was, as my Uncle Lajos and Aunty Loty would send us toys on special occasions.

I was playing tunnel ball on the front oval at school and one of the home kids told me I had to go home as my father was waiting to see me. I ran all the way next door with a mixture of excitement and curiosity about him. There was an old man with grey hair, holding an airways bag, waiting in the children's lounge room. Paul and Chris were already there and Helena arrived just after me. My father greeted me by looking for something on my neck and at my toes. I wondered what he was doing and then he smiled and kissed me on both cheeks.

'Why are you looking at my toes and neck?' I asked my father.

He replied in his thick European accent, 'I'm checking to see if you have a birthmark on your neck and for webbed toes.'

I thought that was funny and giggled. He did the same to Helena and I guessed he must have done the same to the boys before

I arrived. This was his way of identifying if I was indeed his child, since he hadn't seen me for more than four years. I thought that was weird, but I was so excited to see him that I overlooked the strange things he said and did. He had food, lollies and presents in his bag, and we sat around talking until Mr Zander asked him to leave.

My father came daily after the initial visit until Mr Zander told him he could visit only once a month on visiting day. I cried when Mr Zander spoke rudely to my father. I didn't understand why he wouldn't bend the rules as I had waited so long to see him and his daily visits were something I looked forward to after school, especially the presents and lollies he brought for me.

One day, Mr Zander called the police in to remove my father from the premises as he was trespassing, having been told he could only come once a month. I didn't know what the word 'trespassing' meant, but I could tell it was bad. Why else would the police come?

Helena and I cried as our father was taken away.

Paul

I was fourteen when my father unexpectedly returned from Europe.

I was in Year 10, daydreaming (probably about football) and looking out the window of the classroom when I saw a man in the grounds who looked a lot like my father. I couldn't be sure as I hadn't seen him in four years, but his features were familiar, and he was carrying an airways bag slung over his shoulder. It was the airways bag that threw me – my father's trademark accessory. But then I thought, My father's in Europe; that couldn't be him.

The sighting troubled me until lunchtime, when someone came up to me and said, 'Ban, there's a guy at the school gate who says he's your father.' Chris had obviously received the same message and together we arrived at the gate to find our father waiting for us. Not surprisingly after so long apart it was an emotional but awkward reunion with him kissing us on both cheeks Hungarian-style. With a group of teenage schoolboys standing nearby to observe this uncomfortable exchange between two sheepish adolescents and a middle-aged man with a heavy accent, it's fair to say we were more than a little self-conscious. We went to sit under a tree by the oval outside the school. Thinking that we could not have been properly fed in the four years since he'd last seen us, my father had brought with him a cooked chicken, tomatoes, salami, bread rolls, cheese, apple pie and drinks, and proceeded to make us eat.

What do you talk about in a situation like this? How was your day? Or rather, how were your last four years?! In any event, normal conversation wasn't my father's style. He quickly began what became a lifelong campaign of warning us that our minds were being controlled by 'air pushers', and instructing us to be on the alert for 'electrical interference' with our thoughts. Memories of life with him after our mother died – when he told me the police commissioner was responsible for her death – came flooding back. But being older now, I was less confused by his stories, and I knew for certain that what he was saying wasn't true.

After the first of many bizarre conversations centring on his conspiracy theories, over enormous European-style lunches, I had to readjust my whole sense of self. I had become a home kid with an established place in the large extended Silky Oaks family. My emotional connection to adults was to the Abrahams, who had given me the love and boundaries I'd been wanting when I arrived at Silky Oaks, and had allowed me to engage with them at my own pace without expecting me to regard them as parents. Now it came back to me that I was the oldest child in the Ban family, with a Hungarian father who had mental health problems. And it suddenly hit me that although he had been away for a big portion of my life, he loved us and wanted to see us and be a part of our lives.

It was difficult to piece together exactly where my father had been during his four years in Europe, and what he had done in that time. This was not the era of emails or Facebook; we'd had no regular updates about his life on the other side of the world (not that my father would have trusted social media – I'm sure it would have only fuelled his conspiracy theories about corporate surveillance).

But his stories suggested he'd been engaged in constant battles with authorities while he was away, tirelessly working to have us returned to him or sent to live with his Hungarian family. It seemed that after four years, he had run out of avenues to pursue, and decided it was time to come back to us – as a stowaway on an aeroplane!

Helena

Two weeks after the moon landing, I was at netball practice after school, when Kim came racing through the gate from Silky Oaks and made her way to the court.

'Helena,' she screamed, 'your father is in the lounge room!'

I was annoyed at the interruption. 'Yeah, sure, Kim.'

'It's true!' she said. 'He's in there with Paul and Chris and Lizzy!'

There was no reason to believe her. After all, it had been four years since I'd seen him. I continued playing, but stopped after a couple of minutes. 'Do you cross your heart and hope to die?'

'Cross my heart and hope to die,' she said, making the sign of the cross over her heart.

'Miss, I have to leave early,' I told the sports teacher.

As I walked through the gate I decided I was going to kill Kim if she'd lied. But near the entrance to the lounge room, I heard a familiar voice. Could it really be him? Had my dream come true?

In the lounge, he was holding a picture postcard of an airplane and flying it around the room making engine noises. My brothers were amused as they watched the pleasure and fascination on my sister's face. It was him. This was no dream. I ran into his arms and he kissed me on both cheeks before holding me at arm's length.

I'll never forget his first words. 'Let me check you are not an imposter.'

He checked my body for identifying features. The few moles on my neck; the scars on my right hand from the dog fight on the footpath; the one on my forehead from when I fell down the back stairs – these were almost the proof he needed. But it wasn't until he inspected my second and third toes that he hugged and kissed me again, accepting that I was his third-born child and firstborn daughter. We had all inherited webbed toes.

'He's already checked us,' Lizzy assured me. He called her Bessie and it seemed normal for us to revert to that name.

'How many languages do you speak?' he asked.

The boys piped up that they were learning German at school.

'You should be speaking half a dozen languages by now!' he said. 'How many musical instruments can you play?'

'I play the fife in the school band,' I said proudly.

'I play the drums in the school cadets,' Paul said.

'Can any of you play the piano or the violin?' he asked.

'No.'

'Then you must all be physically and mentally handicapped!'

There was a donated piano and organ in the lounge room, but playing it would have landed any kid on the mat. Aunty Jean and visiting members from the church played them occasionally while Roslyn had weekly lessons on the piano.

'What about Jesus Christ?' he asked. 'I'm sure you know a lot about Him?'

He picked up a Bible from the nearby bookcase and opened it. 'I have read this book from beginning to end.'

I was impressed. I had memorised the names of the sixty-six books of the Bible and in recognition received a badge from the

Girls Rally Club. To read the entire Old and New Testaments was a daunting prospect. He continued to amaze me.

'Did you know that I am a prophet sent by Jesus Christ?' he asked.

'I thought a prophet was someone like Moses or Abraham from the Bible,' I said. 'You would have to be more than one hundred years old if you came from the Bible!'

'That's right. I'm a 400-year-old prophet!'

I wasn't sure whether to be impressed or suspicious. Nevertheless, I found it somewhat uncomfortable to call him Daddy after that!

The dinner bell rang and Aunty Jean popped into the lounge room. 'It's time for the children's dinner, Mr Ban.'

'I'll wait here until they are finished,' he said.

'I'm afraid that's not possible,' she said. 'You will have to leave now.'

'Then I will come again tomorrow afternoon,' he said.

'No, Mr Ban, visiting day is the first Saturday of every month, between the hours of two and four. You are welcome to visit then.'

He kissed us before we headed off to the dining room. I had a niggling feeling he might not abide by the rules. And when he returned the next day, my emotions were mixed. I was happy to see him, yet concerned he was breaking the rules.

It had been four years since I'd had any physical contact with him and I had a yearning to sit on his lap. He was talking to the boys when I eased my arm around his neck and slithered ever so discreetly on to his lap.

'Hop off, love, you'll crush my trousers,' he said as he gently pushed me away.

His words hurt. Yesterday had been so overwhelming. I'd had only twenty-four hours to process it. What I craved was what any little girl craved – to sit on her daddy's lap. His trousers didn't appear ironed and his clothes needed a good wash.

He'd brought along a box of food, including chocolates and sweets. He also brought two guinea pigs and a cage which we placed on the lush green grass beside Donny the draft horse. Donny was far too old for anyone to ride and was donated as a pet to see out his final days. He loved the shade of the mulberry trees during the heat of the day and at night sheltered near the chook pens. It was comforting for many kids to stroke Donny while eating mulberries. He was a great listener and successful therapist. Unfortunately, wild dogs roamed the vacant land mass behind the home and the guinea pigs and their offspring were regularly killed. Eventually, even our dad couldn't bear the stress of losing any more and stopped bringing them.

'Are you sure you are all right?' he asked. 'Does anyone hurt you here?'

We assured him we were fine. He checked us for bruising or markings caused by a stick. I thought it best not to mention wire coat hangers, the leather strap or cakes of soap being forced into my mouth.

The bell rang for dinner and Mr Zander entered the lounge room. 'Mr Ban, my wife told you yesterday that you weren't allowed to visit the children today.'

'But visiting day is almost four weeks away.'

'I'm sorry, but all the other visitors have to wait until next month. We have rules here, Mr Ban, and we can't have you breaking them.'

'We'll see about that, Mr Alexander.'

He next came on Saturday. We were about to head off to the SGIO Theatre to see a puppet performance. I raced to greet him as he walked up the long driveway, under the oaks and dates palms.

Mr Zander was told of his arrival and made a phone call before approaching us. 'I told you previously, Mr Ban, you are not allowed to visit the children outside the set visiting hours.'

'I'll visit my children any time I want to, Alexander,' Zoli said.

'That's Mister to you,' Mr Zander snapped back.

'Well, M-i-s-t-e-r Alexander, my home is wherever my children are.'

I was visibly upset by this stage and more so when the police car arrived. Mr Zander spoke to the policemen, while occasionally glancing at my father.

The officers walked over. 'I'm sorry, sir. We have to ask you to leave these premises. You're trespassing.'

Before things got out of hand, Mr Zander ordered us to our rooms. I raced to my building, flew up the stairs and down the hallway. My window had a vantage point of the situation. My breathlessness slowly dissipated as I witnessed the despair and helplessness of my father trying in vain to be understood. I despised what I was seeing. The police were forcing my father into the car, the car was turning, and then it was gone. Tears were streaming down my face and anger was building within me. I'd never felt such a great and evil sensation before. If this deep anger within me was communism, then a communist I had become!

On Sunday, 10 August 1969, the headline of the *Sunday Truth* was 'Tragic Bid For Family', accompanied by a large photo of our father and a smaller one of us four children. The caption below our photo said 'The four motherless children – Paul, Christopher, Elena (spelt incorrectly) and Elizabeth'. The story began on the front page and continued on page nine. 'For six years the youngsters have lived in a Queensland children's institution.' It covered the period after our mother died and our being taken from our father to live in a

State home. It explained how Zoli stowed away on a ship sailing for Europe to bring his mother back to Australia to help him look after his children. The final two paragraphs were quoted by my father:

> I would not mind going anywhere – Budapest, Zurich, Brisbane – as long as we are together again. All I want is to have my family back. Surely that is not too much to ask?

Newspapers were not available for us kids to read and the first I heard about it was at school the next day. The only time it was mentioned at the home was when Aunty Jean reminded me a few days later that Silky Oaks was run by the Christian Brethren as a haven for children. After reading the story and my father's plea for his children, she said, 'How dare your father call Silky Oaks an institution?'

How Zoli came back

In Hungary, Zoli had done everything he could think to do, and nothing had worked. In 1969, he made his way to Switzerland, feeling his only option was to convince his brother Lajos and Lajos's wife, Loty, to return with him to Australia.

By the time he arrived in the capital city of Bern he was penniless, sleeping in forests and parks and collecting empty bottles in exchange for cash. The distance between Bern and Basel, the town where Lajos lived, was forty-five miles, so he called his brother. His sister-in-law answered. He should have written in advance that he was coming, Loty said, so she was prepared. Little did she know how ill Zoli was – at that stage he wasn't sure if he was alive or dead. Anguish over his struggle to regain custody of his children had left him disorientated and suspicious of everyone he came in contact with.

In Bern, Lajos told Zoli that everything had changed. He had applied for Swiss citizenship. He wouldn't uproot his life. Zoli was furious, knowing if his new plan for Lajos and Loty to migrate to Australia failed, custody of his children would be delayed further.

It seemed it never entered his mind that he might never regain custody of the children. And now – in his illness – he felt betrayed by the brother he had loved and nurtured as a youngster.

The brother he relied upon to save his life, a life rapidly spiralling downwards. So he did the only thing he could think to do. He would make his brother's life so unbearable he would have to change his mind. He threatened and harassed Lajos at his workplace. He demanded his brother's employer grant Lajos leave for Australia immediately. He warned his brother that should the Australian authorities not grant him custody of his children he would remain in Switzerland. He would then more than likely be admitted to a mental hospital and Lajos would have to pay the costs for the rest of his life.

Finally, he sent a postcard to the President of Switzerland, Ludwig von Moos, suggesting von Moos be the one cared for in a psychiatric institution. An article about it appeared in the newspapers. His relationship with his brother swiftly ended.

The International Social Services interviewed Zoli, finding him disoriented. The ISS thought the Swiss authorities would try to have Zoli admitted to a psychiatric institution. They felt it would not be humane to force his return to Hungary in his present state, nor would immigration to Australia be appropriate. The information was forwarded to the Department of Immigration and to Mr Zander and Aunty Jean. A translation of the interview was sent to Charles Clark, director of the State Children Department.

Zoli made one final plea for help. A photograph of the family, including his wife Jean was splashed across the front page of a newspaper, detailing his plight for custody. The headline: 'Drama of a Refugee Family'. Zoli was quoted: 'An Australian, who visits a Country behind the Iron Curtain, loses his nationality'. The translated article ended: 'How long will the four children be waiting in the Orphanage of Manly – where the authorities have placed them? How long will they cry when is our daddy coming home?'

After Zoli had again spent an ice-cold night in the forest, the Bern police picked him up. In the Hospitz sur Heimat he was given a bed and daily meals, the cost of which was paid by a charity.

Zoli bought a cardboard replica of a cigar from a tobacconist. At the post office he wrote a brief note and slipped it inside a parcel addressed to the governor-general of Queensland.

> I do not hold any grudge towards you for not assisting me in my request for a passport or a visa. To prove this I am enclosing this cigar as a token of my sincerity. I suggest that you light it immediately. By the time you enjoy your last puff – I will already be in Australia.

Some of his post-war friends offered financial assistance. The Swiss Government issued him an Identity Card enabling him to obtain a tourist visa for Ceylon (now Sri Lanka). Not surprisingly, Lajos was more than willing to pay for a one-way ticket to Colombo, Ceylon, but not on to Australia. With the flight delayed for several hours in London before its first stop in Zurich, frustrated passengers from various flights were added to the flight, and many were not issued with a boarding pass.

When the plane landed in Colombo, passengers transiting through to Perth, Western Australia, remained seated. Once the plane was refuelled, Zoli paced up and down the aisle while new passengers boarded and settled into their allocated seats. He observed the fresh flight crew and just before take-off chose an empty row. He had no ticket or visa for Australia. The flight was uneventful.

The plane landed in Perth on Monday 4 August 1969. As is the norm, international passengers were required to disembark for customs clearance but Zoli was having none of it. He remained firmly in his seat awaiting the next destination, Sydney. From Sydney he planned to travel by bus or train to Brisbane. It was paramount he remained on the flight.

'Excuse me, sir, you will have to disembark here,' a hostess said.

'I am going on to Sydney,' he said.

'That's fine, sir, but you are required to clear customs first. You can then re-board the plane.'

'I don't want to leave the plane,' he said, now agitated. 'I want to go to Sydney.'

'May I see your ticket and passport, sir?'

He carefully went through his plan and explained the confusion in Zurich with delayed flights and boarding passes not being issued. His ticket and passport must have been misplaced by airline staff during the ordeal.

Customs was notified and a telex sent to the Department of Immigration in Canberra. They were well aware of the passenger, albeit surprised at his arrival. However, they not only allowed his entry into Australia but allowed him to continue on to Sydney.

As the plane slowly made its way to the terminal in Sydney, Zoli realised how close he was to being reunited with his children. It was one month shy of four years since his departure from Australia to bring the children's nagymama to Queensland. The plane came to a halt and the steps lowered for passengers to disembark. Zoli wasn't prepared to risk 'escorts' awaiting his arrival so he grabbed his airways bag from the overhead locker and hastily made his way to the exit. A recently landed plane parked parallel was all he needed as camouflage. He crouched behind its baggage trolley as it headed towards the terminal. Then he raced to the nearby fence and scrambled over it. He spent that night at the St Vincent de Paul shelter for the homeless, where he retired to bed after sharing his story over a meal with a bedraggled man. Before he managed to close both eyes a group of men approached him. Eyeing them suspiciously he grabbed his airways bag. Unbeknown to him, his dinner companion had shared his story around the shelter and those who could manage it scraped a few dollars together to assist his passage to Brisbane. They handed him the money and shuffled off to bed.

By morning the police had suspected where he may have spent the evening and arrived just as he was preparing to leave. They escorted him to the Rosebery Mental Hospital near Woolloomooloo. By the day's end he had escaped by climbing the fence. He hitchhiked to Newcastle, a good two-hour drive north of Sydney. From there he caught a train to Brisbane. He was determined that no person, no police officer nor government agent, would separate him from his children any longer.

Liz

Not long after we'd seen the police take our father away from Silky Oaks, Helena called a meeting with me and a few other girls.

'How dare they take our father away!'

She told us we needed to run away to show them how upset we were. I had been upset, but the thought of running away hadn't entered my mind. I was eight years old, I was scared, but I sure as hell wasn't going to show that to Helena or the other girls. Helena made all the plans for the 'runaway' and I listened without questioning her. I loved my sister more than anything.

On the chosen morning we packed our lunches into our school ports, and lined up to collect tuckshop money from Aunty Em. She handed Helena her coin and Helena hugged her tightly and kissed her goodbye. The others followed suit.

'To what do I owe the pleasure of all these kisses this morning?' Aunty Em asked.

'No reason other than we love you,' Helena said.

I felt I was going on a big adventure with Helena and the other girls. We went into the school, and some of the girls pulled out, leaving Helena, Jenny, Kim, Christine, her little sister Vicky and me headed for the back oval. The school was set on ten acres and it was a fair distance getting to the end of the grounds. We went out the school gate, turned right and followed the road. We walked for what seemed like a long way and I was feeling a bit scared, but Helena was happily talking and telling us where to go. She looked to be in control, or so I thought. After ages, we ended up on the main road and Kim said, 'Look, there's the school and Silky Oaks up there.'

'What do you mean?' I thought we were running away and, if we were, why was the school and home within sight of where we were standing?

A few minutes later, Kim screamed, 'Shit! Mr Zander and Roslyn are driving towards us!'

I nearly wet my pants.

Helena

The only thing I could think of was to yell, 'Quick, everybody, hide behind the tree!'

The tree was, in fact, a small shrub and six young girls huddling behind it must have looked pathetic. Mr Zander's Kingswood pulled over with his deputy sheriff Roslyn beside him. He yelled at us to get in and drove the short distance home before sending us to our rooms. We'd been caught because Kim's little sister Michelle had dobbed on us when Kim wouldn't let her come.

After what seemed like an eternity, Aunty Em announced we were to be interviewed by some child welfare officers.

'When you girls spoke to me this morning, I had no idea you were planning to run away,' she said. 'I feel dreadful. I should have known.'

'It's not your fault,' I said apologetically.

Before we'd said goodbye for the day, one of the little sisters had opened her big mouth and asked Aunty Em what the punishment for running away was.

Aunty Em was pottering about and supervising our chores. 'Oh, I'm not really sure.' She hesitated before adding, 'None of you are planning anything like that, are you?'

Before anybody else opened their mouth, I jumped in, 'No! We were just wondering, that's all.'

She thought about it for a moment. 'I suppose they would have to go to the office and Mr Zander would deal with them.'

I'd been relieved. If the consequence was to face his wrath, get beaten with the strap and confined to the mat for a couple of hours then it was worth it. After all, we were familiar with that punishment.

'Enough of this silly talk now, girls. Hurry up and finish your jobs or you'll be late for school!'

I felt bad lying to Aunty Em.

We were escorted to the lounge room. So much had transpired in the three weeks since I'd walked in there to be greeted by my father. And again I hesitated at the door.

Mr Zander ordered us to sit down and introduced two men and a woman dressed in sombre suits. They were from the Children's Services Department and had come to discuss the morning's incident.

My defensive shield went up. There was no way I would allow them to break me during the inquisition.

'Hello, girls, we're here to ascertain what led you to run away this morning. If we could begin with someone telling me whose idea it was . . .'

Five fingers, including Lizzy's, pointed in my direction. It was a betrayal that connected me with Jesus that day. He was betrayed by his disciple Judas, followed by Peter three times. I had five of the buggers ready to crucify me!

All eyes were fixed on me as Mr Zander and the child welfare officers warned us that any further attempts at running away would be punished. They talked in detail about a different kind of home for girls who misbehaved: with bars on the windows, security surrounding the premises and no outings or privileges.

Somebody asked if it was like being in jail and the reply was that it was similar.

Jenny, Christine, Vicky and Kim were granted permission to leave the room and I could see the fright in my eight-year-old sister's eyes as she stayed with me.

What had I been thinking? they asked me.

'When the police took my father away—' I began.

Mr Zander interrupted me immediately to remind me that the police had only escorted him off the premises. My shield went back up and I blanked them out.

Years later, I read the incident report placed on my file:

> . . . at this point Helena became emotionally involved wanting to leave with her father feeling sorry for him and wanting to help him. Elizabeth because she loves her elder sister wanted to go with Helena. In Mr Alexander's presence we generally talked through dad's situation of not having a home, nor an income, nor a housekeeper and that it would be an added difficulty and responsibility for him to have the two girls or the whole family with him. I feel that if it does happen, it will only be intermittent-emotionalism that will turn Helena to anti-social behaviour.

We returned to our rooms for the remainder of the day.

They would have recorded my nasty communist streak, I was sure. One day, that streak would guide me to the Children's Services office, where I would demand to see Mr Clark himself. I would put into action the swear words we often said in the privacy of our room. I would demand he allow my family to go home. Somebody had to pay dearly for my anger. I didn't care about living in a home with bars on the windows. I didn't care about losing privileges. I would gain control of my peers in jail just as easily as I had in the home. After all, it was only another institution.

The next morning, during washing up duty, we all agreed that it hadn't been worth the effort to run away. But I was still angry.

When I got to class that morning, Miss Hickey said the new, interim, principal wanted to see me. His office was across the hallway. As I walked there I thought how unfair it was that I was about to get the cuts – a caning across the open palm of your hand was a common punishment. I'd been punished enough. Maybe not physically, but emotionally I was drained.

I knocked quietly. Mr Boyland hadn't met me before and was still acquainting himself with the school, teachers and students.

'Come in and sit down,' he said kindly. 'I wanted to meet you personally.'

It was odd to be sitting down to receive the cuts. It would be much easier for him if I stood up and held out my hand. But he was new and he would soon learn.

'Mr Alexander phoned to explain why you weren't at school yesterday,' he said.

'I'm sorry, Mr Boyland, for running away and not coming to school!'

'You don't have to apologise to me,' he said. 'I know you have problems. If there is anything you need or if you just need to talk to someone then I want you to know that I am here. Now, off you go back to class and remember my door will always be open for you.'

Mr Boyland was true to his word, never turning me away, and letting me empty his rubbish bin, deliver freshly picked flowers to his desk and buy his lunch at the tuck shop. I had a true ally in him, and, for the short time he was our principal, I had a friend and a confidante.

Paul

My father's return created problems for the smooth running of Silky Oaks. Parents and relatives were able to write and send presents to their children in between the official visiting days, but otherwise it was more convenient for the running of the home if parents remained in the background. As an adult, I discovered this was a widespread approach in the residential care system at the time. Once the State had become your legal guardian and found a suitable placement for you, there didn't seem to be any rush to work with the parents and extended family to see if you could return or reconnect with them.

During the time I lived at Silky Oaks, I didn't come to know the family stories of my peers or the reasons that they were brought into State care. But over the years I pieced together information based on who came to see their children on visiting day. I was pretty sure the ones who didn't have visitors weren't orphans, as the Bus and Tramways Association signage suggested. It seemed more likely that their parents were not able or willing to maintain a connection with them. After my father returned from Europe, I realised – not for the last time – that despite his limitations as a parent, I was lucky to have a father who cared so much about us.

In fact, the Ban children were soon at the extreme end of the visiting spectrum. Except for when he was an involuntary patient at the mental hospital, he didn't miss a single visiting day. My father was so eager to see us that he was initially given special dispensation to visit us outside of the official hours. But after a while, when he started to push the boundaries of this privilege, Mr Zander again called me into his office. This time, he wanted to know why my father kept coming to see us outside normal visiting hours, and why he couldn't abide by the rules like the other parents. I was fourteen at the time, and initially lost for words. All I could manage in response was, 'He's our father and he wants to see us.'

On Australian soil

Since being back, Zoli had continued fighting for custody. Charles Clark, director of the Children's Services Department, John Tarbath at Immigration, the Housing Commission, the police – all continued to play a role. Apart from Tarbath's, a thread of anxiety ran through the official records: Were the children safe? Was Mr Ban a danger to them?

He was certainly unwell. Zoli was happy he had returned to the sunshine of Australia, he told Mr Tarbath, but the social worker noted that Zoli's English appeared to have deteriorated and he seemed somewhat delusional, 'talking a diatribe of nonsense including Queen Elizabeth's relationship with his children'. He talked of fathering a child with Princess Anne, which would place him on the diplomatic list and entitle him to a house. He still wanted to bring his mother to Australia to help care for the children. There were reports of Russians living to one hundred and fifty years while Adam was supposed to have lived for nine hundred and ninety-five years, he said, when Mr Tarbath raised the problem of Zoli's mother's age. Although he was not fit enough to work full time, he felt he could earn sufficient money to support his mother. Furthermore, he maintained that after having been a victim of Nazi aggression, concentration camps and of an industrial disease in

Australia (he believed his schizophrenia was caused by working in zinc and copper oxide fumes), he had the right to be reunited with his children and it was the State's responsibility to arrange this and to maintain them.

The Housing Commission were concerned that Zoli might become violent – he had made a general threat against the staff. They contacted Mr Clark who contacted the police, requesting the Commissioner 'cause enquiries to be made to ascertain if Mr Ban's mental and physical condition is such that action should be taken to have him dealt with under the Mental Health Act.'

The girls were due to spend some holiday time away from Silky Oaks. 'When this takes place,' Clark said, 'Ban's reaction may be violent' though, in the same report he said: 'Ban had visited the day before [and] did not cause any disturbance.'

Was Zoli a danger? Or was he merely an inconvenience?

'Normally the Alexanders are fairly strict with visitors,' reported a child welfare officer, 'and insist on them adhering to visiting hours but in Mr Ban's case they felt they could relax their rules somewhat, but this has led to Mr Ban making a nuisance of himself. Mr Alexander feels he is undermining his authority. Mr Ban always starts off being polite but keeps taking increasing liberties . . . Mr Alexander said that as soon as possible he intended to write a letter to the Director pointing out the upset and inconvenience that Mr Ban has caused him and the home.'

Clark noted:

> His persistent visits are becoming an embarrassment to the home. On one occasion he had brought a guinea pig which incidentally has died – and a duck.

There were insufficient grounds to issue a warrant, the police told Charles Clark – unless Zoli threatened the staff at the Housing Commission again, which he didn't. But things that weighed against Zoli continued to mount up.

One Friday afternoon, a staff member from the Children's Services Department recognised Zoli as she passed the Government Printing Office on her way home. He was walking in the direction of the department's offices. When she arrived home, she telephoned the senior child welfare officer. He said that, in all probability, only the cleaners would be in the office and no one could ever contemplate the motives for any of Ban's actions. He said it would not be beyond Ban in a state of derangement to burn or blow up the department. The senior officer telephoned Charles Clark who rang the night watchman to advise him of the matter. The night watchman reported no sign of Mr Ban at the office. But the information was placed on a file as evidence against Zoli. Was paranoia becoming contagious?

Mrs Scott, the family's old neighbour, telephoned the department to warn them she suspected Zoli was planning to abduct the children again. He'd approached her over the weekend and asked if she could provide a room for him where he could be near the children.

'It is difficult to proceed against Mr Ban under the Mental Health Act,' the police told Clark in response to this, 'because on each occasion he was interviewed by a Police Officer or other persons he was quite rational and gave no signs of mental instability.'

It was proposed that a staff member at the Housing Commission who'd received threats from Zoli (he admitted he hadn't taken the threat personally as it was directed to officers in general) and Max Alexander (Mr Zander) appear before the clerk of the court to give testimony on an application for a warrant to have Ban examined under the Mental Health Act. Before this could happen, the girls ran away from the home, and, shortly after, the police did issue a warrant under the Mental Health Act, and Zoli was taken to Lowson House, a ward for mental patients in the Royal Brisbane Hospital.

After two weeks at Lowson House, Zoli was transferred to Wolston Park Hospital – previously the Brisbane Special Hospital – on the Brisbane River in Wacol. He wouldn't be able to see the children for some time, his doctor said, as he was 'quite mad and still suffering from delusions about the royal family'.

A couple of weeks later Zoli absconded from the hospital, visited the boys in their lunch hour at school then disappeared. A few weeks later he applied to the Supreme Court in Sydney to issue a writ against Silky Oaks to surrender his four children. (The court told him to appoint a solicitor to act on his behalf.) The United Nations for Refugees, the Member for Sydney Mr Jim Cope, the Housing Commission of New South Wales, the International Social Service and T M Nulty, director of Migration in the Immigration Department were drawn in. Zoli approached the media and an article appeared in the local newspaper.

On 19 November 1969, a Detective Young from CIB picked him up in Albion Street and admitted him on a Section 12 1(e) to Rozelle Psychiatric Centre at Callan Park Hospital, in Lilyfield, Sydney. On 4 December, Zoli was committed on a Schedule 2 under the Mental Health Act and would remain an inpatient at Callan Park for the next eight months.

Helena

It was a weekday evening late in the year when Aunty Jean told me to dress in my Sunday best. The superintendents were taking my brothers and me on an outing on a school night. Unusual. We met at the Grey Cottage with none of us any the wiser as to our destination.

'Tonight,' Aunty Jean said as we got into the Kingswood, 'we are going to the city to a missionary conference at Festival Hall.'

Not another bloody missionary conference! I didn't understand why we were the chosen ones, but then Aunty Jean said, 'Missionaries are going to speak about the persecution and atrocities committed by communists!'

At Festival Hall, we watched a long film, telling the story of a missionary who had not only been imprisoned by Chinese Communists but also tortured for attempting to preach and convert the peasants to Christianity. The graphic evidence of swords slicing into human flesh and muscle left me deeply affected and horrified. During the drive home, Aunty Jean said she hoped we understood why communists were so dreadful. I couldn't concentrate as I felt physically sick. Aunty Em thought I was coming down with something later that evening when I vomited in bed. I was eleven years old and unable to grasp any connection between these communist torturers and my father. They were violent and evil. My father was gentle and kind.

Sometime after this, a storeroom in the Big End was converted to a small bedroom and I moved into it with Elly Vogt, one of five German siblings at Silky Oaks. We were into hide and seek at the time, and the best spot to hide inside was in one of the many large wooden wardrobes. Our converted storeroom had a modern built-in wardrobe so my hiding spot was in a bedroom down the hall. One evening, Mr Brennan stomped down the hallway to find the cause of the unbearable noise we were making. He belted everyone on the backside with his hands and sent them to bed. He didn't touch me.

He shouted, 'Children should be seen and not heard!'

A couple of nights later I woke up to discover him lying beside me. When I asked what he was doing in my bed, he said, 'Aunty Em is sleeping down the other end of the dormitory looking after Aunty Alice's girls. I'm lonely.'

I rolled over and returned to my dreams. By the light of day he was gone. It never occurred to my eleven-year-old self that his actions were inappropriate. I don't remember what, if anything, happened. He was lonely. He was a strict religious man.

Where was our father? He'd come and then gone again. The boys told me he'd been to see them at school but that was ages ago, and he was missing visiting days.

Nineteen sixty-nine came to an end.

My body began to mature during my final year of primary school. I wore a 'training bra' and used deodorant. There was a brand of deodorant called 'Ban' advertised on television with a catchy jingle. One day in class I was chatting when the teacher slammed his fist on my desk and sang it: 'Ban won't wear off – as the day wears on!'

I inherited Jenny's bedroom in the Big End when she suddenly disappeared. Often, without a word of warning, we discovered a vacated bed when we returned home from school. Some kids would return with harrowing tales. Others were never to be seen or heard of again. For the first time in my life – after it was scrubbed from top to bottom – I had my own room. It may have been small but the prestige that accompanied it was tremendous.

True to my school principal's word, Her Majesty the Queen and His Royal Highness the Duke of Edinburgh came to Brisbane. The visit was part of the bicentenary of Captain James Cook sailing up the east coast of Australia in 1770. I was disappointed to learn she wasn't coming to my classroom to hear me read poetry. Nevertheless, I was thrilled I would finally see her in person. Over time, I'd come to accept she wasn't my real aunty or my sister's godmother. Yet a glimmer of hope lingered that she would eventually restore my broken family.

Where was my dad? Not a word from anyone as to his whereabouts. Was that really him in the lounge room that day? Did I run away for nothing?

Brisbane schoolchildren piled into buses to go to the Royal National Showground, where the Ekka was held. A lined route was roped off where the Queen and Prince Philip would be driven. Schools were allocated an area behind the rope. The Manly West State School and Wynnum State High School students were placed opposite each other. I waved to Brenda who was a year ahead of me in school and dressed immaculately. She wore with pride a straw hat, grey gloves, thick grey stockings and grey shirt underneath a bottle green tunic. I couldn't wait until I wore that uniform. As we settled into position I was determined to make eye contact with the Queen. I ensured my vantage point was front and centre.

An almighty cheer sounded as her vehicle arrived at the entrance to the showground. The Queen and her Prince were standing at the rear of the vehicle enabling their loyal subjects to view them clearly. I waited patiently as the screaming and cheering grew louder. The vehicle turned down my path. It would only be a matter of time before we came face to face.

My mother was British and a staunch royalist. She often stood outside the gates of Buckingham Palace to catch a glimpse of the Queen or members of the royal family.

It would only be a matter of seconds. There was so much I needed to say to her. So much I wanted to say.

The noise was now deafening and I looked up to see the most beautiful and immaculately groomed woman I had ever seen. She wore a simple dress with matching handbag, shoes and hat. Prince Philip was tall and handsome. He smiled and waved and I thanked God he didn't block my view of the Queen. I screamed at the top of my lungs, 'Queen Elizabeth! Queen Elizabeth!' Time stood still for a moment as she looked directly into my eyes. My heart melted with love and adoration. There was no need for words. We'd made eye contact. The special bond connecting us would never be broken.

Later that afternoon, Prince Philip and his entourage drove past Silky Oaks on his way to the Manly Yacht Club. We lined the footpath in front of the sign 'Silky Oaks Children's Haven'. I wasn't an orphan, a spastic, underprivileged or a communist that day but a loyal subject of our Monarch . . . and maybe a distant relative. The Prince waved as he passed by and again on his return. I wondered if he was aware of what this Haven was. I wondered had the Queen accompanied her husband that afternoon would she have stopped to speak to me?

Not long after the royal visit, I was introduced to my own sexuality. I wonder what Mr Brennan's reaction would have been if he discovered it was due to his youngest son. Jeff was a bricklayer, good-looking, a chain-smoker and rebellious. I thought he was wonderful! I met him at the rendezvous point, the entrance to the family unit down the hallway. He handed me the plastic bag which I hastily snuck into the privacy of my bedroom. The bag contained several magazines of naked women. I couldn't recall seeing my mother naked. Nor had I seen any of the female workers naked. I'd witnessed Aunty Alice in her underwear and petticoat while frantically organising her charges in the morning. I flipped the pages amazed at the various shapes and sizes of breasts. I eyed my own developing body in the mirror and knew I had a long way to go. But I was maturing physically and knew I was on the verge of becoming a woman.

One school morning I woke up with severe cramps in my stomach and told Aunty Em I couldn't go to school. She sent me off to Aunty Jean. The workers didn't have the power to decide whether you were sick enough to stay home from school. No matter how ill you were, you had to walk down two flights of stairs, out the back door of the building, the hundred yards or so to the Grey Cottage, where you had to politely knock on the door and wait to be addressed by Aunty Jean. Most of us had attempted a sickie from school and were quickly cut down with a stern warning about telling fibs.

I dragged myself out of bed, wrapped my dressing gown around by aching body and went down the hallway. Some of the girls were panicking as they had fallen asleep after Bible reading and prayer and still had chores to complete before breakfast.

'How come you aren't dressed?' Michelle asked.

'I'm feeling sick and I have to tell Aunty Jean.'

'Helena Ban, you just want to get out of going to school!'

Aunty Jean was in the kitchen at the Grey Cottage with the teenage girls living there at the time. They were cleaning up after breakfast. Patricia noticed me in my dressing gown. 'Aunty Jean, looks like there's a sickie at the door!'

Aunty Jean came to the screen door. 'What's the problem?'

'I'm not sure but I have these bad pains in my stomach.'

She thought about it for a moment. 'How old are you now?'

'Almost twelve.'

'Have you got your periods yet?'

'No.'

I didn't understand what having your periods really meant. I knew that some of the older girls at school had them. I knew that Jenny had them when she was sleeping in the room on her own.

She then announced to everyone in the kitchen: 'I think Helena is growing up and is about to get her first period! What do you think, girls?'

A short discussion ensued behind the screen door as to what age each girl was when she started. I waited for the discussion to end and permission to be granted.

'You can go back to bed for the day but I wouldn't be surprised if that's what it is.'

The following morning the cramps were worse and I felt moisture between my legs. I hoped I hadn't become one of the wet bed kids so I raced down the hallway to the toilet. There, I was frightened to discover blood rather than urine. Thoughts began to swirl around my head. Was I dying? Is this what had happened to my mother? Did I have cancer?

I was interrupted by a loud thump on the toilet door. 'Hurry up, I want to do a wee!' It was Kim. 'Who's in there?'

'It's me, Helena.'

'You've been there for ages!'

'Go and get Aunty Em,' I cried. 'I'm bleeding and I think I've got cancer!'

I was put into a warm bath while Aunty Em assured me I wasn't dying. 'You have your first period, that's all. There is nothing to be frightened of. You are now a woman.'

She disappeared and returned with an elastic belt with hooks and a thick modess pad. After instructing me how to wear this odd contraption I was horrified to learn that this would continue for the next few days and recur every month!

I was relieved I hadn't inherited my mother's cancer, and I wished she was with me during this frightening experience. Nobody could replace the woman who carried me in her womb for nine months and nurtured me until the tender age of four and a half. She would have been proud of my transformation from girl to woman. I missed her terribly.

I ended the final months of primary school joining the other 'women' in the toilet block during little and big lunch breaks. Having a little sister finally had its merits. She became my mule, meeting me outside my classroom and unquestioningly carrying the brown paper bag containing my womanly needs across the quadrangle. Away from prying eyes, the package was handed over. It wasn't until she experienced her first period that the contents of the package finally clicked!

*

Miss Gibson announced our Girls Rally Club was heading to a Christian Youth camp built on the hill overlooking the caravan park at Burleigh Heads.

I wore my newly created hot pink paisley pant suit. I had struggled with it for so long in sewing class that the teacher kindly completed it for me. The flared pants were matched with a round-necked mini dress with short sleeves. This was by far the most outrageous and groovy outfit I owned to date. It wasn't appropriate for Sunday school or church. (Unlike my aqua crocheted mini dress I wore with witches britches (long-legged frilled underpants) and white fishnet stockings! Go figure? I never did get any Nancy Sinatra boots made for walking.)

We arrived at camp and were ushered into the main dining area where we were allocated huts. It was fun to choose the top of the triple bunks for sleeping. The weekend was filled with the usual Christian fellowship and outdoor activities including swimming at the beach. On Sunday morning, a brief church service was held followed by an activity of your choice. The list on the noticeboard included swimming, rollerskating, hiking or board games.

'Miss Gibson, what activity will you be doing this morning?'

'It's such a beautiful day, I think I'll go swimming at the beach.'

That was good enough for me. I changed into my togs and waited in the hall.

'What do you think you're doing?' Brenda asked.

'I'm going swimming.'

'You know Mr Zander and Aunty Jean will kill you!'

'Well, they're not here, are they?'

'Roslyn is, and she'll tell them for sure!'

'They can all go to hell. Miss Gibson is a good Christian woman and if she chooses to swim on a Sunday without fearing the wrath of God, then I can too!'

In addition to not playing physical games or bathing on a Sunday, swimming would have been the ultimate sin. We were given no reason other than it was God's holy day. The homey kids elected hiking around Burleigh Bluff and when word spread I was going swimming they warned me of the consequence. Oddly enough, Roslyn joined my group and walked to the beach, though there was no way she would defy her parents. I walked alongside my new ally, Miss Gibson.

We arrived at the gently rolling surf, the backdrop to the white sandy beach. Everyone discarded their towels and ran into the water. Roslyn remained fully clothed with her eyes on me. The Mexican stand-off began. Whatever I did, I was dead. If I chose to swim I was dead when I got home. If I chickened out I was dead in the eyes of the homey kids. So I did what was best for my survival. I discarded my towel and ran to the rolling surf. As I dived below the first wave I prayed, 'God, if you think this is a sin then strike me dead now!' I spent the rest of the morning grateful to be alive, even though I knew that my coffin was being prepared elsewhere.

That evening at home, Aunty Em said, 'By the way, Helena, Mr Zander wants to see you in his office.'

Sympathetic eyes gazed at me. It took a few minutes for me to scrape up the courage to attend my trial.

'Good luck!' the girls said as I disappeared down the hallway.

I walked past the lounge room and came face to face with Mr Zander in the hallway.

'Where have you been?' he asked. 'I've been waiting far too long!'

He grabbed me by the ear, dragged me into his office and slammed the door. It was probably too late for me to pray to Jesus for assistance – I expected a good beating with the strap and a lengthy confinement on the mat.

'I've been informed you went swimming today,' he said. 'What have you got to say for yourself?'

I almost asked who the informer was, but thought it best not to. 'Miss Gibson went swimming too.'

'I don't care who else went swimming!' he yelled. 'Sunday is the Lord's day and we do not allow anyone to swim on His day!'

I thought for a moment before replying, 'If swimming on a Sunday is a sin then Miss Gibson, who I thought was a good Christian, must be a sinner too.'

His face turned bright red and I thought he was going to explode. The leather strap remained in its place. When his anger subsided, he said, 'I will allow all of the girls who went to camp to stay home from church to rest. You will be the only one attending this evening.'

I left his office and returned to the dormitory to a hero's welcome. Not only did I not receive a beating but because of my insolence they didn't have to go to church that night!

Paul

Like many other child welfare institutions at the time, the second half of the 1960s saw Silky Oaks embrace the idea of providing children with a more family-like atmosphere than could be achieved in large-scale dormitories. For Silky Oaks, this involved building a comfortable 'suburban' home on one side of the grounds – the Grey Cottage was a few years old now.

With its modernist design, the cottage always seemed futuristic to me. It consisted of two main sections. The first contained a living room, dining room and kitchen, and the second two-storey part of the building housed the bedrooms. The top floor of this part was reserved for Mr Zander and Aunty Jean and their two daughters, along with a bedroom designed to accommodate three teenage girls. On the ground floor was a bedroom for three teenage boys, a small lounge room with a TV, a laundry, a garage and a room for the Alexanders' adult son, Michael.

I moved into the Grey Cottage in 1970, when I was fifteen, with Chris who was fourteen, Kenny 'Whizzer' Marshall and his sister Brenda. Chris, Kenny and I had the downstairs bedroom to ourselves. The following year, Helena, who was about to start high school, and Petra Vogt joined Brenda in the upstairs bedroom. It was a momentous new direction in my life. I had lived with the

Abrahams since I was ten, and it was hard to leave them behind. But I knew I was ready for the cottage experience, and Aunty Rene would not be far away, so I could still drop in to have a cup of tea with her after school.

The Grey Cottage ended up being my home for the last three years of my Silky Oaks life, and over that time the inhabitants of the boys bedroom remained pretty stable. The only change happened the following year, when Chris turned fifteen and left the Oaks to begin his apprenticeship as an electrician. Following his departure, Kenny's brother Peter moved in to the cottage, continuing the Ban–Marshall family-mix.

Although Chris was also a tenant of the Grey Cottage during my first year there, he never seemed to be around much. He had recently acquired a girlfriend – the first of us boys to venture into that terrain – and we didn't see a lot of him after that. Beth's family was part of the Christian Brethren congregation, and she and Chris had met through church – our only authorised off-campus social activity. We couldn't work out why Chris was so tired in the mornings and kept falling asleep during the stories that Michael Alexander regaled us with as we got ready for school. It was only after Chris left the home that he told me he had a pushbike hidden outside our bathroom window, which he used for nocturnal trysts with his new love.

Living together with Chris and Helena and the Marshall siblings in what was essentially a suburban home helped to provide us with what was intended – a more family-like environment. They had managed, almost, to bring together two sets of siblings. But Liz, who is six and a half years younger than me, and three years younger than Helena, was considered too young to live in the Grey Cottage. And it seemed that the real purpose of the cottage was to cater for the growing independence of kids who had reached adolescence, and that this function trumped any thoughts of raising siblings together. I never did live under the same roof as Liz after that day the police collected us from the Inala Civic Centre when I was nine years old.

But living in the Grey Cottage opened up a whole new world for me. For one thing, I actually enjoyed my school lunches for the first time. For some reason, the homely atmosphere of the cottage affected the quality of the sandwiches we were given each morning. Back in dorm life, the girls made the school lunches – the girls dorm equivalent of feeding the chooks and the ducks before school. But I don't think they put as much love into their work as I had done as duck boy. The bread always seemed to be dried out and I was never sure what was spread between the slices. One sandwich usually had some form of jam – the kind that contained little, if any, real fruit – while the other was a complete mystery.

Over the years, I put my hastily wrapped sandwiches in my schoolbag for the short journey to the nearest bin. Consequently, I was always begging my school friends for a share of their more appetising-looking lunches. I was fortunate to have good friends who sympathised with my troubles (or felt sorry for me because I was a home kid), and they readily gave up one of their sandwiches. However, the tables turned when I moved to the Grey Cottage. For the first time, my school friends began to ask me if they could have some of my lunch. I couldn't refuse – I had debts going back a long way.

One of my favourite experiences of the Grey Cottage was the evening meal. Instead of eating in an industrial-sized dining room, with an array of tables and a horde of children, the six of us teenagers sat around a large dining table with the Alexanders. We had a table-cloth and serviettes and there was a gong to announce dinner instead of first and second bell. But the best thing was that the Alexanders would occasionally invite guests for dinner, which meant that we got to interact with adults who were part of 'the outside world'.

One dinner guest visiting from Tasmania, where the Alexanders had lived before 'being called by God' to run a children's home in Brisbane, enjoyed travelling and described some of her many trips to exotic and far-flung places I had never heard of before. Her curiosity about other cultures struck a chord with me – I was desperate to find out what lay beyond Silky Oaks and the Wynnum Gospel Hall. That does it, I thought, I'm going to travel the world!

Another memorable dinner guest was a psychiatrist, who must have been a member of the Christian Brethren church as well. He explained to us why he had chosen a profession that explored 'the mysteries of the mind'. That's it – I am going to be a psychiatrist! I remember asking him about his qualifications and writing the long list of letters after my name in practice for when I had my own shingle.

Another time the dinner guest was a mechanical engineer, who confessed that he had chosen the wrong profession. What he really wanted to do was work with people, and he regretted not studying something in the 'helping professions'. This guy fascinated me. He was already someone important, having completed a degree in a respectable field, and yet he wanted to be a social worker! What was a social worker?

There seemed to be so many options to choose from, and so many experiences ahead of me.

Paul

After not having visited for eight months, our father showed up again without explanation. It was July 1970.

Kids who didn't have visitors used to hang around us on the first Saturday afternoon of the month. While we were fed well at Silky Oaks, our father would arrive with boxes filled with food. Even though he routinely overfed us, there were always plenty of leftovers for the curious onlookers.

I didn't feel comfortable calling him Dad. I'm not sure why, as there were no other rivals for that title. But he'd been absent for so long during my formative years that it just didn't come naturally, and the term didn't seem to fit such an unconventional father anyway. Between ourselves, Chris and I started to refer to our father as the 'old fella,' and over time it became shortened to Offla, which was how 'old fella' sounded if you said it fast. So that was what we called him, and over time Offla accepted the name we'd bestowed on him. The name stuck until his death almost fifty years later and is written on his gravestone.

Offla soon realised that he could extend his time with us by seeing Chris, Helena and me at school lunchtimes, as we were all at the same secondary school. While it was good to see him, and we appreciated the volumes of food he brought us, after a while I began to wish that he wouldn't turn up quite so often, so I could play touch football with my friends. I think he must have realised we sometimes wanted to do other things at lunchtime instead of sitting under a tree outside the school grounds listening to him explain how our minds were being controlled by radio waves.

Our main time together, however, was on those Saturdays. The Ban family tram was located behind the kitchen in the back yard of the home. We did try out the other tram on one occasion, but it just didn't take us on the same journey.

It didn't take long before Offla appeared one Saturday with some guinea pigs in a box. If he couldn't have us live with him, he could at least bring us the things we'd had at home in Inala. Fortunately, Mr Zander approved of the guinea pigs, and they were given their own home in an old chook cage in the far back yard.

But Offla's most lasting contribution to forging our identity as a family were the countless photos he took of us on visiting days. There were group shots, ones of the boys, ones of the girls, individual shots, as well as family photos that included Offla. He used a timer on a chord for the family photos. After clicking the timer, we would all hold false smiles for ten seconds or so before realising there was some technical fault with the timer. Offla used to develop the black and white photos himself. I could picture him in his makeshift darkroom somewhere surrounded by the images of his children he could only see for a brief period every month.

Liz

My father came every visiting day and it was these occasions that brought us together as a family. When I was eight, I remember being proud of Paul as I watched him dressed in his army cadet uniform playing the drums. I wondered if he really noticed me like I did him. I liked Chris's sense of humour – he used to clown around and make me laugh – but I didn't see him as much, so I enjoyed seeing him on visiting days.

It was only for a couple of hours, but it was a time where we shared our stories with each other about what we did at the home. My father's airways bag was always full of lollies and tubes of Nestle coffee with condensed milk, which Helena and I loved, and comics. One time he brought me a duckling, and another time two guinea pigs, a male and female, which I was allowed to keep. It was unusual for parents to bring pets for their children and I was surprised I was allowed to keep them.

Offla's love of animals was instilled in me from a very young age, at our home in Inala before we were taken from him and again at Silky Oaks.

I loved the guinea pigs and would spend most afternoons with my friends playing with them down behind the tram and the dug out area that was meant to be a tennis court. I had straight-haired and curly-haired guinea pigs. There were always new babies being born. They were vulnerable little creatures and I loved nurturing them. I was devastated when a dog managed to rip the chicken wire from the cage and kill some of them.

My father was full of stories of Europe, the war, his family and his beloved mother. He was forty-five years old when I was born, and had grey hair. At first, calling him 'Offla' felt disrespectful and, besides, I enjoyed calling him Dad. It took me until I was about thirteen before I began to call him Offla too. By then, my father would introduce himself to people as Offla and over the years people thought it was his real name.

Helena

My brothers began calling our father 'Offla' and I followed suit, assuming it was Hungarian for 'daddy' or 'father'. The name stuck until one day I questioned Paul as to whether the name was, in fact, Hungarian.

He laughed and said, 'No way, I just made it up.'

'But what does it mean?'

'When you say the "old fella" really quickly it sounds like "Offla", doesn't it?'

'So is that what we're going to call him from now on?'

'That's what I'm going to call him,' he replied. 'You can call him what you like.'

I liked 'Offla'.

The Brisbane City Council donated two trams to Silky Oaks when they moved to buses for public transport. They were fixed on concrete posts, one near the swings and the other near the mulberry trees. We originally claimed the one near the swings, but quickly found the other tram was our preferred one for visiting day. This claim was respected and no other family boarded between 2 p.m. and 4 p.m. In that two-hour period my father transformed himself into the driver and conductor, taking his passengers on a bewildering and often amusing two-hour journey.

From his airways bag came second-hand comics, including *The Phantom*, *Superman*, *Richie Rich*, *The Archies* and *Jughead*. Unusual toys were pulled out: boxing puppet figure-heads, figurines that moved or collapsed depending on how far up you pushed the button and a variety of battery-operated barking dogs. Coca-cola, fruit tingles, sugar cubes, tubes of condensed milk and blocks of chocolate filled our sugar quota for the month tenfold. Back in the dormitory, I did a roaring trade at swap meets.

Offla had a variety of box brownie cameras and a slightly more modern camera with a tripod, and took almost a whole roll of film on each visit. We lined up beside the tram or under a mulberry tree while he painstakingly measured the six feet between camera and subject. Once satisfied that the distance was perfect he often discovered one of his subjects had disappeared through boredom and so he commenced his routine all over again. Finally, he counted to three very slowly before saying 'Mickey Mouse' or 'cheese' to encourage laughter. Invariably he hadn't wound on the film and the routine would begin again to laughter and frustration. It was hysterical when he began using the timer on the camera to join us. We egged him on while he frantically got into position before the timer went off. The early days produced many a blurred image of him, but he mastered it over time and we have many family photos taken on those memorable visiting days.

On one visit he brought along a poster of the great Polish pianist Stanislas Niedzielski, who was famous for playing Chopin. Niedzielski's hands were resting above the keyboard of a piano. Offla taped the poster to the side of the tram and asked Bessie to stand in front of it with her hands raised.

'Bessie, keep your hands still!'

'Why do I have to have this stupid photo taken?' she asked.

'Niedzielski's talent will be superimposed into your hands,' he replied. 'Soon you will be able to play the piano like a genius!'

He reminded us how handicapped we were not playing musical instruments or speaking several languages, though apparently Bessie's lesson with the great Niedzielski was all she needed.

Offla said there were people filming information into his brain, making him do things that were out of his control. He talked about cryogenics, where in the future human beings would have their body or head frozen after death awaiting a time when scientists were able to defrost them and bring them back to life. Laser beams filmed messages into people's brains, leaving Offla particularly upset when they began to be used for security in stores.

He suspected someone called 'Smitbachi' was behind the kidnapping of his children and certain information filmed into his brain. Along with some colourful Hungarian language, Smitbachi's name was used as a curse each time Offla stubbed his toe or something didn't go according to plan. I learned years later that he was in fact a real person and my father's neighbour when he was growing up in Budapest. Smitbachi was an insurance salesman. My father's interpretation of our tragic circumstance was that we were victims of a triple insurance fraud between Hungary, England and Australia and that was the reason why the government kidnapped his four young children. The government would be eligible to claim the insurance on our lives should something happen to us. He said the government and the insurance industry were in a conspiracy playing mind control games with everyone on the planet. Our brains were all connected to a main frequency through individual codes. He heard voices and saw visions I couldn't comprehend and copied quotes and references from books he read in the State Library on to scraps of paper. He spent hours researching anything and everything, including electronics and radio frequencies. 'Direct hearing is known where people can hear radio frequency directly without necessitating conversion to audio frequencies.' 'Ability – No one knows what he can't do until he tries. Crime – Steal money and you're a thief. Steal a country and you're a king.'

At 4 p.m. the journey ended and we disembarked.

During the year it was announced that Aunty Jean won the Queensland Mother of the Year award. She also received an Order of the British Empire (OBE) for her services. There was much ado and fuss made, resulting in a gala dinner to celebrate the occasions. Various dignitaries, deacons and elders from the Christian Brethren congregation were invited to the event to be held in the main dining room. The room was prepared in a manner never seen before, with Aunty Jean and her family sitting with dignitaries at the head table. We pubescent girls weren't party to the preparation of the meal but we received an etiquette lesson on how to wait on tables – we would be amateur waitresses for the night.

A guest commented how lucky I was to have such a wonderful mother figure and I smiled politely. Speeches were held in the Mother of the Year's honour. It was explained that Queen Elizabeth had given her the OBE for her many years of service working with underprivileged children. I understood the Queen's kindness and gratitude. However, after making discreet enquiries I was unsure of the other award. If it wasn't any of us kids who voted her Mother of the Year, then who the hell did?

When I transferred to the Grey Cottage over the Christmas vacation I bid farewell to the woman who had been my mother figure for the previous three years. It was difficult to leave Aunty Em but I was eager to start my new life as a high school student and a teenager. I was reunited with Brenda, and my brothers shared a bedroom on the lower level with Brenda's older brother Kenny. This was the first time in a little more than six years that I slept under the same roof as Chris and Paul. Lizzy remained in the safe and loving hands of Aunty Em in the main brick building. Mr Zander and the Queensland Mother of the Year became my new parent figures.

At first, I found the adjustment to high school a difficult one. The school was a little more than a mile away and I was used to walking through a connecting gate. But it became an adventure travelling to and from school and it gave me some of the freedom I had long yearned for. Petra (Elly's older sister), Roslyn and I commenced Year 8 while Brenda began Year 9.

There were chores in the Grey Cottage, as there'd been in the main brick building. Aunty Jean prepared the cooked breakfast while we girls set the table, swept floors and made beds, then she led Brenda, Petra and me in a Bible reading and a prayer before the boys arrived from attending to chores in other buildings. Roslyn attempted to join us for Bible reading but often slept in – Aunty Jean said she was too tired for chores in the morning. I suppose she was entitled to special benefits given her position. However, it was difficult for me to grasp as Aunty Jean often said they treated us kids they way they treated their own. Maybe she'd won the competition on that basis.

The boys arrived hungry and ready for a hearty breakfast. We sat at a large rectangular table with discussions far more interesting than I was used to. After dishes were done we dressed for school and collected our bikes from underneath the boys dormitory. Petra and I received hand-me-downs from kids who had recently graduated from high school and their life in the home. We sped down the long driveway before stopping to dismount to cross the busy main road. We rode alongside each other on the safe and almost straight road.

Once we hit Peel Street the challenge was on. We lifted our feet off the pedals and flew down its steep hill like birds with the wind in our hair. Sometimes we were interrupted by a horn warning us to slow down. It was Mr Zander as he drove his two daughters to high school.

The uniform had changed since the Queen's visit. A plain bottle-green skirt with a short-sleeved grey shirt replaced the pleated pinafore I'd looked forward to wearing the previous year. It was paramount that the skirt length was no shorter than four inches above the knee when kneeling. Thick grey stockings with shiny black leather shoes, short grey gloves and a cream straw hat with headband completed the look. Our principal was Mr Jack Guy. The headmistress, Miss Elizabeth Nixon, looked like a kindly grandmother and was nicknamed 'Gran'. But I discovered that looks are deceiving when she found me on the parade ground during my first week. She held a ruler in her hand and marched up and down the line of students just as a general would inspect his troops.

She stopped directly in front of me. 'What is your name, dear?'

'Helena Ban, Miss,' I answered, eyeing the ruler nervously.

'Kneel down so I can measure the length of your skirt.'

As I knelt, I felt hundreds of eyes watching me. I straightened my back as she had ordered and waited for the results of the measurement.

'Just as I thought, your skirt length is four and a half inches above the knee and not the regulated four. Now stand up straight.'

When I did, she ripped down the hem of my skirt. Unfortunately, the hem was triple-layered as the sewing ladies allowed room for me to grow. When she was finished, my skirt dangled around my ankles. This added to my unnerving introduction to high school.

And for the first time I felt pitied when teaching staff or students discovered I was a home kid. I was often asked, 'Do they feed you enough?', 'Do they beat you?' The most humiliating question: 'What are you in for?' Some students thought I lived in one of those homes with bars on the windows where there were no privileges. My reaction to this was to misbehave in the classroom and I enjoyed the daily challenge of being thrown out of class, and mixed with normal girls who shared this challenge. My music teacher said that I wasn't a bad person, but a follower. She had no idea of the leadership qualities I'd gained since I'd been institutionalised.

We were expected to be part of the inter-school Christian fellowship group which met once a week during the lunch hour. The group consisted of kids of crunchies from our church, homey kids and a few normal kids. We homey kids slotted everyone into categories. 'Crunchies' were religious'. Kids on the outside were simply 'normal'. We were orphans, spastics and underprivileged. And, of course, there were four of us who were communists. If a homey kid was saved by Jesus Christ and baptised, they turned into a crunchie. Some kids got baptised for attention but reverted to their original heathen state sooner or later. A 'homey' longed to be 'normal' while being raised by 'crunchies'.

My English teacher was a member of our church and ran the meetings in her classroom with an occasional guest speaker. A camp retreat was organised at Petrie, an outer northern suburb of Brisbane. It was a similar set-up to the church campsite at Burleigh Heads but beside a creek rather than a beach. The bus left from the church grounds and upon arrival we were allocated huts.

My brother's friends who were seniors and A-grade footballers decided to attend camp even though they weren't regulars of the club. Paul was surprised at the interest his friends took in me and the fact that they nicknamed me 'Chesty Bond'. It related to the white singlet top I wore most of the weekend and my developing breasts. My brother, however, preferred to revert to his chosen nickname for me – 'Ox', as he said I was built like one.

A thick rope hung off the branch of a large tree at the side of the riverbank. We lined up before taking a running jump and landed in the creek below. I borrowed a friend's bikini for the weekend and wondered what punishment would befall me upon my return. A two-piece with a short dress attached to the top was acceptable. I suspected a bikini was not something my new workers or God was ready for! I wore it and enjoyed the attention I received.

I teased an older boy as he walked near the rope swing resulting in being chased into the bushes and along the river bed. I turned around laughing when I came to a dead end. He grabbed both my upper arms and pulled me towards him. I thought he was about to throw me into the river when he planted his lips on mine and gave me a lingering kiss. I had no idea what to do so I just held my breath. As soon as he withdrew his lips, I ran away. I had a crush on this son of a church elder and senior board member of Silky Oaks for years after that kiss. He was fourteen and I thirteen. However the barrier between us was far too great. He was normal. I wasn't.

And just as the weekend was progressing perfectly, Offla turned up at the campsite. It was the first time I was embarrassed by his presence. My brothers and I sat on a log under the shade of a tree for about an hour and once he was satisfied we were safe he disappeared.

On the bus trip home we sang along to popular songs on the radio. 'Chirpy, Chirpy, Cheep, Cheep', a song by the Scottish band Middle of the Road was the flavour of the day. I sang it all the time and wondered whether a link existed between a little bird searching for its momma and poppa and me.

I had become popular with boys, received my first kiss and was entering a new stage in life. No punishment eventuated from the bikini-wearing episode. Neither Brenda nor Petra had experienced their first kiss when I confessed to receiving mine. They, too, were in a quandary as to the correct way to do it.

'I'm pretty sure you're not supposed to hold your breath,' Brenda said.

'I heard from the girls at school that you're supposed to stick your tongue in their mouth,' Petra added.

'How disgusting!' we all said.

'I suppose the only way we're going to learn is to practise on each other,' I suggested.

'Okay, but I'm not sticking my tongue in either of your mouths!' Brenda said.

Paul

After my father's return from Europe, contact with him became regular and predictable. But we never did have the kind of father-and-son conversations I had hoped for. Instead, they tended to centre on his conspiracy theories, and usually involved him instructing me about how knowledge could be filmed in through radio waves without the need for formal education. He would become excited as he explained in detail the research he had uncovered about this topic, along with the signs and symbols he saw in magazines and newspapers that only he could decode.

Despite my father's life lessons, I maintained my desire to gain entry to university. My academic achievements in my senior years of high school weren't too bad, especially considering I had chosen to study Pure Maths, Applied Maths, Physics and Chemistry, only to discover I wasn't really cut out for maths and science. I had been steered into those subjects by a careers counsellor at school, based on my reasonably good results in my early high school years and on my belief at the time that I wanted to be an optometrist like Teddy Green.

By the time I was in Year 12, my imagination had been stirred by this degree called 'social work', which seemed to focus on understanding people and society and then went beyond simply understanding to wanting to improve people's lives. It sounded like such a great course that I couldn't understand why everyone didn't want to enrol in it. In my years living at the Grey Cottage I saw a number of caseworkers from the State Children Department, much more frequently than had been the case during my time in the boys dorm. During the period in the dormitory, a 'Man from the State', wearing a white shirt and skinny black tie, would bring us comics once a year and ask us how we were going. I think that was our yearly check-up with our legal guardian or, at least, the comic-bearing representative of our guardian.

At the Grey Cottage, visiting caseworkers noted my interest in studying social work. It was a profession that was slowly making its way into the child welfare landscape at the time. However, none of the people I had contact with had a social work degree themselves. They had a range of tertiary qualifications, some being lapsed teachers. The worker I got on with best had a degree in biochemistry. But he admitted to me he should really have studied social work, given his job and his interest in child welfare. Alec Lobban was my assigned caseworker during my final years of school, and he made it his mission to find a way for me to be able to attend university if I didn't receive a Commonwealth scholarship. This was before the Whitlam Government brought in free tertiary education, and obtaining a scholarship was not going to be easy. I had to not only get into Queensland University, which had the highest entry of any tertiary institution in the state, but obtain a substantially higher score than the entry marks to be eligible for the scholarship.

Then, at the end of my Year 12, Queensland University increased the entrance requirement. My results fell just short of what I needed to get in. It took me less than a minute to realise that I would have to repeat Year 12 and try for a higher score if I was going to realise my dream.

Repeating the year was one thing, but staying on at Silky Oaks while I did was the real killer. I had mentally prepared myself for independence and had bought a motorbike during the Christmas holiday break, courtesy of a holiday job in a hardware warehouse. However, Mr Zander told me I couldn't have the bike on the property until I received the approval of my legal guardian. To my surprise that wasn't Mr Zander, but some guy in the city who I didn't know and who, I was pretty sure, didn't know me. I assume Mr Gough was a representative of the Director of the State Children Department. He smiled the whole time as he told me that I couldn't have the motorbike because he 'wouldn't allow his children to have one'.

Until that time my knowledge of 'the State' as my legal guardian was very limited. It was more of an abstract notion than anything practical, with Mr Zander and Aunty Jean calling the shots (or so I thought). I knew the clothes we were outfitted in when we arrived at Silky Oaks were from 'the State,' and was aware I would receive another outfitting when I left the home. I recalled the man with the comic books and the man who had asked me if I wanted to live in Europe. Until Alec arrived, they had been my only real contact with my legal guardian.

My father knew I was disappointed that I didn't get into the University of Queensland and, of course he was no believer in the need for formal education. So he decided to apply for a job for me without consulting me about it.

'Paul, you have an appointment at the Language Laboratory at the University of Queensland next week.'

'What appointment? What's a language laboratory?'

'Never mind, you can find out about it when you get the job.'

I was stunned that Offla had lined up a job interview for me in an area I knew nothing about. But then remembered that was how Chris had got his apprenticeship as an electrician – Offla went to the Queensland Railways without telling him.

'It's a job as a technician at the language laboratory. You can find out how languages are filmed into your mind.'

What was I going to do? I knew his intention was well meaning, and there was an 'Offla logic' to his desire for me to be on the inside track regarding access to knowledge 'filmed in'. It was pointless arguing with him that I didn't want the job and that I was prepared to sacrifice a year of my life, both at school and Silky Oaks, if it meant getting into the university course I wanted.

'I'll meet you at the bus stop in the city so we can go to the interview together,' he said.

There was no way out of this. I was going to have to tell the interview panel the truth.

On the day of the interview, Offla sat in the waiting room while I went in for my allotted thirty-minute appointment. The panel consisted of a senior academic from the faculty – whose area of expertise was completely unknown to me, as I hadn't even read the job description – along with two others from the lab.

'So, Paul, what attracted you to this position, and what do you think you can offer?'

I didn't even try to fudge it. 'Actually, I don't know anything about the job. I'm only here because my father wants me to be here.'

Their faces registered surprise and curiosity in equal measure, and I realised I would have to tell them the whole story. I carefully explained that my father had been diagnosed with paranoid schizophrenia and that one of his delusions involved a belief that languages were being directly 'filmed in' to people's minds, making them instantly multilingual.

'He thought I shouldn't be denied this opportunity, so that's why I'm here. He's sitting outside in the waiting room.' I didn't want to add that he didn't trust me to get this far without him leading me by the nose.

To my great relief, the panel members were sympathetic to my situation and asked me lots of questions about my father and our relationship. I told them that I couldn't leave the interview early, because he would find it suspicious. The panel was obliging and we talked about my father, and about Silky Oaks and being in care, and even a little about the job itself. When the thirty minutes was up they said goodbye and wished me the best of luck for my future.

'How did it go?'

'It went well, I think. They'll let me know next week.'

Despite my charade, I had the feeling Offla knew I hadn't really tried to get the job. But he didn't let on. I was just grateful he hadn't asked the panel if he could sit in on the interview with me!

There were a number of things that helped get me through that final, extra, year at Silky Oaks. Kenny and Peter were still there in the Grey Cottage with me. And Alec Lobban, my biochemist caseworker, had become more of a friend than a worker. We used to sit in his sports car on the property when he visited, and he would talk to me like I was an equal, not just one of the kids in his caseload. He certainly didn't seem like 'the State' to me.

Like Aunty Rene and Mr Abraham before them, Aunty Jean and Mr Zander allowed me to be myself, which was the best thing they could have done. I negotiated with them to allow music to be played during the evening meal, putting my case that music was a good outlet for teenage angst. I thought Simon and Garfunkel would be a safe start.

Even though I had chosen to stay on at school for another year, I was desperate to find out what life offered me beyond the bounds of the home and Wynnum State High School. I was beginning to struggle with the constraints of the Silky Oaks rules, the Christian Brethren narrowness, and still wearing a school uniform when I was seventeen. I worked hard to get on top of my science subjects, determined to improve my grades.

It was my German teacher, Mr Ramsden, who saw education as being not only learning the subject for exams but preparation for life. I don't even know why I chose German in Year 9. But Mr Ramsden used his class to teach us about the power of language, using some of Adolph Hitler's speeches to make his point. He also taught us the poems of Rilke, Schiller and Goethe. My favourite poem was 'Wilkommen und Abschied' ('Coming and Going') by Johann Wolfgang von Goethe. It was about a man whose lover lived some distance away and he could only see her on weekends. He spent all night Friday riding horseback to see her and all Sunday night riding back home. The poem was about his anticipation of the weekend ahead on his outward journey, and his sense of satisfaction combined with loss when riding home. It was the first time I'd considered the idea that anticipation might be better than the event looked forward to. I really hoped that wasn't going to be my experience when I left Silky Oaks.

Mr Ramsden knew my situation and gave me extra tuition for no charge in the couple of months leading up to my 'Year 13' exams. He would arrive at the home every Wednesday night after dinner, still dressed in the jacket and tie he had worn at school that day, and spend an hour or so tutoring me. The only drawback was that he chain-smoked, something I had never seen him do at school. As no one smoked at the Grey Cottage, Aunty Jean had to buy him an ashtray. Despite her views about smoking, she was willing to put up with it because she was so impressed by his commitment to me, and didn't want to discourage him.

And then, finally, Alec arrived with the best of surprises. 'You've been promised a Queensland Public Service Scholarship if you gain entry to the University of Queensland.'

Alec looked both happy for me and exhausted by the efforts he'd made to argue my case for a scholarship. Back then very few children in care went on to university, so there had been no real precedent to follow. Alec had argued passionately on my behalf that the State, as my legal guardian, had a responsibility to provide me with the best possible opportunity to prepare me for adult life. He wrote submissions on my behalf stating that if I lived up to my part of the deal and gained entry to the University of Queensland, my guardian should reward my commitment. As it was not possible, apparently, to award a one-off 'Paul Ban scholarship', Alec had to find an existing category for me to fit into. A Public Service scholarship was the category he seized upon, and the department accepted it.

At last, my being in care was paying off!

The Public Service Scholarship was a particularly good one for me. It covered all my fees and gave me a book and living allowance, as well as guaranteed work with the public service during university breaks. In addition, I was offered the chance to live at one of the university residential colleges, as Manly West, where I had lived for the past eight years, was a considerable distance from the university campus in St Lucia. However, my enthusiasm for living at a college diminished the moment I was shown through one of them, and saw the common dining room and dormitory-style sleeping arrangements. I'd had enough of that life.

It was time to think of a different way of living, which ended up being a shared house a couple of kilometres from Silky Oaks with Chris, Kenny Marshall and another uni student.

The wait for round two of my Year 12 results was excruciating. On the day they were published I decided I would read them in the *Courier-Mail* with my father, who I was meeting for lunch in the city. The results were the key to my future, and I wanted to share the experience with him. For once he stopped talking about air-pushers and having knowledge filmed in directly to my brain. I think he realised how important this was for me. Hidden among all his experiences of growing up in Budapest and being in a Russian prisoner-of-war camp was the fact that he had once been a student of Economics at the Franz Josef University. Somewhere in his earlier life, before the war and his mental health problems, he had valued formal education.

We opened the newspaper.

I'd been accepted.

Helena

The area near Donny's final resting place and the abandoned chook pen was now a construction zone. A new house, Bay Cottage, was being built for Mr Zander, Aunty Jean and their family. It would be more spacious and opulent than the other buildings at Silky Oaks and had sweeping views of Moreton Bay.

But the build kept hitting problems and the Alexanders were forced to co-share the responsibility of the teenagers at Grey Cottage with their replacements. Bruce and Lesley Fleming and their young family took up residence in a makeshift room on the lower level. I quickly grew to love their three-year-old son, Jono, and baby daughter, Jane.

Fourteen years my seniors, Bruce and Les were younger than the usual workers. They were pioneers for change too: their main aim was to push for siblings to live together in group cottages. I took an immediate liking to this new concept and to them. But change and new ideas were not welcome in this institutionalised haven and months of tension between the old and new followed.

The Flemings were prepared to stand up for what they believed was best for the children. They had opinions on administration and wanted to replace the staid committee members – all elders of the local Brethren Church – who oversaw Silky Oaks along with the Department of Children's Services.

As soon as Bay Cottage was completed the five members of the Alexander family moved in. I was filled with mixed emotions when the woman who officially replaced my mother left me. In my fourteen years of life, Aunty Jean was one of many mother figures to me, yet the only one to receive an award. But I didn't love her as I did my biological mother. I didn't love her as I grew to love Aunty Alice, Aunty Joan, Aunty Em or Lesley. I had affection for her that yearned to grow to love, but I didn't feel it was reciprocated. Maybe she wasn't capable with so many children.

In my final year of primary school we'd shared a special moment. It was a Sunday evening at church following several baptisms. This time I'd opted out of placing bets on which victim would arise coughing and spluttering after being submerged. The deacon was keen to recruit new followers of Christ. It was his job to convince sinners to give up their lives to the Lord Jesus Christ and be saved. He asked the congregation to refer to their hymn book. The mundane yet eerily hypnotic song always sent shivers down my spine.

> Just as I am, without one plea, but that thy blood was shed for me,
> And that thou bidst me come to thee, O Lamb of God, I come,
>   I come.
> Just as I am, and waiting not to rid my soul of one dark blot,
> To thee whose blood can cleanse each spot, O Lamb of God, I come,
>   I come.

'The Lord God Almighty is stretching out his hands to you tonight!' the deacon announced. 'He's ready, willing and able to forgive you of your sins. Please make your way towards the pulpit and the Lord God will save your soul!' When he gave the nod, the congregation proceeded to sing the next verse.

> Just as I am, though tossed about with many a conflict, many a doubt,
> Fightings and fears within, without, O Lamb of God, I come, I come.
> Just as I am poor, wretched, blind, sight, riches, healing of the mind,
> Yea, all I need in thee to find, O Lamb of God, I come, I come.

The congregation paused awaiting the deacon's next response. During the second verse a young man and woman had made their way towards the pulpit. An elder or senior member of the congregation always joined the sinner at the front for support as they awaited salvation. 'Do not be frightened to come forward to ask God's forgiveness. We have members here to pray with you after the service.' A few more members made their way towards the pulpit and salvation. At that moment I felt a presence and my heart began to beat rapidly. More sinners and elders were moving forward.

> Just as I am, thou wilt receive, wilt welcome, pardon, cleanse, relieve;
> Because thy promise I believe, O Lamb of God, I come, I come.

I was frightened. I had never felt like this before. Not only was my heart thumping, I also felt a tremendous impulse to head towards the pulpit. I thought how the homey kids would be shocked by my conversion to a crunchie. I remembered my shock at others who had trodden this path. Something had an enormous and frightening hold over me.

> Just as I am, thy love I own hath broken every barrier down;
> Now, to be thine and thine alone, O Lamb of God, I come, I come.

There was silence, both pleasure and tears on the faces of those who'd been brave enough to seek redemption and salvation. They held hands with each other and unashamedly wept with pure joy. What was wrong with me? Why couldn't I do the same? I knew I had much to forgive.

It was now or never, though I struggled with thoughts of how the homey kids would taunt me. During the final sentence of the hymn, with my heart pounding, I walked past my peers. Their mouths fell open as I made my way to the pulpit and to salvation.

Now, to be thine and thine alone, O Lamb of God, I come, I come.

As I wept at the pulpit, someone kindly, lovingly, put their arm around me.

'Let us pray!' the deacon said as he surveyed God's new recruits.

I closed my eyes, feeling the comfort of being held. When the prayer ended, the congregation sounded out an almighty 'Amen!'

I was held more tightly, then I heard a familiar voice. 'I am so proud of you, Helena, and so is Jesus.'

I looked into Aunty Jean's smiling eyes and witnessed a transformation. She led me downstairs to a quiet corner of the hall where she prayed for me.

'You know, Helena, you have always been one of my favourites,' she said, inviting me to sit beside her. I hugged her tightly.

She would never again refer to my nasty communist streak; perhaps it had been exorcised that night. And the saving of my soul seemed to be the turning point in our relationship, yet, afterwards, still nothing grew.

For a while I held my own religious services in the dormitory, with baptisms and all! The kids were in awe of the miracle that occurred that night. I now aspired to become a missionary or even a nun.

Eventually, though, I realised that religion wasn't my calling in life and I reverted to being a homey kid.

With change came emotional upheaval. After two years of living with Paul and Chris, it was time for my brothers to move on. Paul went to university and Chris became an apprentice electrician. With Brenda's older brother, Kenny, they rented a house a mile or so away.

Offla was far more settled and content once my brothers left the home even though they remained officially under the care of the department until they were eighteen. My father's health improved. So much so that he would never be admitted to a psychiatric hospital again. His illness would continue but in a far less disturbing way.

He was missing his ageing mother and wished to see her, but his status was still shaky. The Prime Minister, Gough Whitlam, supported the idea of an inquiry into the federal public service to have its structure and procedures reviewed by an outsider. So Offla applied for citizenship directly to the Prime Minister. Mr Whitlam's office forwarded the application to the Department of Immigration. Mr Len Keogh MP followed it up with a phone call to Immigration, who advised him that every endeavour was being made to complete the remaining formalities. Offla was sent an application for a Certificate of Identity to facilitate his travel should he wish to leave prior to his citizenship's final consideration.

But the Hungarian Government would not issue a visa on the Certificate of Identity. Offla sent a letter to the Commonwealth Director of Migration advising that the director's work ethic was below the standard required for such work. It was my father's considered opinion that the director was not suitable to continue in the position and he should report within seven days the reasons why his appointment should not be annulled. He signed it Z. Ban (Public Service Inspector).

At the Grey Cottage, Brenda and I moved into what was once the guestroom while Petra shared with her sisters Elly and Kim. Lizzy came. For the first time since our arrival years earlier my sister and I ate at the same dining table. She shared a bedroom downstairs with other younger siblings.

This was the beginning of what would be known as group homes. It replaced institutionalised dormitories by providing care for smaller groups of children. Re-acquainted siblings would not only live under the same roof but dine at the same table. Life as we knew it changed dramatically. We may very well have landed on the moon. One small step for siblings. One giant leap for siblings in institutions.

After my brothers went, as history dictated, there were more brothers to fill empty beds. Brenda's brother Peter transferred across with Robert (Woodchuck) and Noel from the boys dormitory.

Woodchuck was the eldest in a family of three and given his nickname shortly after his arrival. He continually repeated the tongue twister 'How much wood could a Woodchuck chuck if a Woodchuck could chuck wood?' His two sisters also transferred across adding to this large new family.

Brenda started work as a clerk typist in the local hardware store. It was owned by three brothers who were elders of the Brethren Church. My old roomy Elly and I often dressed and danced in ridiculous clothing entertaining the family group. We smuggled in cigarettes from school and smoked them in the bathroom. I'm not sure who was responsible for most of the butts outside the windows, the boys or us. One day, Les pretty well caught us red-handed when smoke began to smoulder from the rubbish bin.

Brenda continued her new life as an employee, quietly maturing while I continued to test boundaries.

One day after Sunday school, Woodchuck changed into a pair of shorts and a t-shirt and shocked us by announcing he'd had enough and wasn't going to attend any more morning services.

'If you're so against attending church, you should meet with Mr Zander to explain your reasons,' Bruce said.

'Okay, I will,' Woodchuck said and set off to the Bay Cottage.

A short time passed and we expected him to rush back to get changed for church. At least we expected to see a couple of welts from the leather strap. Instead, the bus arrived with Mr Zander driving and no sign of Woodchuck. A rumour went around the bus that Woodchuck couldn't walk.

We had various way of dealing with boredom during morning service. I tried and failed to convince Mr Zander I was reading a religious book when he caught me reading *The Nun's Story*. It was about a young nun who worked and fell in love with a doctor in the Belgian Congo, and was made into a movie starring Peter Finch and Audrey Hepburn. Woodchuck, however, once masterminded the ultimate entertainment. He painstakingly cut out a square hole in the pages of his Bible leaving a neat compartment to slot in a small transistor radio. He connected one end of the earpiece to the transistor and threaded the wire up through his sleeve and out his shirt collar. He slipped the other end into his ear and pretended to read the Bible. I'm not sure whether one of the workers grew suspicious of his sudden interest in the Bible or one of the kids dobbed him in, but they were disgusted when they found what he'd done and he'd been in a lot of trouble. For some time afterwards our Bibles were inspected prior to boarding the bus.

After the morning service we found Woodchuck reading a magazine on his bed.

'What happened? What did Mr Zander say?'

'I told him I wasn't going to church anymore.'

'What did he say?'

'He said that I had to.'

'What happened then?'

'I told him that he would have to drag me into church himself, and then I left.'

Woodchuck was almost fifteen, with a stocky build, and, at times, an aggressive temperament. It was difficult to imagine anyone dragging him into church. I was amazed at his guts in confronting Mr Zander. No child in the history of Silky Oaks had been that determined to follow such a serious threat through.

The outcome of Woodchuck's rebellion was that we were given a choice of attending the morning or evening service, though Sunday school remained compulsory. Most kids chose the more family-friendly and shorter evening service. With Bruce and Les's support, times were changing. Woodchuck became a hero.

Where did I fit in? Trying to figure it out as a teenager was difficult.

I wanted to be like my peers at school but was rarely given permission to go out with them on weekends. I wanted to mix socially with my church peers but not at church. I wanted to live a normal life. I wanted to be a normal person. I wanted to rid myself of all the labels: orphan, spastic, underprivileged, homey kid, communist, crunchie and abnormal. My true label, I felt, was that I was abnormal.

A good education wasn't my priority. My teachers thought I

was capable of completing my senior years, but I was desperate to leave the home and this wouldn't have been possible if I remained a student. My Year 10 Junior Certificate would be my final year.

During the final weeks of school, I received a letter from the department store David Jones. It thanked me for applying for a position with the company as a junior administration trainee and asked me to attend an interview. Offla had applied on my behalf without my knowledge. I was offered the job immediately. It started in the New Year, and I'd be trained in various departments of the administration office. I had two weeks of school remaining, with a job already lined up!

Bruce arranged a lease on a two-bedroom flat in Manly for Brenda to share with her brothers. Peter had just completed his senior year at school and Kenny and Brenda were employed. She was so excited. I couldn't help but wonder what the future held in store for me. Where would I live? I wanted to live with Brenda but didn't have any financial support. I wasn't due to commence work for several weeks and it would take time to save money. My worst fear was to remain at Silky Oaks for another year.

I was playing with little Jane one day when Les said she had something to tell me. I followed her into her bedroom and sat on the bed.

'We'll be leaving Silky Oaks shortly.'

I was silent, wanting to burst into tears. I had to remain strong. This had happened to me before. I should be used to it by now. Throughout my life, people I loved either died or abandoned me. But it was difficult to hide my shock and disappointment.

'We want you to come and live with us.'

'What do you mean?' I couldn't help but remember the similar conversation years earlier with the Mattresses.

'Bruce and I have grown to love you very much and the thought of leaving you behind would break our hearts.'

I hugged her tightly remembering the ultimatum I gave to Fred and Norma. 'What about Lizzy?'

'Of course we want her to come. We love you both very much.'

I couldn't believe my ears. I wanted to yell and scream and jump for joy.

'You must keep this a secret for the moment' she said. 'Things aren't finalised. We're waiting on approval from the department to foster you before you can leave with us.'

Bruce walked in on our conversation and saw the excitement on my face. I hugged them both before I went to my bedroom, where I immediately confided in Brenda who 'crossed her heart and hoped to die' that she wouldn't reveal the secret to anyone.

'There's one more person I have to tell.'

'Who's that?'

I opened the bedroom door and yelled, 'Lizzy – get in here!'

As the Department of Children's Services was releasing us from their care we were entitled to be outfitted with one last suitcase of clothing and shoes. Les drove us to the Warilda Assessment Centre at Wooloowin, the new name for the old Depot. It had been many years now since my family arrived there by police escort.

Ten days before Christmas of 1973, Brenda and her brothers moved into their flat and my sister and I were released into the care of our new foster parents. Geographically the move was minimal – Bruce and Les's new house was diagonally opposite the home. However, emotionally, the transition from the life I'd known for so long left me veering from euphoria to insecurity.

It had been almost eleven years since my mother died and nine and a half years since my siblings and I drove up the long date-palm-lined driveway.

There were no dramatic farewells. I thought Aunty Jean might have sent a note to say goodbye. She didn't.

I received my cheque for $89.68 on the day we left Silky Oaks, my one-sixth share of our mother's land, sold by the public curator so long ago. The beautifully embossed letter from Her Majesty Queen Elizabeth II was also released to its rightful owners.

With the euphoria of the last few weeks I'd almost forgotten how the most important person in my life was feeling. Twelve months earlier my father was thrilled when my brothers left the home and he was welcome to visit them without threat or altercation. His daughters were now departing an existence he abhorred. He found it difficult to understand why we were released into someone else's care and not his. But he accepted the situation graciously. The alternative – for us to remain institutionalised – would be detrimental not only to his sanity but also to mine.

Liz

I was twelve years old and going to the Grey Cottage was my seventh move. The first was from my family home to the Depot, the second to Silky Oaks, and the rest in Silky Oaks itself. Paul and Chris had already left Silky Oaks, but they came back to visit sometimes. There were about eight children living in the Grey Cottage and it felt more like a home than the Big End, where there were fifteen girls to one set of house parents.

What stands out for me during that period was the little blue record player that Paul passed down to me. I loved that record player and it started my interest in music. A bit later I saved enough money to buy my first single. I gave the money to Helena and asked her to buy Carly Simon's 'You're So Vain', but she came home with Paul McCartney's 'My Love' instead and I was very angry with her, despite her trying to convince me that I would love Paul McCartney just as much.

In the Grey Cottage I slept in a small room with a set of bunk beds with Kim Vogt – sister to Elly and Petra, who Helena had shared with. Kim was one of my best friends at the home and we used to talk about living together in a flat when we left Silky Oaks. I whizzed around on the roller-skates that Offla gave me – the ones where you put your shoe into the skate and adjust it to your size.

We played spin the bottle at school during lunchtimes and kissed one of the boys when the bottle pointed to them. I would hold my breath and close my mouth and kiss for as long as I could while the other kids counted. It was a competition to see who could kiss the longest. Some afternoons we would hide in the bushes at Jackie Singer's place and resume the game. I was keen on Alan Kirkgaard who was twelve and in my class. He had light red curly hair and smattering of freckles. Alan gave me a silver bracelet with my name etched on it as a gift at the end of Year 7 and a love note which I kept for many years.

I went to the Farrells again that Christmas. The Farrells were my holiday people for about three years, a lovely family who treated me with respect, love, and kindness. They lived in a suburb of Brisbane. Keith drove a taxi and Dorothy was a nurse. They had four children: Kylie, Evatt, Lewis and Clive. I looked forward to the school holidays, so I could catch up with them and the other children in the neighbourhood. Although, after the long summers, I was excited to return to Silky Oaks as I missed my friends.

The Farrells treated me as one of their own children. Kylie was my age and she and I were good friends. We would lay awake in bed at night and whisper about all sorts of things. The night before the Ekka was especially exciting, and we'd lay awake talking about showbags and the rides we wanted to go on. At the Farrells I could be 'normal' and do what other 'normal' kids did at the time. We roamed the streets in gangs with other kids from the neighbourhood, played in the park, fished for guppies in the creek and collected bottles for money. The thing I loved the most was dressing up and putting on plays with the neighbours' kids. We spent the summers in and out of the different houses. They were happy memories. At Christmas, the Farrells bought me presents.

That last Christmas I spent with them was at the end of Year 7 and I will always remember it. They gave me a gold signet ring with my initials engraved on the love heart and my name etched on the inside of the ring. It was the 'in' thing with girls my age, and I still have it today. They also gave me a second-hand bicycle they'd repainted, with streamers on the handles and a new seat. I loved that bike. They made me feel so special.

I used to spend the whole summer holiday with the Farrells, but that last summer was cut short as I moved to live with the Flemings. They were very upset when I left. I had mixed emotions. I wanted to stay with them for the rest of the holidays, but also wanted to go to the Flemings to start my new life there with Helena. I felt so guilty.

Helena

For the first time in many years I shared a bedroom with my sister. I chose the décor. The lilac walls and carpet, with purple and black patterned bedspreads went perfectly with the ornate white furniture Les selected. Lizzy accepted whatever I wanted. She loved the new bedroom designed for a princess . . . and her little sister.

On my first day at work, in the New Year, it was a pleasant surprise to discover a familiar face in the training room. Jane attended my high school and lived along my bus route. We were to be trained in each department of the administration office on a two-month rotation. Every Friday afternoon we met to discuss the week's events. Workshops were run with motivational videos and scenarios to act out. It was a satisfying and safe way for a young girl to commence employment in the corporate world. At 5 p.m. I caught the bus home near the Story Bridge. The first couple of weeks of this were uneventful. Then I spotted him at the bus stop.

'Excuse me, Jane, there's someone over there that I have to talk to.'

I was angry he was invading my working life. Yet I was pleased to see him. 'Offla, what are you doing here?'

'My beloved daughter Helena, I have some food and toys for you and Bessie.' He produced a small plastic bag from his airways bag and handed it over.

'Couldn't it have waited until we saw you at Paul's house on the weekend?'

Offla had bought a second-hand movie camera and recommenced filming his favourite subjects. We were teenagers and not prepared to co-operate as we once did. The director put up with our antics for a while. He laughed then cursed Smitbachi while punching his fist in the air. He filmed us driving around Paul's back yard in his Mini Minor and on the boys' motorbikes. We did anything to deter him rambling on about air pushers and governments filming information into our brains via laser beams.

'I have to go now,' I said. 'The bus is coming.'

I was pleased Jane didn't ask who he was.

Offla's days were spent frequenting op shops in the inner city. He bought odd broken toys which he mended and gave to us. We in turn donated them back to the op shops or threw them in the bin. He loved the challenge of chess and was a regular player with the senior citizens at City Hall. He now had no teeth, a combination of the effects of war and lack of personal hygiene. He blamed the electric shock treatments he received in hospital. He received a free set of dentures from the government which he tried in vain to get used to. They were not only painful and uncomfortable to wear but looked ridiculous. He reminded me of the British comedian Dick Emery's buck-toothed Church of England vicar. He decided they were best kept in his bag.

Offla continued meeting me sporadically at the bus stop after work. One afternoon he handed me a plastic bag while I bid him a hasty hello and goodbye before joining Jane on the bus.

'I've been meaning to ask you something for a while,' she said.

'What's that?'

'Who is that funny old man?'

I had been dreading this question and her reaction if I divulged who he was. 'He doesn't frighten you at all, does he?' I asked.

'No, of course not!' she said. 'He just looks – different.'

'He can't help that,' I said defensively. 'He's a friend of my parents and gives me gifts to take home.'

She accepted my deceit while I contemplated my denial of my father. Memories of the Bible story of the disciple Peter's denial of Jesus came flooding back. Peter was asked three times by the Roman soldiers whether he knew Jesus and three times he denied it. Jesus was handed over to Pontias Pilate before being crucified. When my father had returned from Europe years earlier, he'd confessed to me that he was a 400-year-old prophet sent by Jesus Christ and, later, that he came from a place in the heavens called Planet 5. I had just denied my father's existence, albeit once, and the guilt of my betrayal was swirling in my gut.

I loved my father dearly. I just didn't know how to love him. Words from the musical *Jesus Christ Superstar* filled my head and I imagined myself as Yvonne Elliman singing 'I don't know how to love him'. Dressed in a flowing white robe and armed with the voice of an angel I strolled down a deserted street. As I turned the corner, an angry crowd followed an elderly man struggling to carry a large wooden cross. They were laughing and jeering, 'Crucify him! Crucify him!'

To my horror I recognised the elderly man. It was my father.

'I'm so sorry, Offla,' I cried. 'I'll never deny who you are again!'

The crowd jeered even louder. Vibrations filled my body from head to toe.

'Helena, what have you got in that bag?' Jane asked.

I returned to reality and the back seat of the bus. People were staring at me and the plastic bag on my lap. It was vibrating, and emitting a laughing noise. I opened it to discover a battery-operated laughing box that had been set off by a bump in the road. My face was deeply red as I pulled out the battery. I wondered whether a certain prophet from Planet 5 had predicted my denial of him. Touché, Offla, touché.

It was not working out with the Flemings. Once I drove down the driveway of Silky Oaks for the last time, I thought I'd bought my freedom. But there were rules even in a small family. I was expected to attend at least one church service each Sunday and was banned from watching the new weekly soaps *Number 96* and *The Box*. Admittedly, the shows were risqué for that era, but all my friends were watching them. A few months in, I was rebellious, focused on making Les's life miserable, confused and angry. I wasn't sure whether I loved or hated my father, my foster parents, my job and this new normal life. I was so mixed up that I'd forgotten I was actually living the dream I had longed for. One night, Les told me that a social worker was coming to visit to discuss my problems.

'I'm not talking to any stupid social workers!' I said as I slammed the door to my bedroom. The last time any of them had bothered about my existence was when I'd instigated the 1969 Runaway Incident. And all they did then was threaten to put me in another home behind bars.

The following evening, Miss Davison tried in vain to befriend me. Yet she managed some progress during the interview. I told her I was unhappy about my living arrangements and that I was regretting leaving school and working so soon. She understood my embarrassment when my father visited me after work, yet as soon as she inferred something negative about him I told her that she would be angry if her kids were taken from her, too. I confessed that I resented Bruce and Les trying to play the role of my parents.

I already had a parent, even if not a good one. I felt it was too late to have that kind of relationship with anyone else.

Miss Davison returned a week later with my brother Paul. She was concerned that I'd felt threatened the week before. He was now in his second year at university.

'I suppose you've come to spy on me as well!' I said to him.

'I'm here to support you as my sister not as a social worker,' he said.

I told him I was better expressing myself in writing than in talking.

'Do you have anything for me to read?'

I handed him a piece of paper full of my worries.

What am I doing here? Why did my mother have to die? Why couldn't we have lived with our father? Why isn't he normal like other fathers? Why aren't I normal like other girls? Why is life so complicated? Why am I so unhappy?

My immediate future was discussed at length. I had four options: I could move into a flat with Paul; I could go to a girl's hostel; I could live in a boarding institution with a family of the department's choice; or I could return to Silky Oaks.

I chose to move in with Paul, although I said I would have preferred to move in with Brenda!

I was fifteen when my brother and I moved into a modest two-bedroom flat on the hill in Manly. Between my meagre earnings and his small living allowance from his scholarship we somehow managed. I was left to fend for myself although Bruce and Les remained in the background.

Liz had to stay with the Flemings.

Offla

In early 1974, a memorandum 'Representations by Mr LJ Keogh MP' was sent to the Secretary of Immigration. It gave a brief history of Offla's applications for citizenship.

> ... Notwithstanding Ban's lapses into illness and notoriety over the years he has in many respects had a difficult life. Having arrived here as a refugee in 1950 he lost his wife in 1963 and was left with four small children. They were in effect taken from him and many of his troubles over the subsequent years could be attributed to his over possessiveness towards the children.
>
> He is a resident in Australia and will remain here although he is still drawn to Hungary where his mother resides. He intends to visit her when he can obtain an Australian passport.
>
> He complies with the conditions of the Act and it is considered that the application should be approved. I am however, in view of past publicity and interest at varying times displayed by other organisations, seeking your concurrence to the grant of Citizenship to Mr Ban.

One week later a telex was received from Canberra authorising the application to proceed. Mr Keogh was advised that special arrangements were being made for Offla to take the Oath of Allegiance. And Offla finally received the letter he had waited twenty-two years for. He'd applied fifteen times for a Certificate of Identity and/or citizenship and finally his efforts were about to be rewarded.

On 2 April 1974, he swore an Oath of Allegiance in a private ceremony.

> I, Zoltan Ban renouncing all other allegiance, swear by Almighty God that I will be faithful and bear true allegiance to Her Majesty Elizabeth the Second, Queen of Australia, Her heirs and successors according to law, and that I will faithfully observe the laws of Australia and fulfil my duties as an Australian citizen.

He received the precious piece of paper – a Certificate of Australian Citizenship signed off by Timothy Ronald Sullivan as Authorising Officer and the Minister for Immigration, The Honourable Al Grassby.

Zoltan Ban's file began in May 1950 in Switzerland under the Resettlement Scheme for International Refugees. No one could have guessed how large and complex it would become. Twenty-four years after it began, the Immigration file was closed and archived.

That same month, Chris married Beth. He was eighteen.

A week before Christmas 1974, Beth gave birth to a baby girl. Melissa Jean was the first of nine cherished grandchildren. Their grandfather's pet name for them was 'littlie sparrows'.

Liz

I loved living with Les and Bruce and the freedom it gave me. The Flemings' place wasn't far from Silky Oaks, but it felt a world away. Bruce's parents lived next door, on a couple of acres of farm land. Bruce loved growing vegetables and I had a stint at growing sweet corn.

I started high school at Wynnum and would either ride my bike, the one the Farrells had given me, or walk the two kilometres to school.

It was fun to finally share a room with Helena. She worked in the city and was full of exciting stories of what she did and the new people she met. I loved hearing all about it. I got my period and was too embarrassed to tell Les, so I asked Helena to tell her. Helena wanted me to look feminine, so she plucked my eyebrows and made me shave my legs. I was now twelve and a half and I thought she was so mature at fifteen and a half.

I saw my father weekly at Paul's place. Paul was now sharing a house with a couple of guys on a big property in Whites Road, Manly. He and Chris had motorbikes and they would ride around the house with us girls on the back and Offla filming us. Offla was always taking photos or movies of the four of us, so he could send them to his mother, his brother Laszlo in Budapest and his brother Lajos in Switzerland.

I was thirteen when Helena moved out. I really missed her, even though I saw her every week with Paul, Chris and Offla. I was now alone with Les, Bruce and their two young children. Jono was six and Jane was three. It was a difficult time for me emotionally. My siblings were all working and living independently and I was living with Les and Bruce who were nice, but still not my own family. Around that time, there was a movie called *Sunshine* which I went to see with Carol. It was about a mother who had cancer and died when her daughter was about eighteen months old. I cried a lot during and after the movie and it got me thinking about my own mother and the sadness of not remembering her. I think I was grieving the loss of not living with Helena, or with my friends from Silky Oaks. I also had doubts about whether Les and Bruce really wanted me. It was Helena that they were so close to at Silky Oaks, and I questioned whether they took me from the home only because I was her sister. They wanted to foster Helena, but did they really want to foster me? The love they had for their two kids made me reflect on the love I had missed out on from my own parents. Jane was the age I was when taken from my father, and seeing how much love and nurturing she needed from her parents reinforced my sense of loss. I wished I had parents like Jane and Jono.

I lived with the Flemings for a year after Helena left. There were some happy times and some sad. One night, Les told me they had decided it would be good for me if I went to live with my brother Chris and his wife. Chris and Beth were both nineteen and I was fourteen and a half. I cried. It wasn't fair – they were just kids themselves, and they hadn't been married that long. I pleaded and begged to stay with Les and Bruce. I would go to church on Sundays without any complaints. But it was too late. They had made up their minds.

I moved to Chris and Beth's place with mixed emotions. I was happy to live with my brother, but felt guilty as they had to look after me, as well as Melissa, who was six months old. I loved my niece, who looked like a doll, and enjoyed playing with her.

We lived on Mount Joy Terrace, Wynnum, in an old house on the corner of a large block. It was close to Manly train station and a short walk to school. Kathy, my friend from school, lived with her older sister just around the corner. She could relate to me and what I was going through, as she had spent a year in a children's home in Toowoomba after her mother died.

I missed Les and Bruce and the routine that helped me feel secure. I loved Chris, but he was more relaxed in his parenting, and I was determined from the outset to maintain the same bedtime rituals and study routine I'd had with the Flemings. Chris and Beth allowed me to go out with my friends, and were not too worried about what time I got home. I think I was my own police at that stage.

Once I moved, the Flemings visited me only a couple of times and then stopped. Each time a car pulled up outside, I hoped they had finally come to see me again, only to be disappointed when it was someone else. I longed for them to reassure me that they did love me, but it didn't happen. I would see them sometimes on Sundays at church. I kept going when I first moved, but then I stopped: it was too painful to see them. I cried many tears in bed at night, wondering why they wouldn't come and visit me.

When Chris worked on his car engine, I would hang out with him and tell him about my friends at school and what we got up to. He had an old bomb of a car and, as money was scarce, he would often work on the engine on the weekends. The humidity in the air was stifling and he usually wore stubbies and thongs, and no shirt. After many frustrating hours, he'd be covered in sweat and grease from the car, but would emerge happy after solving the problem, if only temporarily until the next thing broke. I liked spending that time with him. Beth, though, felt left out. One time, she was so angry she told me she was sick of having me live with them and that I had to move out. Six months had passed and I agreed with her. But where was I to go?

I had a meeting with a social worker about what I was going to do. He explored the option of me living with Paul's parents-in-law, moving back to Silky Oaks, or finding a new family. I was fifteen and in Year 10. Two weeks later, the Cash family came into my life.

They lived in Wynnum, not far from the wading pool where my parents took Paul and Chris as toddlers. I met them a few times over two weeks. They had their own two boys, who were nineteen and ten, and an adopted daughter who was six. They were friendly and were excited to have an older girl to complete their family. But that wasn't what I needed at the time. I was polite with them, but never really shared my feelings. I would say hello when I came home from school and then withdraw to my bedroom. They were disappointed – they'd wanted someone who was going to be a 'fit' in their family and engage with them. But they wanted more than I could possibly give, with all the hurt I was feeling.

During that time, I rang Les Fleming from a phone booth most days after school on my way home. I wanted to share my day at school with her. After a few weeks of phoning her, she told me I didn't need to call as often anymore. I was living with a new family and I should tell them about my day. I said goodbye to Les, hung up the phone and never called her again. I was so upset. I felt so rejected. And it confirmed my belief that Les and Bruce had never wanted me as their foster child. It took me a long time to work through that pain.

I was at an age when teenagers naturally withdraw from their own parents, let alone their parent figures, and become more focused on their peers. But that was not what the Cashes wanted or could understand. I felt I was under a microscope and that everything I did or said was being magnified by them. They were too interested. They were moving too fast. I'd started to feel miserable. My only escape was school or my bedroom, and the more I spent time in my bedroom, the more upset they became. Finally, we had a meeting with the social worker, and I asked to go back to Silky Oaks.

That was not an easy decision. I'd spent my whole life wanting to leave the home and now I needed to return.

Helena

Not long after I moved in with Paul I was transferred to the Queen Street department store to be trained in reception duties. One of the buyers invited me to dinner, and I said yes. I was more nervous about eating at a restaurant than dating a man ten years my senior. I was sixteen and had eaten out only once before at the bistro in the Brisbane Arcade.

My date picked me up from the flat and I introduced him to Paul. I wore the outfit I'd bought for my brother Chris's wedding. It fitted me snuggly and accentuated my figure.

David was a gentleman and fascinated me. I introduced him to my family and extended family at a barbecue on the Wynnum foreshore. My father remained quiet while silently studying this new man in my life. Within a week he was armed with information.

'What do you know about this man you are seeing?'

'He likes me and I like him!'

'I don't like him,' he said.

'It doesn't matter that you don't like him.'

'I suppose that's how all prostitutes feel,' he mumbled.

'What did you call me?'

'A prostitute.'

'I'm not a prostitute and you'd better watch your mouth!'

'What else would you call a young girl who has sex with a married man?'

I'd almost died of embarrassment months earlier when Offla had offered to advise me on menstruation and women's problems. He was now way out of line discussing sex. My childhood had instilled in me that a man's duty was limited to supervising chores and dishing out punishment. But then what Offla said sank in. A work colleague had warned me that David was married but when I'd asked him he denied it.

'What makes you think he's married?'

Offla pulled out some paperwork from his bag. 'I've searched the state and federal electoral rolls. He has a wife.'

I was hurt. 'Oh, really, and what else have you discovered?'

'He has a son and a daughter.'

David finally admitted he was estranged from his family. Our relationship cooled then ceased altogether when I transferred back to the Valley office to continue my training.

My new job with Tony Yeldham's T-Shirt Printing Shop kept me at David Jones still, working in a leased area beside ladies hosiery and the cosmetics department. The shop backed onto a doorway, which concealed the busy security department.

I'd served my father with a verbal restraining order now that I was on the shop floor and in public. He was banned from my workplace. I'd had enough of being embarrassed over his vagabond appearance.

Over my time there, I witnessed many store arrests. You knew the inevitable when two or three security guards scrambled through the door and passed my counter whispering on walkie-talkies.

Within minutes they'd return with the alleged thief proclaiming their innocence.

One day, after the lunch hour rush had subsided, the door behind me flung open. Two guards warned me their cameras had spotted a suspicious character hovering behind the hosiery stands. No crime had yet been committed and they were planning on sneaking closer, hoping to catch the culprit red-handed. It was a bit of excitement to fill in the afternoon and I stood on the tips of my toes to peer over the hosiery stands. Oh my God! How embarrassing! It was Offla! I could have killed him right there on the spot. I was crimson-faced as I explained to the security guards who the vagabond was and his reasons for hovering behind the stands.

Offla wasn't the only person keeping watch over someone.

Woodchuck, the hero of the anti-church uprising, was now sleeping on the couch of the flat Brenda shared with her brothers, Kenny and Peter. Brenda had been losing weight and suffering with aches and swelling to her legs. Les had taken her to the doctor but she went home without a diagnosis. One day she collapsed at home. Fortunately, Woodchuck was there and took her back to the doctor. She was hospitalised and a blood clot was discovered. Brenda's kidneys had failed and her future looked bleak.

She was placed on a waiting list for a transplant. In the meantime, she needed to go to the hospital regularly for dialysis treatment.

Months later we rejoiced at the success of a transplant. To mark the occasion I bought her an identity bracelet engraved with our names and the date of the surgery. It cemented our bond further. But the celebration was short-lived. A month later her body rejected her precious new gift. She returned to dialysis treatment.

*

I was still coming to terms with one brother married at eighteen when the other announced his engagement. Paul was mature beyond his years so I figured if it was good enough for one then it should be for the other. 'Congratulations, but I think you're crazy!'

Six months before his twenty-first birthday he married Helen in the church they attended as children. Liz and I were bridesmaids, along with Helen's best friend, Heather. Chris, Ken Marshall, whose bed was beside Paul's for eight years at Silky Oaks, and Helen's brother Evan completed his side. Helen was one of nineteen cousins and had a storybook grandma. Paul's first 'date' with Helen was to visit her grandma who lived in Montville, in the ranges at the back of the Sunshine Coast. While Helen thought Paul was giving her a lift to see her grandma, he thought they were on an outing as a potential couple. When he got there they were greeted not just by her grandparents, but by a number of aunts and uncles who also lived in the ranges and must have heard that Helen was bringing a boy home.

With both my brothers marrying daughters of local crunchies I was determined my partner would come from further afield. My first kiss was by courtesy of the son of a crunchie. And the son of another regularly found ways to catch me off guard to fondle my breasts. The latter left me confused. Did I have a crush on this older boy? Or was I merely a victim? Homey girls craved attention and love. We were easy prey for men connected to the church. Homey boys equally craved love and attention and weren't excluded from this. No, a crunchie's life was not for me. Neither was marrying young, or so I thought.

I met Ray Wilson during a stormy trip to North Stradbroke Island. As heavy rain and large swells tossed the barge about, Ray and his mates – highly trained, enthusiastic volunteer lifesavers at

Point Lookout – continued their weekly ritual of guzzling beer and rum during the voyage, while my friend Kathy and I clung to our seats.

When my nausea wore off, my attraction grew, and, undoubtedly, there was some chemistry between us during the first of what were to become many weekend visits to the island.

Ray was four years older, a carpenter, and, unlike my secretive first boyfriend, freely showed his adoration in public. He would become my saviour on so many levels. I introduced him to my family and was pleasantly surprised to find that Offla was genuinely interested in him. It came as a relief when my father failed to provide evidence of marriage, offspring, jail convictions or acts of terrorism.

I spent Christmas with my family and joined Ray on Stradbroke Island to celebrate New Year's Eve of 1975. Kathy and I planned to go to the barbecue at the surf club, where Ray was clubhouse director, before heading off to the pub for a dance. The pub had spectacular panoramic views overlooking Moreton Bay with distant views of the sand dunes of Moreton Island.

We were still at the surf club, a talent quest underway, when Kathy glanced at her watch.

'It's 11.30. We'd better head to the pub if we want to make it by midnight.'

'I'll tell Ray we're leaving and see if he wants to join us.'

But he didn't.

'I want you to stay with me at the club,' he said.

'But it'll be more fun at the pub.'

'There's something I want to ask you at midnight,' he said. 'If you leave now I may not get the opportunity again.'

'What is it?'

'You'll have to wait and see.'

By the time I found Kathy it was nearing midnight so she left without me. I went back into the clubhouse, jealously believing her evening of dancing would surpass the talent quest finale. My boyfriend of six weeks grabbed me. 'Come in here so we can be alone.'

He closed the door and turned the light on. We heard the roar of the countdown to midnight.

'Happy New Year, Helena,' he said before he gave me a lingering kiss. 'How about we get engaged?'

I surveyed the tiny room with its shelves stocked with flour, sugar, rice, canned foods and an assortment of items. A proposal of marriage had never entered my mind. If it had I might have dreamed of a more romantic venue than the surf club pantry!

'But I'm only seventeen,' I said.

'I know,' he answered. 'You don't have to give me an answer tonight. But will you at least think about it?'

'Of course.'

I remained on the island for a few more days. Among other things, we discussed raising a family together. Ray was one of seven children and his family had been devastated when his brother Jimmy was killed by a drunk driver on the island two years earlier. His three older sisters were married and I knew his younger twin brothers from the surf club. Ray adored his mother and father. I loved that he was from a normal family. So I based my decision on security and my need to belong to a normal, functioning family. They may not have been the right reasons, but I wanted these things so badly. I surprised most people with the news, including myself. 'How do you know when you're in love?' I asked Bruce and Les during the excitement.

I was now working for a firm of solicitors on Wickham Terrace as a law clerk. My father's aptly named residence – 'Dracula's

Castle' – was nearby. The 120-year-old two-bedroom cottage sat behind Ballow Chambers Medical Centre and was believed to have been a shepherd's house. Made of wood with a tin roof, stone fireplace, and criss-cross woodwork on the verandah, it was the last house of its kind remaining between Wickham and Astor Terraces. High-rises had almost surrounded the old cottage, dwarfing it with its few shrubs and one large tree.

My father first boarded with its elderly tenant. When Tom passed away it didn't take him long to fully claim the cottage and flaunt his eccentricity. He decorated his home with witches riding broomsticks and hung plastic skeletons from the ceilings. Spiders were ignored and webs left intact. Dusting and mopping were completely out of the question. Offla swept the floors regularly only to clear a path through the house.

It was on the cleared path that he taught me to waltz to his beloved classical music. His favourite was 'The Skaters' Waltz' by Émile Waldteufel. He often hummed the tune while doing a little jig. He also had a soft spot for Johan Strauss's The Blue Danube, a waltz named after the magnificent river running through the city he was raised in. He had an amazing collection of books, magazines and newspapers piled high around the edge of the rooms. It didn't matter what any of us thought about his living conditions, his home was his castle. He told us our family ancestry could be traced back to Transylvania and to Count Dracula himself. Hence the new name given to Tom's old cottage.

A stray cat wandered into the castle one cold winter's day and snuggled behind the refrigerator near the warmth of the motor. My father named him Penguin although the pronunciation sounded more like Pengwah. We all thought Pengwah was a male until she gave birth to several litters of kittens.

A carpet python named Cleo, Offla's only true friend, also lived there. The snake wrapped himself around its owner to pose for photographs and was rewarded with a plump mouse. It was wise to carefully scan the premises before entering on the chance Cleo was released on good behaviour. If I discovered his evening meal was sitting in a cage, I opened the latch for it to scurry away. Invariably, the temptation to return was too good to refuse and the stupid mouse was plated up to Cleo.

I often dined at the castle for lunch, meeting Brenda and Lizzy. A diary on Offla's cluttered kitchen table recorded our arrivals and departures, as precise details were imperative. Laid out was a banquet of stale bread, kabana, canned sauerkraut, boiled eggs and coca-cola. Over-ripe bananas sufficed as dessert and on special occasions an out-of-date apple pie from Coles.

One day, I arrived at the castle's entrance at midday. 'Is the coast clear?'

'Don't worry, he's in his cage sleeping,' came the reply from within. I hesitantly leaned over the cage to find Cleo there. And, to my horror, huddled in the corner, a frightened albeit well-fed pigeon! It looked at me and then at Cleo, seemingly accepting its fate.

Offla had been feeding the birds in Anzac Square and had managed to catch one.

'That's the last straw!' I said. 'If you don't let the pigeon out of the cage right now I'll never speak to you again!'

'Okay, okay, don't get so upset,' Offla said.

'I mean it this time. You'd better let him go before that stupid snake wakes up!'

'Cleo isn't stupid,' he said defensively. 'He is my best friend and the only one I can trust.'

I stormed out of the castle, threatening that I would never return unless the snake and the pigeon were gone!

It was at the castle that my Prince Charming and future husband asked my father for my hand in marriage.

On my eighteenth birthday, I received a letter from the director of the Children's Services Department.

> I wish to advise that as you have attained eighteen years of age on 30th July 1976 you have automatically been released from the Care and Protection of this Department as from that date. This Department will have no further jurisdiction or authority over you.
>
> Wishing you all the best for the future.

Twelve years earlier, I'd discovered I was owned by the State. All these years later they relinquished ownership. Just like that. I wondered whether any of the child welfare officers or the director really knew me. They knew my mother was dead. They knew my father suffered an illness while fighting a hopeless custody battle. They knew I was the ringleader in the 1969 Runaway Incident. Maybe that was all they needed, for I was one of thousands of children in care under their jurisdiction. I was a statistic, a name on file. If they'd made the effort to understand the little girl within the file, I wondered whether their final letter might have been more personal. My almost ten-year-old personal file held at Silky Oaks consisted of only three pages. The first was a Form 2 – Register of Children in an Institution under The Children's Services Act, including my date of admission, date of birth, religion, parents' names and whether they were living or deceased. The second and third pages noted I had visitors ten times from the period October 1966 to October 1967 and had been taken temporarily (day trips or holidays) from the institution twelve times. There were no personal details of an often frightened and sometimes troubled little girl.

On the eve of my wedding I discussed plans for the big day with two of my bridesmaids, Brenda and Lizzy. There were hairdressers booked for the morning followed by make-up and a quick lunch. The formal photographs would be taken in Bruce and Les's lounge room and their splendid garden.

As we prepared for bed in Brenda's flat downstairs, I said, 'When you marry, Brenda, I hope I'll be your bridesmaid.'

'Of course you will,' she said. 'I wouldn't choose anyone else.'

'Don't worry, Helena,' Lizzy said. 'You'll definitely be mine.'

After a busy morning, Paul's wife Helen arrived dressed in her apricot chiffon ankle-length tiered dress. She completed my treasured trio of bridesmaids with five-year-old Jane Fleming dressed in floral chiffon as my flower girl. Jono, at eight, refused to be a 'sissy pageboy'. Chris arrived with the father of the bride. I was breathless as I gazed at Offla's clean-shaven handsome features. He was dressed in a smart suit, necktie and shiny shoes. The sparkle in his ice-blue eyes had returned. A few months earlier he'd received word from his brother that his beloved mother had died from heart failure. She was eighty-six, and my siblings and I would now never meet our Nagjmama. It was a pleasure to witness that sparkle again.

Les fussed over me in place of my mother. She was a fine replacement. She would one day present me with a book on behalf of my mother titled *Always*. It is the answer a mother gives to her child when asked 'How long will you be my mother? How long will you love me?'

I placed the delicate white lace handkerchief inside my bra. It was handed to me in an envelope with a note from Aunty Jean the day before.

Offla's Children

Helena dear,

Just a special little "Hanky" for you to use on your wedding day. We have always thought a lot of you and wish you every happiness.

Much love, Aunty Jean xx

The photographers raced ahead to the church as the bridesmaids and flower girl climbed into one white Mercedes, and my father and I into the other. I felt as close to royalty as possible as I waved to motorists and pedestrians during the drive to St Stephen's Cathedral at Coorparoo. I was the princess I aspired to be, with my father direct from his castle beside me. He appeared calm but I suspected he was anxious. If only he could find the strength to ignore Smitbachi and the 'air pushers' while he walked me down the aisle.

The church bells were ringing as the cars pulled up at the entrance. More photographs were snapped before the veil was placed over my face. My white chiffon dress fell into its three tiers as I stepped out of the car. The organ played and Jane took the lead down the aisle followed by Lizzy, Brenda and Helen.

'Are you sure you're okay?' I asked Offla.

'Yes,' he answered softly. 'Let's go.'

I put my arm through his as we slowly made our way towards my future husband. It had been ninety-eight days since I was released from the care and protection of the State. Now the only man who had proven without doubt he was genuinely devoted to me was about to hand me over to the care and protection of another. This time it was with his blessing.

I was determined to acknowledge my guests as we made our way to the altar. These included friends from the surf club, workmates, family and extended family including Bruce and Lesley Fleming, Aunty Jean, Mr Zander and their daughter Roslyn, Ken and Peter Marshall and Robert 'Woodchuck' Krojs.

When the minister asked, 'Who gives this bride away?' I turned and gave him an encouraging smile. His eyes moistened and a tear fell gently onto his cheek. He knew more than anyone the importance of such a question. He said, 'I do.'

Now there were only three years left before Liz turned eighteen and the Children's Services Department's twenty-year-long Ban file could finally be closed.

Seven months later Brenda died of a cerebral haemorrhage. The doctors said it wasn't related to her kidney failure or her body's rejection of the transplant. How could this be? It wasn't fair. She was only nineteen. I loved her as my sister. She was my confidante through all the difficult years of growing up. She was my blood sister, my roommate and best friend. She had recently been my bridesmaid and promised I would one day be hers.

Brenda Lorraine Marshall experienced the saddest childhood of all. She grew up without the nurturing and support of parents. She had just begun to spread her delicate wings when her life ended. And just like a butterfly she flew out of our lives forever. Her brothers Kenny and Peter were devastated, as were we all; they remain part of my precious extended family.

Liz

It was 1976 and I was fifteen when I returned to live at Silky Oaks. I had been an 'ex-home' kid for two and a half years and had lived with three different families. I felt like a failure. Although I was embarrassed to return, there was also a comforting feeling of familiarity. I'd tried to make it work outside the home, but when you are young you are powerless to make big decisions, and, besides, I had no way to make people want to keep me, let alone love me in the way I needed.

I was back in the Big End with the Quelches as my new house parents. Aunty Pam was Aunty Jean's sister. The Quelches were a nice couple. They allowed me time to settle back into the home and didn't place any pressure on me, apart from doing my daily chores. I was free to hang out in my room, which I shared with Karen and Kerrie, who had grown up with me in the home since we were little kids. There were no expectations placed on me to fit into any family.

Most of the kids who went to high school were dropped off in a mini-bus, but I didn't want to be seen in it, so I would ride my bike, whether it rained or not, through winter and summer. I didn't want anyone apart from my close friends at school to know I lived in a children's home, let alone had returned there. I didn't want anyone's pity for being a 'home kid'.

My friends at high school were my saving grace. They smoked on the school oval and told me about the different boys they kissed on the weekends at the parties they went to – things I didn't do. But they accepted me for who I was. I thought they were cool and I wondered why they liked me, as I didn't push boundaries like they did. Six years later, when one of the girls, Rhonda, invited me to her twenty-first party, I found out. We had all dispersed at the end of Year 10 and I had lost contact with them. Rhonda tracked me down by looking up our family name in the local phone book and found Chris's number. I was surprised and asked her why she wanted me to go. She told me she always admired me for not going along with the girls if I didn't think it was the right thing to do. There were many times when I lived at Chris and Beth's where I had to make excuses to avoid going to parties where I knew there would be alcohol or boys. It wasn't because I was a 'goody two shoes', but because I didn't feel confident in those environments. I was taken aback by what Rhonda said and it gave me a confidence boost.

Life in Silky Oaks had changed a bit since I first left. We didn't have to do all the morning readings and prayers before breakfast. There were not as many children in the home and there was an emphasis placed on smaller group homes with everyone eating in their own buildings rather than in the main hall. We only had to go to Sunday school and not the morning or evening services.

I lived at Silky Oaks for six months and was allowed to visit my family regularly during that time.

The only real trouble I got into was when they didn't allow us to go to the school dance towards the end of the year. One minute they'd said we could go and then they changed their mind, as one of the girls who was a year older said she hadn't been allowed to go the previous year and didn't think it was fair that we should be allowed to. I thought that was ridiculous. I tried to reason with Aunty Pam, but she wouldn't relent. I talked Karen into going with me. We ran the two kilometres to school and sat outside the venue and listened to the music, longing to be inside with our friends. We returned to a furious Aunty Pam. She had tried to find me during the evening because Paul had phoned to arrange a time to pick me up to visit Offla. When she asked where we were that evening, we told her. Our punishment was one week's washing and drying the dishes for twenty people.

Towards the end of Year 10, Paul and his wife, Helen, lived in the Old Building for a short time before they moved to Cairns to live. I liked school and was above average academically, despite the emotional upheavals in my life. But I talked with Paul and Helen about leaving school at the end of the year so I could get a job and so leave Silky Oaks.

Throughout my time there I had been good friends with Carol, who I met on the first day of school in Grade 1. The Weeks family lived half a kilometre down the road. At the end of the year, Carol's mother, Jean, asked if I would like to live with them. She knew I wanted to leave the home and get a job. I jumped at the opportunity. Jean and Alan had four children, two boys and two girls, just like my own family.

The school holidays were six weeks and I planned on enjoying them before looking for a job. Offla, however, had other ideas. On a visit to Dracula's Castle, he told me I needed to look for a job at the CES (Commonwealth Employment Services) office. Nothing I said could convince him otherwise, so I reluctantly went with him and pretended to look at the noticeboard. Just as I thought we were finished he found a job advertised for an office junior at an insurance firm. I had to ask the person behind the counter about it and, before I knew it, I had an interview lined up. On the day of the interview, Offla came with me. He followed me to the building and I let him catch the lift to the same floor on the condition that he hid at the end of the corridor while I went in for the interview. I got the job and Offla was very happy.

I was excited and nervous at the same time. I earned my own money, caught the bus to and from the city and wanted to go out with my friends on the weekend or visit my family. I was fifteen and a half years old. Carol was in Year 11 and spent her evenings studying. Over time, Alan became upset with me coming and going and felt I was treating the place like a hotel. It started to create more tension between him and Jean, adding to their marital problems, which I was unaware of at the time. After about three months Jean told me it was not working for them as a family, and I would have to find somewhere else to live. I was gutted. So was Carol. I remember lying on the bottom bunk in her bedroom where I slept and crying myself to sleep. I was happy living there and was unaware my going out was destabilising their family. Alan was concerned I would affect Carol's studies. That was the last thing I wanted to do.

I told my family what happened and Helena and Ray said that I could live with them till I found something else. The size of their flat in Coorparoo and the length of time they'd been married (six months) always meant it would be for a short while. I was nearly sixteen and Helena nineteen. I was so happy to live with her again, even to share her with Ray, who was a great guy, very understanding and easygoing. Helena and I would laugh and reminisce about what we did at Silky Oaks. We caught the bus to and from work together, and would meet most days for lunch at Offla's place in the city. I was emotionally needy and Helena was a great support. She was bubbly, happy with her life and lots of fun. I, on the other hand, had no confidence and was trying to find out who I was and where I fitted in the world. I lived with Helena for about three months, and moved out two weeks after my sixteenth birthday, into a share house in Buranda, with a girl I found through an advertisement in the newspaper. My bedroom was in a sleep-out and I had to walk through her bedroom to go to the bathroom. On my second night, I woke up during the night to go to the bathroom and walked in on her having sex. I was so embarrassed. I told Helena the next day and she arranged for me to live with her friend Kathy.

I was sixteen and Kathy twenty-one. The flat was in a great location, on the corner of Gregory Terrace and Brunswick Street, Fortitude Valley, a short bus ride to the city, where I worked. The flat was attached to the side of a big block of flats that her family owned, and built above two car bays. The floor sloped and you could roll a bottle down it. When it rained I had to put six pots out to catch the drops that leaked from the ceiling. Kathy's parents and relatives all lived in the flats within the complex.

Living with Kathy was great: she was lots of fun and she let me do my own thing. I lived with her for six months before she went to Europe to travel. She planned to be away for a year and told me I could stay in the flat. Because her family owned it, the rent was cheap and I could afford it on my own. I loved that flat: it was homely, and I felt secure knowing that I was not going to be asked to leave. While Kathy was in Europe, her parents would regularly invite me for dinner and I would watch television with them. On the weekends, Kathy's sister Maria, who was in Year 11, and I would go to the local swimming pool. My friends would often sleep over, especially Sue, my best friend at the time, or I would go to their place if I wanted a decent feed. Life finally took a turn for the better and I felt happy. Throughout that time, I regularly saw my siblings and Offla.

Finally, I felt I was taking some control of my life. I had the freedom to do what I wanted without worrying whether I was upsetting someone. I enjoyed my work and had moved from an office junior to receptionist. My boss, Helaine, who was ten years older than me, took me under her wing. Helaine's husband, John, was a social worker and they invited me to their place on weekends with their friends, where we water-skied. I went camping on Stradbroke Island with Sue and her sister, Sharron, on other weekends. We scuba-dived on the island, at Byron Bay or on the Sunshine Coast, and hung out at the beach most weekends.

After a year and a half in my flat in Gregory Terrace, I decided it was time to move on. Yes, it was my decision. For the first time in my life. I was due to go to New Zealand in a few weeks for a one-year working holiday with Sue. In the meantime, I thought it might be fun to live with Offla at Dracula's Castle. I'd always felt sorry for him not being allowed the chance to have us live with him when we were children. And I thought he might like having me around.

I slept in Tom's old bed, and it gave me the creeps knowing he had died in it. The toilet didn't flush and I had to fill a bucket of water to flush it. The hot water didn't work in the bath, and I would heat water up in the kettle or on the stove top before I could bathe. It was a camping experience without the tent.

Living with Offla was an interesting experience. He was set in his ways and his paranoid beliefs had a way of creeping into our conversations. I'd have to tell him I didn't believe what he talked about and steer the conversation in another direction. He loved cooking things that I thought were strange at the time. Pigs heads, ox and sheep tongue, lots of kabana, salami and bacon. He would buy a chicken carcass for 50 cents and boil it up for broth and make soup.

He loved BBQ chicken, and apple pie for dessert. He had bread with most of his meals. He drank loads of coffee with four heaped spoons of sugar. He loved chocolate and always had a tub of ice cream in his freezer. The fridge was stocked with coca-cola as he didn't like drinking water. It was an unhealthy diet and I was amazed he lived as long as he did. He must have had a stomach of cast iron, or maybe the experiences he'd had during the war in Europe had toughened him up. Offla saw food as a means for survival and didn't spend much time cooking. Eating was a practical experience based on a daily need.

I had two budgies in a cage that I hung from the ceiling on the veranda. One night Offla heard a commotion outside with the birds, and when he went out he found a nine-foot carpet python trying to get into the cage – Cleo. He caught it and kept it in a wooden box under my bedroom window. I'm no fan of snakes and I was not happy he kept it. One day I said to him that I'd had enough. Either the snake went or I went. He loved that snake, as he did all animals, so I moved out. It was only a week or so until I was leaving for New Zealand, so I stayed with Helaine and John. Paul, Helena, and Chris were all married at that stage and I didn't want to ask them for any more favours.

Liz

Sue and I spent about a year travelling in New Zealand. We had a flat in the centre of Christchurch, in Armagh Street, above Roley's milk bar. It was in a perfect location for two young girls who loved going out on the weekends. We were friends with the owner, who we knew from Brisbane, who said we could stay there as long as we wanted. I worked in different jobs: a factory hand cutting out pantyhose, a tea lady for the Department of Transport, and a waitress in a Chinese restaurant. All hard work and lots of fun.

I turned eighteen a couple of months into the trip. The only person I now belonged to was myself. My mail was waiting for me, post restante at the GPO in Christchurch – birthday cards from Helena and Ray, Paul and Helen, Chris and Beth, and Offla. There was no phone in the flat, so I called Helena from a pay phone on my birthday.

What I liked about New Zealand was the freedom to do what I wanted, without any expectations being placed on me. No one knew me or my past experiences – living in the 'home', the multiple moves and the struggles I'd had. Listening to people tell me about their lives made me realise that not everyone has a perfect upbringing. Perhaps I wasn't that abnormal. Perhaps I wasn't the only one hurting. In Australia, I felt ashamed, judged, or embarrassed to tell people my story, but I didn't feel the same way in New Zealand. The first time, I felt self-conscious and it still felt raw and brought up emotions inside me. However, the more I told my story, the more it started to free me and the less emotional I became.

Towards the end of the year, I returned to Brisbane, and to my family. But it took me a little while to settle back in; it was all too familiar and I quickly reverted to being the 'little sister'. I lived with Helena and Ray in Sunnybank for five months to save money, before going to South-East Asia. My bed was in a sleep-out by the front door.

I travelled through Java, Bali, Singapore, Malaysia and Thailand with Gerry, a good friend of mine. We hired bicycles in Yogyakarta and cycled to the beach through small villages and were amazed at how friendly the people were. We stayed in a simple dirt-floor home-stay and when I scooped the water to pour over my head to wash my hair, there were fish swimming around in the tub. The fish must have come down the bamboo pipe from the river. In Malaysia, people thought we were poor as not many people hitch-hiked. Most people who picked us up would take us to a restaurant and buy us a huge meal. Everywhere we went we were shown kindness and hospitality. In Thailand, we trekked for five days into different hill tribe villages. People slept on mats on dirt floors, and lived simple but hard lives. I remember reflecting on the comforts of life in Australia and how unhappy some people were, chasing elusive happiness through material objects.

After our return to Australia it took me some time to readjust to the lifestyle and need to conform to society's 'norm'. I didn't rush to get a job and spent the summer with Sue, going to the local pool or to the beach, before moving into a flat with Carol, my best friend from primary school. Carol and I lived in Highgate Hill in Brisbane for two years. We planned a trip to Europe together and I worked two jobs to save the money. During our time in the flat, Offla would regularly come over for dinner. It was a Monday night ritual, with Offla bringing chicken and ice-cream. I felt a sense of responsibility for him because of all he had done for us, and I was sorry for him that he had had such a hard time. I saw my siblings and occasionally had Chris's two eldest children, Melissa and Jeremy, for sleepovers.

Carol and I left in 1982. We wanted to travel for two years throughout Europe and see as many countries as we could. We had no real plans apart from arriving in Athens, Greece. If it was cold and raining in one place, we'd travel to another city or country where the weather was warm. I loved this freedom, and I felt connected to Offla, through his stories of Europe after the war, when he worked in France and Switzerland.

One city we travelled to was Budapest, where we met my cousin, Laszlo, and his wife, Eva, and their daughter, Brigitta, who was three years old. Meeting Laszlo was amazing as he was the first relative I had met other than my siblings and Offla. He had dark curly hair, which I thought was natural; it wasn't until years later, when I visited him again, that I found out his hair was naturally straight, like mine. Laszlo is the same age as Paul and is an only child. His English was limited, in fact he only spoke a few words of English and Eva spoke Hungarian and some German. Carol and I learnt German in school and we conversed in German with Eva and used a Hungarian dictionary with Laszlo. Also, the odd pantomime came in handy at times. We stayed with Eva and Laszlo for two weeks while we looked around the city where Offla grew up. His mother died some time before I went to Budapest and I regretted not being able to meet her, to see whether any of us resembled her, to see for myself the special, strong person Offla told us she was. Perhaps because I'd never met her, I always thought of her as Offla's mother rather than as my grandmother.

Years later, on another visit with my husband Ed and our children, Jasmine and Austin, Laszlo took us to my grandmother's house. It was the house where Offla had stayed when he returned to Budapest while we were at Silky Oaks. I tried to picture him there, pleading with his mother to leave Hungary and travel to Australia, where she could help him look after his children.

Laszlo had arranged for Carol and me to meet his father, also named Laszlo, and Laszlo's wife, Elizabeth. I was excited at the idea of meeting my uncle, to hear what he had to say about his brother, my father. I had hoped to hear stories about them as boys growing up and the things they did. There was definitely a family resemblance – with the Ban nose being the most obvious. Offla had a big nose, and I realised through meeting Uncle Laszlo it was a family trait, which he had passed on to me and my two brothers. Helena was the lucky one who missed out.

It was a difficult visit as they could not speak English and I could not speak Hungarian and my cousin, Laszlo, with his limited English, tried to interpret. Hungary was still a communist country in 1983 and my cousin and uncle didn't have much in the way of material wealth. My cousin lived in the inner city of Budapest and Uncle Laszlo lived on the outskirts of town in a small one-bedroom apartment in a high-rise building. I remember Uncle Laszlo asking why I couldn't speak Hungarian. I was surprised by that question, as I was sure he knew we hadn't lived with Offla, and I was frustrated he didn't or couldn't understand the difficulty we'd had not living with him. I hoped he would be excited to see me and be full of stories about his older brother. He didn't appear interested. I met Uncle Laszlo and Elizabeth twice and both times it felt strained and

I left feeling disappointed. They were strangers and the language barrier was too great.

Laszlo and Eva were different. They were younger and as interested in finding out about me and my family and life in Australia as I was about finding out about them and their life. Budapest is a beautiful city, more beautiful than I had imagined from the stories Offla told me. And being in the city was special for me as I tried to imagine my father growing up there and the life he would have had before the war broke out. Years later, Laszlo came to Australia to visit his uncle Zoli, Chris and Paul. Helena was staying with me in Oxford, England, at the time of his visit in 2002. That same year we met his daughter Briggi again, who was now an au pair in England, where she studied English.

Carol and I travelled to Lugano, Switzerland, where we met my Uncle Lajos and his wife, Loty. After my visit with Uncle Laszlo, I tried not to have high expectations. Lajos was Offla's youngest brother, now sixty. He had flecks of black in his hair, unlike Offla and Laszlo, who were completely grey. Lajos spoke limited English, whereas Loty's was quite good. We spent a week getting to know them. They were quite rigid in their ways. Loty was particular about meal times. Lunch was at midday and dinner at 6 p.m. sharp. She clapped her hands to make a point. I thought she was strict and seemed to boss Uncle Lajos around. They didn't have any children together. Lajos had been married before in Hungary and had two children to his first wife. He left Hungary in the 1956 uprising and fled to Switzerland leaving his wife and two children behind. He worked in a bank in Lugano.

One night, Lajos pulled out some letters he had kept from my mother and some photos she had sent him of my family. I was moved to think he had kept them all those years. Had he hoped one of Offla's children would collect them one day? Perhaps he was more sentimental than I gave him credit for at the time. There were eight letters that dated back to 1959. I read them and re-read them and I guess Uncle Lajos could see how important they were to me, so he gave them to me along with the photos. Reading those letters was like getting to know my mother. I got a sense of who she was through them and it was a gift from heaven to be able to connect to her that way. She seemed gentle, loyal, and understanding as she wrote to Lajos and Loty, trying to piece together any information to help her understand why her husband was sick.

I found out I was a surprise baby and that she hoped I was a girl and named me after her mother's second name. I also found out just how unstable Offla was during the years we lived with him and how my mother was left caring for us for long periods of time, while Offla was in and out of mental hospitals. I had never heard those stories before and all sorts of emotions came to the surface: It wasn't fair, my mother was taken so soon; Why didn't I have a 'normal' father? I could empathise with my mother, and the difficult life she had lived, not that she said one bad word about my father. It made me realise I didn't want to be bitter about my experience of living at Silky Oaks and not with my family. I wanted to take some strength from my mother. There are some things we just have to accept. Through my mother's letters, I realised that it was better that I had grown up at Silky Oaks. I would not have had a stable environment if I had lived with Offla. The few weeks I'd lived with him before travelling to New Zealand had been enough to confirm that.

I knew my siblings would be just as moved as I was to read the letters and so I posted them to Helena in Australia to look after while I continued my travels around Europe.

After I left their place, Uncle Lajos wrote me a letter and said I would not be welcome again. What had I done to upset them? I was upset myself. Some time later, I found out that Offla had written to Lajos prior to my visit and told him I was there on Offla's behalf inquiring about how well-off they were. Of course, I had been innocently asking questions about life in Switzerland and comparing it to Australia as any tourist would do. But Lajos must have thought I was spying on him. I was furious with Offla.

In 1984, Helena came to Europe, and we went to Budapest where she met Laszlo and Eva.

After Helena returned to Australia, Carol went to the UK with her mother, and I bought a bicycle, planning to ride through Germany, Luxembourg, and Belgium before catching the boat to England. It was the first time I had spent any significant time alone. The first two weeks of cycling it was cold and often wet. I cycled between eighty and one hundred kilometres a day, along the Rhine and Moselle rivers. I stayed in campgrounds and some nights in youth hostels. It was so cold one night that I slept in all my clothes, winter pants, jumper, plastic rain coat and pants, wrapped in an emergency silver sleep blanket inside my sleeping bag that made a noise every time I rolled over.

Cycling on my own gave me confidence that I could do things by myself and didn't need to rely on anyone. I was used to having people around me as I had grown up with so many kids and had wondered how I would cope being alone with just my thoughts. Would it bring sadness from my teen years to the surface? But I kept myself busy cycling and being a tourist by day, and cooking on the camp stove at night and reading for a few hours before falling asleep. I enjoyed the freedom to decide where and how far I cycled. The trip was a turning point. I realised I could survive on my own in the world.

Offla's Children

After nearly two years, homesickness crept in. And I flew home. Most young people have their parents to rely on, but each time I went away I returned to Helena and Ray's. Then I set about finishing my high school education.

I'd travelled all over the world and I met the love of my life in a dark and noisy bar in Queen Street, Brisbane when I was twenty-eight. Kathy and I had been out to dinner and the movies, and popped in for a quick drink and dance on our way home.

I bought a drink and put it on a table beside the dance floor where two guys were sitting, so Kathy and I could dance. On my way to collect my drink someone bumped the table and knocked my drink over. One of the guys got up from the table and offered to buy me another drink. That was Ed. The other guy was Ned, his cousin from Boston, US, who had just arrived in Brisbane that day. I made a flippant joke about them being 'the Ed and Ned show' and chatted to Ed while Kathy talked to Ned. We talked and talked. When the bar closed we said goodnight and Kathy and I made our way to the taxi rank. I was climbing into the taxi when Ed came up and asked me for my phone number. He was a bit shy and unbeknownst to me at the time his cousin had asked him why he hadn't asked for my phone number as he thought we'd hit it off.

Ed was born in England to an English father, Hoops, and an American mother, Betty. His brother was two and a half years younger. At nine, while I was sharing dorm rooms at Silky Oaks, he went to boarding school at Cheam, where Prince Charles went, and in high school he boarded at Radley College, three miles from Oxford. Ed was doing his masters in Geology in Brisbane. Beforehand, he'd been studying in Austin, Texas.

I was in awe of Ed when we started dating. I'd never been with anyone who had gone to uni. He challenged me intellectually and culturally. He was fascinated by my life, and he supported me during my studies at university.

When I met Ed's family they were warm, welcoming and accepting. His mother was an incredibly positive person, full of beans. When Ed and I got engaged she gave me a cheque for $1000 to open an account so I could have my own 'mad money' to do with as I wanted.

When I married Ed, Helena finally felt confident to cut the apron strings she'd kept dangling between us for years. We became sisters again.

Part 5

After care

Paul

In the late 1980s, after leaving Dracula's Castle in the centre of Brisbane, Offla obtained a Housing Commission flat in the inner suburb of Yeronga. It was a block of ground floor flats built in a U shape, with the open-ended part of the U facing the street. The flats were brick and reasonably new. Offla's had one bedroom, which was not closed off from the open-plan kitchen and dining room. He had a shower, laundry and toilet off the bedroom. While this sounds like basic accommodation, it was absolute luxury compared to Dracula's Castle. The toilet flushed without being assisted by a bucket of water and the shower had hot and cold water.

But it didn't take long before Offla began to turn a typical modern suburban flat into his own version of Dracula's Castle. He was worried he would hurt himself on the sharp edges of the kitchen bench, so he placed small cardboard boxes over the sharp corners for protection. The shower wasn't ever used for its intended purpose. Offla turned it into a pet sanctuary for lizards he kept in a cage. He occasionally had birds in cages too, but not at the same time as the lizards. He wasn't used to having a functioning bathroom and preferred his European-style bird-baths. The laundry sink was a place for frogs to live – an open aquarium. Offla rarely washed his clothes. He preferred to throw them out and replace them with op shop acquisitions. I'm not sure what the trigger was for the change – maybe the weather, as he usually slept in the clothes he wore. However, he was meticulous about cleaning and cutting his fingernails and toenails.

The wall beside his bed had a rough surface, and he plastered tracksuit pants, a top and a beanie onto it so it looked like the Invisible Man was resting there. That way, he could jump out of bed and get dressed straightaway, he told us. But the clothes remained on the wall the whole time. He added to his wall decoration by cutting out the face of a gorilla from a magazine and placing it where the Invisible Man's face would have been.

Helen and I lived in Cairns twice – the first time for a year, the second for three years – and Offla visited us. He'd been travelling to Cairns on his pensioner train pass for some time before we moved there and usually stayed a few months throughout winter. So when we moved there, we were entering Offla's holiday space. He always seemed more relaxed in Cairns and didn't talk as much about air pushers and radio frequencies controlling our minds. He knew people in the boarding houses where he stayed, and he had his own community of friends and routines that seemed comparatively normal to his life in Brisbane.

In Brisbane he had his circuit of opportunity shops, where the staff knew him. When not replacing his clothes, he used to buy old cameras and second-hand books, which I read because they were usually Penguin classics. One of his favourite hobbies was to buy old broken-down watches, which he would painstakingly repair to their former glory. I don't know what he did with them once they were fixed – I think it was just the challenge of bringing them to life again.

In Cairns he would go to the beach and swimming pool, as well as research areas of interest in the library. Usually his research was to confirm his conspiracy theories by linking what others would think were unrelated pieces of information.

He would even have a holiday from Cairns, travelling on the train west to Forsayth, a railway terminus for a defunct mining town. It was a refuge for others like him escaping society. He had friends there who accepted him because they were a little unusual themselves. Once he surprised everyone with a box of penny tortoises and a snake he caught while having his outback experience. The poor creatures had to put up with being crammed into a cardboard box on the two train journeys, to Cairns and then Brisbane. Remarkably, they survived and were handed out to his grandchildren. The tortoises were popular but no-one wanted the snake.

In Brisbane, I'd see Offla at Chris's or Helena's house or his Dracula's Castles. But in Cairns, he'd come to us like a normal visitor. It was a relief to have interactions approximating normality instead of being subjected to a barrage of Offla's conspiracy theories nonstop, as though he'd saved them up to tell me and was bursting at the seams. I remember waking up at his place one morning in Yeronga to find him standing beside the bed telling me something conspiratorial in an animated manner with no breaks for me even to say 'good morning'. In Cairns, when our daughter Lauren was four or five, he used to take her for rides in a seat on the back of his pushbike. He would usually take her to what he called 'Timbuktu' on Sunday afternoons, which was a closed shopping centre. Lauren told me years later that she thought that was the real name of the shopping centre.

Helena

Fourteen years after receiving Australian citizenship, Offla returned to the Autumn of Budapest. It was 1988 and he was seventy-one. This time it was with a passport and a one-way ticket.

It was one week before the birth of my third son and the emotional farewell left me wondering if my baby would ever meet his grandfather.

I swear he was with me in spirit during the birth of my first child when I noticed the words 'Planet 5' imprinted on a machine near the bed. As I painstakingly pushed my firstborn into the world the presence of a 400-year-old prophet was definitely felt. He'd told me years earlier Planet 5 was his home planet. My father had proudly sat at my bedside within a couple of hours of my first two sons being born. So I decided if he couldn't meet my third son on the day of his birth, I would allow his alter-ego to return.

Several months later he met his seventh grandchild, a new littlie sparrow. Without warning, he appeared on my back landing greeting me in his still-heavy accent. 'Helena, my beloved daughter.'

Details of his 1988 trip are scant. I was occupied with raising two toddlers and a baby and couldn't cope with his outpouring of conspiracy theories. Government air pushers playing mind control games in Europe and Australia were too much to bear!

But he *was* deported, from Hungary to Switzerland.

Any future plans of returning to either country were laid to rest when his flight home was paid courtesy of the Swiss Government. I have no doubt he exhausted all avenues to claim the pension he was adamant he was entitled to. Later, Paul told me Offla was well aware prior to this trip that he wasn't welcome at either brother's house. His plan to visit them never eventuated. As only he could describe it: 'The power line was disconnected.'

When he turned eighty in 1997, at his birthday party, I asked, 'How are you feeling today, Offla?'

'Oh, I'm not sure I have many years left.'

'Your mother made it to eighty-six and I'm sure you'll survive beyond that.'

I could tell by his demeanour he was recalling the day he received word his beloved mother passed away. He truly loved her and regretted he had not been able to bring her to Australia. We felt his loss when she died.

'Recently I walked through a graveyard and noticed the age of many didn't reach beyond the age of seventy,' he said.

'Have you forgotten that you are already a 400-year-old prophet?' I asked

He thought for a moment and his eyes sparkled. 'That's right, I am.'

As the subject of graveyards popped up, Liz asked, 'Offla, would you prefer to be buried or cremated?'

He thought for a moment. 'Neither, I want to be stuffed.'

'What for?' she asked.

'In this life I've been a daddy. In the next life I want to be a mummy.'

I'd previously given him two one kina coins from Papua New

Guinea. The currency is silver and round with a hole in the centre. He studied them and asked, 'Will you place these over my eyes when I die?'

'What on earth for?' I asked.

'I want to always keep an eye on things.'

Later as we ate the last of his birthday cake, I asked, 'What has been the most important thing you've learnt in life so far?'

'No matter what anyone says about you,' he replied, 'always believe in yourself.'

The apology

When the Ban siblings were in their late thirties and early forties, the Queensland state government commissioned the Forde Inquiry (Commission of Inquiry into Abuse of Children in Queensland Institutions in 1998-1999) to investigate the treatment of children in licensed government and non-government institutions. Silky Oaks was one of 150 institutions investigated. During the period the inquiry encompassed – 1911 to 1999 – around 1000 children were cared for at Silky Oaks and fourteen came forward to be heard.

Edwin Smith, who was in charge of the boys dormitory when the Ban children arrived at Silky Oaks, was found by the Commission to have sexually abused at least two residents there, one from the age of ten. He was later convicted and jailed. The inquiry found 'that those administering Silky Oaks at the time appeared to not fully appreciate the risks involved in placing individuals in positions of power over children without any mechanism in place to monitor their conduct towards the children in their care' and 'They failed to create at Silky Oaks an environment that was conducive to the disclosure of abuse.' The report acknowledged religious bodies that responded positively to the inquiry. The Council of Silky Oaks was one of these.

Twenty years later, investigations continue and charges are sought for abuse perpetrated in the 1970s.

None of the Ban children were abused themselves, but as adults, Liz, Helena and Paul all heard about instances of sexual abuse at Silky Oaks.

On 16 November 2009, when Offla was ninety-two, Paul fifty-five, Chris fifty-three, Helena fifty-one, and Liz forty-eight, these 'Forgotten Australians' were finally remembered (as were Former Child Migrants). They received a formal apology from the Prime Minister, The Hon Kevin Rudd MP.

> We reflect too today on the families who were ripped apart simply because they had fallen on hard times.
> Hard times brought about by illness, by death and by poverty.
> Some simply left destitute when fathers damaged by war could no longer cope.
>
> . . .
>
> We recognise the pain you have suffered.
> Pain is so very, very personal.
> Pain is so profoundly disabling.
> So, let us together, as a nation, allow this apology to begin to heal this pain.
> Healing the pain felt by so many of the half a million of our fellow Australians who were children in care – children in our care.
> And let us also resolve this day that this national apology becomes a turning point in our nation's story.
> A turning point for shattered lives.

Helena Wilson / Liz Ban / Paul Ban

A turning point for governments at all levels and of every political hue and colour to do all in our power to never let this happen again.

For the protection of children is the sacred duty of us all.

Helena

Offla died on 30 August 2010. He had lived for ninety-three years and eight months.

Ten years earlier, as the year two thousand came to a close, I remembered talking about what the year would be like with my Grade 6 teacher. The space age had definitely arrived!

I was disappointed I wasn't flying around in a spaceship and I didn't have a robot as a maid, but I could defrost, reheat and cook a meal in a microwave.

There had been several manned moon landings since 1969. Computer technology had taken over the world. Children's outdoor games were replaced by a screen and a joystick. Fax machines, mobile phones and email were the preferred form of communication. Was my father right? Was modern technology a worldwide communication conspiracy?

I would never have imagined that Offla's lectures on cryogenics on the tram would come to fruition. But a surprising number of people signed up to have their bodies frozen once confirmed clinically dead. I wondered what sort of world my then 83-year-old father would wake up to if he had the opportunity to sign up for the experiment.

Lasers were used in practically all areas of our lives, including surgery, electronics and entertainment. I took my father to the theatre twice. The first time was to see the musical *Singing in the Rain*. He spent the majority of the show with his back to the stage studying the laser beam lighting as it hit the stage. He said it was important to have one eye forward and the other backward. The second show was *The Man from Snowy River*. He remained facing front and centre due to the lighting fixed above centre stage. He studied every movement of the horses as coloured lighting beamed messages directly to them ordering their next move. A phenomenon I'm certain was not observed by any other member of the audience.

German researchers have now developed a car you can drive with your mind using technology currently found in the latest video games systems. It uses an electroencephalograph headset to measure brain activity which essentially reads the drivers mind when they want to stop, turn and accelerate. Perhaps in the future we will be driving mind controlled vehicles.

My father was an intelligent and knowledgeable man. I used to think many of his peculiar ideas were the result of his illness. I was mistaken. He was just thirty or forty years ahead of the time.

His eccentricity and sense of humour always kept us entertained. As he aged, his bodily functions were switching so regularly with diarrhoea, constipation and vomiting he thought he might turn into a shithead. It wouldn't have worried him as he said he has lived in countries where shitheads ruled for fifty years or more!

Along with being stuffed as a mummy he asked for the inscription on his Epitaph to read the words Julius Caesar announced to the Roman senate 'I came. I saw. I conquered.' I wondered whether he had conquered the government system or his illness and once asked him whether he thought he had a mental illness. True to his character, he replied, 'Einstein had a mental problem – and he worked out relativity.'

I often checked his lucidity on my visits by asking him who I was. His sarcasm was a strong personality trait and he teased me by saying I was one of his grandchildren. He knew how far to push my buttons and pacified me before I threatened to leave by admitting 'You are my beloved daughter Helena.'

When he was hospitalised the nurse asked him if he knew where he was. He said, 'Next to you'. She then asked him what his name was. 'I told you before,' he said, 'and if you don't know by now I'm not telling you again!'

Chris and I met at the cemetery to discuss funeral arrangements. Paul and Liz were flying in from overseas and interstate. Chris and I had been estranged for several years due to individual stubborn loyalties to our father, but we embraced and sobbed in each other's arms. We had shared the responsibility of providing a home and physically caring for our father over several years. Now, our disagreements were replaced with sorrow.

We chose a plot beside a tree-lined fence with a timber seat conveniently placed nearby. Zoli – known and loved by the name Offla – would have approved, for it was close to the road in case there was a need of a quick exit. But this time there would be no escape. This would be his final resting place.

We visited the funeral home and chose a coffin, both painstakingly making an effort not to disagree. Offla would have been proud of our selection. It had no sharp edges – all corners were rounded off to prevent injury. The small bunch of Australian native flowers was perfect. Then the funeral director asked if there were any special requests on the day.

I remembered Offla's wish years earlier for the Papua New Guinean one kina coin to be placed over each of his eyes when he died. The hole in the centre would allow him to keep an eye on things and he would have liked the two crocodiles on the reverse side of the coin. They often featured on his postcards from Cairns – once he carefully pasted a cut-out of his head inside a crocodile's gaping mouth.

Two coins minted in the year 1999 had been set aside. Offla sarcastically referred to everything costing $19.99, which was an outrageous price to pay. The funeral director asked if the coins were to be put on top of or underneath his eyelids.

'On top,' I replied, horrified. 'And I will place them there myself.'

One week after Offla's death, we entered the chapel at the Hemmant cemetery. In his coffin, dressed simply but elegantly with a woollen scarf draped around his neck, he looked serene. He was at peace. The coins were gently placed over his eyelids and we made our final farewells.

Guests entered the chapel listening to 'The Skaters' Waltz' by Émile Waldteufel, a French composer, while a presentation of family photos was digitally displayed on the large screen above his coffin.

Paul, Chris, Liz and I shared the eulogy, before the boys and four grandsons carried Offla's coffin from the chapel, to Hector Berlioz's 'Hungarian March'. It was mentioned during the service how one of Offla's many philosophical statements was 'When times are tough, keep marching.' And so my sister and I marched ahead of the coffin holding a framed photo of our father.

At the graveside, the Cat Stevens' song 'The Wind' was played, followed by 'Father and Son' as the coffin was lowered to its final resting place. Offla often confused English words and referred to Cat Stevens as Dog Jimmy.

During final memories at the graveside, Chris said that living with our father had all the drama and comedy of *Mother and Son* with all the practicality of *Steptoe and Son*.

We sat side by side holding hands and shedding tears. Memories of forty-six years earlier remained raw, when we'd been taken from him.

And then I remembered the comforting words our father offered during many times of uncertainty. 'Everything will come together. Everything will be all right.'

Paul

Offla was going well physically into his mid-eighties and could still travel to Cairns on the train with his pensioner pass. He continued to ride his bike around Cairns. As he grew older, however, he started riding on the footpath instead of the roads and was offended when the police stopped him to tell him he had to wear a helmet. In an act of defiance, he converted an old ice-cream container into a helmet with a piece of string to secure it. I'm not sure what the police thought of the conversion and its road safety value!

In his late eighties he began to experience what he called 'power cuts' and was cared for by Chris, Helena and again Chris in their homes in Brisbane. Chris's house in Manly, Brisbane, was neat and modern, bought new. But after splitting from his wife of twenty years, Chris let the garden go and it was wild and overgrown. When he came to bring the garden back later, he uncovered things he'd completely forgotten about – three little skiffs for sailing around, a couple of old cars with running boards. The hot water system blew up, and for a year he showered in cold water. Like Offla, he cooked stews that would last for days. When Offla moved in they were well-matched: both had an eccentric side, both were stubborn and both had thick skin. They understood each other. As Helena had before him, Chris made Offla feel like part of the family.

Chris's life had changed a lot since his days at Silky Oaks, when he left school early to become an electrician. In his late thirties, Chris went to night school to finish high school, alongside his eldest, his daughter Melissa, who had also left school early. He did an arts degree. Next, he and Melissa studied law together. Both are now lawyers. His son Jeremy is a mechanical engineer, and Brendan is a primary school teacher.

When it was time, Offla went into the hospital section of a retirement home. As the retirement home was closer to Chris than Helena, Chris visited him daily for years. Helena could see him more often than Liz and me, as we lived interstate. We wondered how Offla would cope with the containment of a nursing home, as he valued his independence and only wanted to be with family. Helena and Chris did a great job of providing him with care within his family for as long as possible. The nursing home's solution to his defiant and challenging personality when dealing with officialdom was to medicate him. So it was a subdued Offla we used to visit, with elements of his sarcastic wit coming through every now and then.

I was on a trip in Europe in August 2010 with Helen, when Liz phoned to say Offla had passed away. Although I had expected to receive such a call for some time, it was still devastating.

I sat for a while in the apartment we were renting in Paris, thinking about all his eccentricities. Offla had many quirky responses to things. One of them was to pretend to spit in disgust at something he objected to and pretend the spit had turned to ice, as it would have in Hungary in winter. He would then hum 'The Skaters' Waltz' and pretend to skate around the room. Like all of Offla's trademarks, it contained some level of sarcasm while being amusing at the same time. I played the 'The Skaters' Waltz' on YouTube and a flood of tears welled up.

We flew back to Brisbane for the funeral. Helena and Chris did a great job of overcoming their differences regarding how Offla should have been cared for in his final years to organise a moving funeral. After I told Helena about my association with Offla and *The Skaters' Waltz* and how it had affected me in Paris, she made sure it was included in the service. Chris, Helena, Liz and I all spoke about the impact Offla had on our lives, and our tone was one of humour regarding his behaviour rather than sadness. Our father had managed to overcome the tragedy of the war, mental illness followed by losing his wife and children to death and 'the welfare' respectively, and would still be remembered for his wackiness more than anything else. Offla had the most complex and difficult life of anyone I have ever known and he was finally able to rest. The four of us sat on chairs next to the grave dressed in our finest while Offla was in a box having dirt thrown on him. He'd withstood dirt being thrown at him most of his life, so I thought he could handle a little bit more.

When Offla first came to Australia, he went to an RSL after hearing it was a club for people like him who had fought in a war. There, he was told he wasn't welcome because he'd fought on the 'wrong' side.

Research done in the 1960s and 1980s found very high rates of 'severe psychiatric illness' among eastern European immigrants who came to Australia between 1947 and 1950, and that the incidence of schizophrenia in this group was five times greater than among the Australian-born population. Interestingly, the rate of schizophrenia was highest among non-Jewish immigrants from Czechoslovakia, Hungary and Yugoslavia who had left their countries before the communist takeover. This was the group that Offla belonged to.

The lower rates of schizophrenia among Jewish immigrants, even those who had been in concentration camps, was reasoned to be because they married people who had shared the same experiences, and formed tight-knit cultural communities in Australia. Similar findings were reported about Italian migrants who came in the next wave of migration and developed their own cultural communities in Australia – 'little Italys'. Unfortunately, Offla wasn't blessed with that kind of strong community support in Brisbane.

Those in Offla's position also experienced difficulty in adjusting to life in Australia compared to other eastern Europeans, 'significant downward mobility', and the loss of social status.

The Australian Government's decision to accept non-Anglo migrants after the war was part of an economic nation-building policy, not a humanitarian initiative. So, although the first wave of European migrants (who arrived between 1947 and 1950) had experienced war, they were not regarded as people in need of support and recovery. Offla was part of this first wave.

In return for being allowed to come here, this group of migrants was expected to work for two years after their arrival, typically in low-paid low-skilled jobs such as working in the mines or on major infrastructure projects, including the Snowy Mountains Scheme. For migrants from Hungary and Czechoslovakia, many of whom were tertiary educated, this was a big come down from their pre-war middle-class lifestyle. This was certainly the case for Offla, who found himself labouring in a zinc mine in Tasmania.

'Cultural shock' was also a factor. Unlike the Russian and Polish immigrants of the era (many of whom came from rural villages), most of the Hungarian and Czechoslovakian migrants had lived in large metropolitan European cities before the war, cities that boasted opera, classical music, cafes and fine dining. Australia in the 1950s was a far cry from Budapest and Prague. Australian men drank beer in pubs, not wine in cafes, and the pubs closed at 6 p.m. While Melbourne began to develop a café culture in the 1960s, thanks to the large influx of Italian migrants, Brisbane must have felt like a cultural backwater to Offla, who had grown up in the heart of Budapest close to the Opera House.

Added to this were other hardships that are often part of establishing a life in a new country for migrants. The research says that for eastern Europeans in the first wave, these included difficulties in buying a home and providing economic security for their family when work was irregular and unpredictable and English was not their first language. They also had to contend with misunderstandings, discrimination and rejections from white Australians who were not yet accustomed to or comfortable with living alongside non-English speaking migrants (only 2 per cent of Australia's population had a non-English speaking background in 1947).

I remember a time (it must have been in the year after our mother died) when we were at a train station and Offla told me to ask a man on the platform how we could get to Enoggera, a suburb of Brisbane. It is pronounced 'Ennogra', but Offla pronounced it Eee-nog-geera and told me to say it that way. When I did, the man laughed at me. I remember times when Offla (who could speak six languages) became angry and frustrated when people couldn't understand his heavily accented English.

These stressors would certainly have contributed to the development of Offla's schizophrenia, as the research indicates, or at least they wouldn't have helped. Our mother's letters indicate that his condition was worsening over time in Australia and suggest that the move to Brisbane – which took him away from some of his connections to others who had left Hungary when he did – may have exacerbated it.

I also think – based on my childhood memories – that Offla's mental health deteriorated, and his paranoia increased, when our mother was diagnosed with cancer. He told me the hospital authorities had made her sick. I feel that our mother's illness and death was the final straw for Offla. Before that, he would be admitted to hospital for treatment and come home well again. But after our mother died he was pretty much permanently in his schizophrenic state, and the earlier days of a 'normal' father and son relationship were lost.

I knew that there was another Offla inside the one who talked about air pushers controlling our minds with some special frequency and how we needed to be aware of their influence. When there were gaps, I managed to get him to explain the stories behind the classic operas. He even bought me a book on the topic. His home in Dracula's Castle always had classical music playing on ABC radio and he would tell me about the music and its context.

When I first went to Paris, Offla's eyes lit up and he spoke of a famous nineteenth-century French author, Emile Zola. I sent him a postcard of Zola and started reading his books to see why Offla liked him. Zola wrote about the lives of everyday people in the mid-nineteenth century as they lived through the continual changes of that century – France flipping between a republic and an empire a few times. The average person lived their struggling life irrespective of which ruling system was in power.

This reflected Offla's experience of Hungary being a kingdom before being claimed by the Ottoman Empire and then the Habsburg Empire. After World War I it was stripped of a considerable portion of its land and new countries were created. During

World War II Hungary reluctantly allied with the Germans in the hope of reclaiming their lost land. They were occupied by Germans at the end of the war before being occupied by Russia. Offla had a saying – 'When there is a crowd, stand in the corner', meaning don't go swearing allegiances openly to ideologies, because they are likely to change, as he found out. He had experienced nationalism then fascism then communism, seeing people persecuted at each change and incoming set of beliefs.

I've now read twelve novels by Emile Zola. They featured people on the land, people who worked in the central market in Paris, miners, train drivers, shop keepers and prostitutes. I can still picture Offla's eyes lighting up when he mentioned Zola. I now know why.

Towards the end of his life we were talking about how time passes quickly. He then started quoting fourteenth-century French poet François Villon's refrain 'But where are the snows of yester-year.' 'But where are the snows of yester-year?' from The Ballad of the Dead Ladies. It is about the winter of life, where you can't get back what has already gone. That quote is now on his gravestone. I managed to get him a copy of Villon's poems in Hungarian through my cousin Laszlo, as he only had a French copy. I have an English copy.

It's a tragedy that this cultured and intelligent Offla was buried beneath the mental burden of paranoid schizophrenia. I saw glimpses of that Offla, but would have liked a whole lot more.

I was raised in the care system in Brisbane between 1964 and 1972. Having had a generally positive experience, I was interested when a exhibition called The Forgotten Children came to the Melbourne Museum in 2014. The exhibition explored the experiences of children in care in Australia, including the period in which I was in care.

I thought it would be interesting to see the exhibition so I could reminisce about my past life. For some reason I thought it would be fun, and had completely blocked out why the apology was needed.

When I went to buy my ticket at the museum, the woman at the counter told me it was on the first floor before sighing, shaking her head and saying, 'When will we ever learn?' I didn't know what she meant and wondered if I was going to the right exhibition.

When I entered the display area I was met with a series of stories of abuse and neglect with Oliver Twist overtones. There wasn't one light-hearted display and I felt like I was in the wrong place. 'These aren't my stories' was my reaction and while I acknowledged there was abuse and neglect that accompanied institutional care, I thought there was also light that contrasted with the dark stories.

I felt the need to tell my own story of that era, as I was given opportunities by being in care that I wouldn't have otherwise received. I don't deny the validity of the stories of abuse and neglect that were displayed so clearly. But I thought there needed to be a balance to them for fear that those taking in the exhibition would think there was nothing but misery if you grew up in care during that period.

Was mine a sad story? Was it a story of one person's resilience within an environment that was oppressive to others?

I felt that I was lucky in a number of ways and that particular circumstances contributed to my sense of feeling well adjusted despite being raised in an abnormal setting. To begin with, I was not rejected by my parents and always had a sense that they loved me. To carry feelings of rejection from those who should love you the most into an institutional setting is a bad start.

I benefitted from not being forced into another family's identity. Though I drifted from my siblings for a while, my sense of being a 'Ban' was not diminished in any way. Silky Oaks was too big an organisation to try and restructure family identities similar to what occurs in foster care and permanent care. Although my relationship with my father was not promoted, it was allowed to continue when he returned from Europe without there being any challenger to his role as head of the Ban family.

During the time I was in care I was at the one address for eight years and attended only one primary school and one secondary school. For the majority of the time I had two sets of primary caregivers who were both prepared to give me space to be myself without wanting to absorb me into their family structures. I felt a genuine sense of love and caring from the two women, Aunty Rene and Aunty Jean, and didn't feel like I was simply one of many who were all in care at the same time. I was at the same address as my three siblings and under the same roof as Chris for all of the time and under the same roof as Helena for some of the latter time.

Are these the factors that make for a good care experience? Was I just lucky that my sense of identity was able to develop positively rather than through a fog of neglect and abuse? My personal make-up must be a factor, as I always felt I was a temporary visitor at Silky Oaks and that 'real life' would begin once I left.

I ended up with a successful career in social work and along the way completed a Master of Social Work, Master of Arts (Aboriginal Studies) and a Master in Conflict Resolution. In addition, I was at the right time to become part of an international movement called 'family group conferencing' that eventually allowed me to provide training in this area around Australia and in ten different countries. I provided training at the Depot in Brisbane, which had long closed as a children's receiving and assessment centre and had become a training venue for child protection social workers in Brisbane. I trained social workers in Tasmania, where I was born, and was able to reconnect with a neighbour who used to care for Chris and me and remembered my love of fruit tingles.

The basic principle of family group conferencing is the engagement of extended family, empowering them to become decision-makers regarding the welfare of children who have come to the attention of child welfare authorities, the role of social workers being that of expert information providers so the families can make their own decisions about their children's safety. One of the countries where I provided training was Hungary and another was Switzerland. The training in Budapest, Hungary, was particularly special, as I met my cousin Laszlo, who is my age, for the first time and reflected on how I could have been raised with him if the Queensland child welfare authorities allowed us to go to Hungary to live with our extended family.

Despite my attraction to this new way of working, I do not regret being taken into care even though I had extended family who were not consulted. My grandmother did not speak any English, and had never left Hungary before, and she was almost seventy years old at the time. I suspect that she would have felt very lonely and isolated living in suburban Brisbane, and would, no doubt, have struggled with the challenges of my father's fluctuating health issues.

Once, a 'Man from the State' paid us a visit at the home. He asked me if I was happy at Silky Oaks, to which I replied 'yes'. Then he asked if I wanted to live with my father in Europe. I was twelve at the time – we'd been at Silky Oaks for around two years – and I had little concept of Europe. I knew something about Switzerland from my uncle's postcards, but I knew nothing about Hungary. And

I wasn't going to find out either, not from him – it seemed the less we knew regarding our options the better. Or maybe he didn't know either.

I doubt that sending us to live in Europe was ever seriously considered, but in any event I'm glad I stayed at Silky Oaks. I was settled and happy at the time.

Yet, I was never given an informed choice. This was long before Australia's accession to the UN Convention on the Rights of the Child, and it was rare to ask children for their views about significant decisions that affected their lives. With no information at all about what sort of life might have been in store for me in Hungary or Switzerland, it was inevitable I would choose to stay where I was. What might I have decided if I had been given a detailed picture of my potential life in Europe? I will never know.

I was rescued from what was becoming a chaotic family life with no boundaries living with my father after my mother died and was provided with an environment that had clear boundaries. In addition I was able to experience the calm and gentle parenting style I received from my mother for eight years in the form of Aunty Rene from when I was ten to fourteen. By the time I was cared for by Aunty Jean, from fifteen to eighteen, I had a solid base from my mother and Aunty Rene to move toward independence.

Coming into care worked for me.

When I was nearly fifty-seven I was diagnosed with an aggressive form of Non-Hodgkin lymphoma. When I was diagnosed, while sitting there dazed, it struck me that my mother must have once received news as solemn as this. And at some point she'd been told there was nothing more her doctors could do for her, and she'd been sent home to spend her final days with her family. What must that have felt like for her, knowing she would leave behind her four young children, and knowing that the voices in our father's head were an increasingly regular presence?

I only once heard my mother lose patience with him. It must have been towards the end of her life when she was sick. They were in the kitchen together and Offla was speaking non-stop about our minds being controlled through special frequencies. My mother started pleading with him to stop and I heard her raise her voice and scream, 'Stop it Zoli! Stop it!' I remember it really upset me, because she never normally did that.

I had a great deal to be thankful for. I'd outlived my mother by almost twenty years, and had never had to experience the kind of hardships she'd known.

Later I paid a visit to Aunty Rene and Aunty Jean in Brisbane. Both widowed and well into their nineties by now, the two women were living in a nursing home in Redcliffe run by the Brethren church. Chris, Helena, Liz, Kenny and Peter all came with me, and together we paid tribute to them both for their love and care of us as children.

Aunty Jean was full of energy, while Aunty Rene was frailer. I acknowledged the important role that Jean had played in my upbringing, especially during those last three years as a teenager when I'd lived with her and Max (Mr Zander) in the Grey Cottage.

But it was sitting with Aunty Rene again that gave me a lump in my throat. I was just ten years old when she took me under her wing and gently nurtured and encouraged me and made me cups of tea. I couldn't tell my mother how lucky I had been that I had landed in a safe place, but I could certainly tell Aunty Rene what she had meant to me.

She held my hand and looked into my eyes and waited for me to stop talking about how good it was to see her.

'Paul, it was a privilege to look after you.'

She didn't have to say anything more.

Liz

I was forty-nine when Offla died. I was having a cup of tea with a friend, when I received a call from Chris to tell me he'd died at lunchtime. It didn't come as a shock to me, as he had been slowly fading away since he was admitted to the nursing home eighteen months earlier. But I felt tears well up and an ache in my throat. I'd last seen him in early June. I was in Brisbane for a friend's birthday and dropped in to visit a couple of times over the weekend. On one of the visits he was asleep the entire time I sat there, oblivious to me staring at him and wondering how he looked so frail and peaceful. How different he looked from the Offla of old, whose presence you couldn't escape when he was sharing his beliefs about air pushers or making sarcastic comments about the topic being discussed at the time. The other visit he was awake and had just had a shower. His hair was brushed back and he was sitting in a chair in the common room with the other elderly people. His blue eyes lit up when he saw me and he smiled as he greeted me, 'Hello, Bessie, my beloved daughter.' He had taken to calling me Lizzy for many years and so I was surprised to hear him call me Bessie again. It was his term of endearment. I felt sad and happy at the same time seeing him there. Sad to see him so frail and in a place I knew the old feisty Offla would have hated, but happy to see him. I sat with him and tried to fill him in with news of what Ed, Jazzy and Austin were up to and how my work was going. But I could tell he wasn't really interested in following the story and so I sat with him until he drifted off to sleep in his chair. I kissed him on the top of his head and told him I loved him before I left. I walked away from the nursing home wondering if I would get to see him again, as I had done ever since he turned eighty. I had lived in Perth since 1991 and Offla had asked when was I coming back to Brisbane to live ever since. He was seventy-four when I moved to Perth – strong and fit and full of life. I would regularly go east to see him, sometimes twice a year, especially when Jazzy and Austin were young.

Now, the news was sinking in about his death and the tears flowed. I felt a sadness for him, for the difficult life he had lived. But love and respect for him, too, and for his enduring love for us, his children. It was the end of an era, and Offla's quirkiness and all the funny things he used to do and say came flooding back.

How I miss him and those days he would pop up out of nowhere when you least expected it, carrying his airways bag. He was not your conventional dad, but he was my dad and I loved him.

When I reflect on my life at Silky Oaks, it is with a tinge of sadness for the loss of growing up with my own father, mother, and siblings. My first three years with my family were the foundation of a strong emotional connection to my father and siblings. I can't remember my mother at all, but I can only think she must have nurtured me in a loving way, which has kept me centred throughout my life. The strong bond with my siblings has been an anchor, an invisible, welcome weight that has held me in place in times of rough seas, when I was thrown from one set of caregivers to another. The love from my father, despite his mental illness and his powerlessness at keeping his family together, was a source of my strength. I never once doubted his love for me.

This connection to my family, and Offla's love and determination, enabled me to develop trust and a secure attachment to my husband, Ed, and our two wonderful children, Jasmine and Austin.

Although I had my own family within Silky Oaks, I also had an extended family there. I had close ties to my peer group, and a strong sense of being a 'home kid'. There were lots of happy memories. We had plenty of free time in between our chores and religious meetings to play games and explore our eight acres. I loved racing against the other kids on the front oval, or practising high jumps after school. The home kids had a sense of cheekiness too, and bravado if we got into trouble. I learnt about life through my peers, as we believed it was 'us' against the 'adults'. We came from all walks of life. Some were there because their parents didn't want them, some were neglected, some were abused, physically and sexually, some were taken because their parents did not fit the 'norm' of what was considered acceptable parenting and some because their parents couldn't afford to look after them at the time. We all had different stories and were all hurting in our own way, some more traumatised than others. This bond with my Silky Oaks siblings is one which no one but a home kid can understand.

My life's experiences led me to study social work. Initially, I worked in child protection, where I was a caseworker to children who had been taken from their families and placed in foster families. Two years in, I witnessed two young children being prised from their parents, screaming, after a supervised visit in the office, and realised I could no longer do it.

When my children were five and two and a half years old, Ed resigned from his work as a geologist and we travelled for a month through Thailand before moving to Oxford, England, for eighteen months. Ed was 'Mr Mum' and looked after the children, while I worked for Oxfordshire Social Services in Banbury. My role in the foster care and adoption area was to interview and assess potential carers and adoptive parents. I also supported foster carers looking after children. It was a role I enjoyed immensely, as I felt I had some insight into what constitutes good caregivers. While I was there, I arranged for my brother Paul to present a workshop on family group conferencing. I have fond memories of Paul presenting the workshop and me standing alongside him with one of my cases, explaining how a foster child in care would be better placed within his extended family.

In my early twenties, prior to going to Europe, I told one of my friends about my life growing up in Silky Oaks, and the Farrells, and how I regretted what happened that last summer I saw them. My friend asked me if I had ever thought of going to visit them to tell them how I felt. I hadn't; I had presumed they would not want to see me. My friend offered to drive me there. Initially, I was nervous, but I was glad I went. Keith and the children, who were young adults by then, were home. Dorothy was out somewhere. I felt awkward when I saw Keith but I thanked him for the kindness he and Dorothy had shown me and told him how bad I felt leaving the way I did that last holiday. He was very understanding and I was glad I went. I spent a couple of hours with the Farrells and then showed my friend the places where we played as kids and fished for guppies in the local creek.

After the success of seeing the Farrells, I got in touch with the Cash family. After thanking them for looking after me for those three months when I was fifteen, I explained how I was feeling at the time and that it was not a reflection on them as people. Again, like the Farrells, they were understanding and happy to see me and to find out what I was doing with my life.

While I was living with Helena and Ray, Les Fleming apologised to me and said she and Bruce were having marital problems when I lived with them and she had felt bad for asking me to leave. I accepted her apology and I was happy she'd told me. Les and Bruce divorced when I was in my early thirties. Les still has regular contact with Helena, and I see her from time to time when I'm in Brisbane.

I have always kept in touch with the Weeks family and I am still good friends with Carol, our friendship going back some fifty-odd years now. Jean and Alan also divorced and I visit Jean when I am in Brisbane.

Over the years, the thought of fostering crossed my mind on a few occasions. But I realised that my reasons were selfish. And I wanted to be emotionally present for my own children, which would not be possible if I were to foster a child. It takes a special selfless person to foster and I was not convinced I was ready.

As a social worker, I used to refer children in care for counselling, and, over time, I decided I wanted to be that person the children and families would talk to. On my return to Australia I went back to university and studied a postgraduate degree in counselling, and went on to work with refugees, families, couples and individuals. I use attachment theory in my work, especially with couples, and we explore their families to try and understand why some people are more securely attached, while others are anxious or ambivalent.

Over the years, when I have told people about my life growing up in a children's home, their response is: 'You poor thing. Did they feed you?' and 'You turned out normal.' I sometimes ask myself: What is normal? How come I didn't go off the rails, or become angry and bitter about my experience? Was it the strong attachment I had with my father and siblings? Was it personality? Was it luck? Was it resilience? I think it probably was a combination of all those things. But I also think it was some of the people along the way, who showed me love and kindness, who influenced and helped shape me into the person I am today.

I don't remember my life before Silky Oaks. After the initial grief of missing my mother and then my father, I felt safe and secure. My siblings were close by. I had friends. I knew the boundaries in the home and the consequences if I stepped outside them. I flew under the radar at Silky Oaks – I was a happy-go-lucky child, not a rebel. The problems started when I left at twelve and moved a number of times. Going from a large family of seventy children to a small family group when I was fostered made me stand out more. I noticed what I didn't have and what I had missed out on as a young child. I was lucky I only had a few placements, and that I remained in the same school with my friends during them. Some children are on a merry-go-round with multiple families and schools, losing their friends each time. It is no wonder they have emotional and behavioural issues. I still had regular contact throughout my moves with my siblings and father which helped too.

Through reading my mother's letters, I realised that Offla's mental health would have prohibited him from providing us with a safe and stable life after our mother died. I believe life at Silky Oaks offered me and my family stability. What they couldn't offer was the love, attention and nurturing I needed as a young child. I don't recall anyone at the home telling me they loved me or that I was special to them. I don't recall hugs or wanting to be hugged. I loved Offla and spent my childhood wanting to live with him, but I didn't understand why I couldn't. Offla was not affectionate towards me apart from a greeting kiss. I remember being twelve and Offla holding my hand as we crossed the road in the city. It seemed insignificant, but it stood out – he had never shown me that kind of attention before. I knew he was different to the male caregivers at Silky Oaks, and the Holiday fathers.

I was a ward of the state from when I was taken into care until I was eighteen years old, however, once I left Silky Oaks at fifteen and a half, I never heard from the social worker again. I left the country to travel to New Zealand when I was seventeen and 'the state', my legal guardian, had no idea where I was.

When I reflect on the letters from my mother, I see a strong woman who loved and supported her husband, who didn't complain about the difficult situation she found herself in. She lived in a new country, with four young children and a husband who was in and out of institutions for long periods of time. She had breast cancer and it must have been difficult for her, knowing she was going to die and leave her four children behind. I longed for the love of my mother when I was going through troubled times in my teenage years. I needed someone who loved me unconditionally. Someone who wanted to talk to me, to understand what I was thinking and feeling, to show interest in me, my friends and the things I valued. I would close my eyes and try as hard as I could to recall memories of my mother, to see her face, but nothing, nothing appeared. I didn't even have a photo of her. Did I resemble her in any way? It wasn't until Uncle Lajos gave me the photos and her letters that I could see her and get to know her.

I wonder if losing her affected my ability to attach to the female adults at the home? Perhaps my subconscious protected me from further hurt by not allowing me to get close to anyone else in case they died or left me? I met many young guys as a teenager and in my twenties who showed interest in me, but I had my protective barriers up. It wasn't until I met my husband, Ed, in my late twenties that I let my barriers down and allowed myself to get close to him and trust him, knowing that he would not abandon me.

The feelings of loss at not having my mother resurfaced when I had my two children. I was scared of dying before they turned three years old and leaving them motherless. I realised how much they needed me and their father. I loved them both dearly yet was aware I couldn't smother them to make up for my own loss. Each year after they turned three was a bonus. They are now both young adults and I can sigh a relief: we've made it. I outlived my mother and gave my children a childhood based on unconditional love.

Although Offla was not the 'normal' father I longed for, he was consistent in his love for me. Offla used to say, 'When things get tough, keep marching.' I can hear his voice now. I kept marching through the first twenty years of my life, but somehow, through my travels and my satisfaction at having achieved my goal to work with people and help them to make sense of their own lives and relationships, I find myself skipping more than marching these days. Life has been good to me for a very long time now and I am thankful for the many people who have shown me kindness throughout it.

Every day I give thanks for who I am and where I have come from, and some days I have to pinch myself to make sure that this life I am living now is real. Happiness for me is knowing I come from a family who were always there for me no matter what or where I was in the world.

Helena

In order to make sense of my childhood I obtained our family file from the state government under the Freedom of Information Act 1992.

The Ban family file may well have been one of the most substantial files held on record, for it covered a twenty-year period. It began three weeks before my first birthday and was closed when my sister turned eighteen. The file records incorporated much of our father's file held by the Department of Immigration until he was granted Australian citizenship.

I began the lengthy, cathartic experience of recording events in chronological order. Years of noting down my father's memories paid off for I was able to fill in blank periods between state government letters, memoranda, and what my siblings and I remembered.

I learned of the many years he spent fighting the system to regain custody of his children. It would have been easier for him if he'd walked away. It wasn't in his character.

I learned that after all four of us children left care, he was never again charged with or hospitalised with a mental illness.

I learned he was the inspiration behind the Children's Services Department granting parents regular access to children in care.

And the file confirmed what I already knew. What I dreamed about as a ten-year-old. What I've known ever since.

My father never ever abandoned me.

In the months and weeks leading up to his death his willingness to provide answers to my questions didn't abate.

What began as a soul-searching experience ended up with me recording a tribute to a man diagnosed with a mental illness in an era with little compassion and even less understanding. No one knew how to frame the external factors that fed into his illness – war, stress, our mother dying, a lack of money, of security, of employment, his children being taken into care. It was often easier to lock people away when they became a nuisance to society. He was labelled by the ignorant as a communist because of his country of origin. There, he risked his life escaping from the 'liberating' Russian Army to avoid such a label.

I have no doubt my childhood living in an institution, a children's haven or whatever label I feel is appropriate, was in many ways a godsend. My siblings and I were charged with neglect at an early age. Yet, it appears the only physical assistance my father received after our mother died was from kind neighbours. What would our lives have been if he'd had more help? What would it have been like if our Nagymama Ilona could have come out to help raise us?

I did have a life prior to being institutionalised at six, and it was that life that I clung to during my time in care. Dim memories kept the rebellious spark in me lit for years.

Still, all of this has shaped me into the woman I've become. I now understand that fate plays a part in all our lives. Years of soul-searching have led me to believe that it is a matter of accepting our fate that makes us who we are. If we don't, the healing process may never begin. I understand I was always normal; it was my circumstances that weren't.

In my adult years there have been tumultuous periods, but I've experienced mostly happiness. I grew to love and cherish the man I originally married for security, my lifesaver on so many levels. Ray and I have raised three wonderful sons of whom we are immensely proud. Ryan and Dane are both Commanders serving in the Royal Australian Navy. Callum is working his way up the ladder in the corporate world in the field of telecommunications. We have a cherished grandson, Jacob, who is fast approaching seven years of age, and we celebrated our forty-year ruby wedding anniversary in the south of France almost four years ago.

In addition to the years of playing mother to my sister, there was a time when I hoped for a daughter. I felt I deserved it and still mourned the mother–daughter relationship that was wrenched from me far too soon. As it wasn't meant to be naturally, I looked into adopting when my youngest son was three. The process was demanding but I was determined it was what I wanted. The State government-run organisation was determined to place many of its children already in foster care into permanent placements, regardless of how emotionally disturbed the child was or how many unsuccessful placements they may have had.

Our intended adoptee, Jenny, was fifteen and had been physically and emotionally abused since the age of two. The social worker managing her case equated my young family to a mobile, the kind of decorative structure suspended from a ceiling whose parts are balanced and move freely in the air. Due to Jenny's tumultuous childhood, we were warned her intention would be to unbalance us. And that is what transpired. My dream to adopt a daughter left my family's equilibrium as unsteady as if someone had opened the front door to high winds.

During several weeks of intense discussions with this once-innocent child, I came to understand she was never going to allow someone to take her parents' place. Her emotional outbursts may have often resembled those of a two-year-old, but I sensed the love and adoration she still had for her parents. The system wanted to find permanent placements. But adopting Jenny could very well have destroyed my young family and my marriage. As the date drew closer to legalising the adoption I knew the choice I had to make. So, a new family was sought for her and we were no longer allowed any contact.

I received professional counselling for several months after abandoning this troubled young girl. I knew I'd made the right choice for my family but it took me by surprise to learn that not only was I trying to offer Jenny a loving home, I was trying to save the emotionally troubled fifteen-year-old inside me. She was there when I was a young mother. And I believe she still exists somewhere within my ageing body.

My husband and I spent many years raising our sons and living in various parts of Papua New Guinea for his work. In fact, our twenty-six-year relationship with the Land of the Unexpected is ongoing. When we first arrived in Port Moresby we were captivated by a culture so unlike our own yet less than a three-hour flight from our hometown.

I was particularly fascinated by the *wantok* system. A *wantok* can be family, a member from the village or from the same province. Basically, anyone who speaks the same language can be your *wantok*.

The system enables *wantoks* to look out for each other by sharing their *haus* (home), *kai kai* (food) and kina (money) with those in need. It can be a blessing as well as a strain depending on which end of the system you happen to be on at the time. *Pikininis* (children) are raised not only by their parents but are often the responsibility of the whole village. Should a parent not be capable of raising their child then the *wantok* system comes into force. The child becomes the responsibility of an aunt, uncle, sister, brother, *bubu* (grandparents), cousin or, perhaps, a village elder. There is much merit in this system. I believe the old proverb 'It takes a village to raise a child' has been attributed to African cultures. It is certainly also alive in Papua New Guinea.

Family group conferencing, one model of care, involves the inclusion of extended family members in decision-making for children needing care. What a different world it might have been for many with whom I shared a unique childhood if this concept was born earlier. I wonder if there would have been a need for so many institutions if extended family members shared the load. For us, though? My father was a migrant with limited English, a widower, jobless, with citizenship deferred due to his illness. My siblings and I not only needed a village, we needed a miracle.

At Silky Oaks, my father's homeland was often referred to as 'that place over there'. I admit it may have been difficult for an Australian Christian Brethren woman to comprehend a country in landlocked Central Europe under Soviet rule.

When my sister and I stayed with our father's nephew Laszlo in Budapest in 1984, the country was still under Soviet rule and would be for another five years. Its dismal economic structure was evident in the sparsely stocked shelves in department stores, the horrific conditions for exotic animals in the city zoo and lack of available cash. At one stage we unwittingly became part of the black market sitting in the back pew of an historic church secretly exchanging American dollars for Hungarian forints.

Being in our father's birthplace was both emotional yet disappointing. As a child, I'd imagined the exotic lives our Hungarian relatives led. Laszlo had had a similar idea of us. We were both mistaken.

I returned for my fiftieth birthday. Ray and I met up with cousin Laszlo, who by now was looking more like my father. We spent a few days with him showing us the historic sights of this now renewed metropolitan city and tourism mecca. The Berlin Wall had fallen, Hungary was now a republic, and making the difficult, gradual transition to a free-market economy. One afternoon we visited Nagymama's old suburban duplex. Its elderly new owner, Miha'ly, welcomed us inside with open arms and a bottomless homebrew of schnapps! Several hours and several shot glasses later we staggered back to our hotel. Miha'ly couldn't speak a word of English and Laszlo only 'little bit'. Yet it was one of the most memorable occasions of my life. I felt the presence of Nagymama Ilona while sitting in her small kitchen. I hoped she approved of her granddaughter even with a belly full of schnapps. She was a huge presence in my life even though I never met her.

My husband and I joined our river boat cruise and sailed down the magnificent Danube River into Bratislava, Slovakia, forty-seven kilometres from the town of Felso'szeli. This is where my Nagypapa Ferenc was born and his parents before him. We continued along the picturesque Danube River through Austria, Germany and on to the Rhine River into Amsterdam, Holland. We then flew to the United Kingdom, the birthplace of my mother.

My sons have visited their grandfather's homeland and met Laszlo and his daughter Brigitta. Since my fiftieth birthday I have returned three times, the last being for my sixtieth birthday, each time eager to learn and see more of a place that is not 'over there' anymore, but in my heart forever.

I've travelled to London several times and each time felt a sense of pride and belonging. During my second trip, Liz and I tracked down the house our mother was born in. We caught the train to Fulham, west of London. As we stood on the street corner and looked up at the street sign, Ellaline Road, I wasn't prepared for the enormity of my feelings. As I sobbed loudly, my sister put her arm around me. She was more subdued than I was. 'You know,' she said, 'I don't remember our mother at all. I wish I had experienced the five years you had with her.' We walked quietly to number nine. I wanted to bang on the door and demand my right of entry. Nobody appeared to be home. After spending what seemed an eternity stalking the premises we giggled at the thought of being arrested should somebody think we were potential burglars. The only things of value to me inside were my mother's memories. If I could steal them, I would do so in a second. As her parents did before her, my mother entered the world in the family home. With no living family members from her side that I was aware of, I'd found my English roots, albeit brick and mortar ones.

My mother died six months shy of forty years of age. I struggled with guilt to survive my thirty-ninth birthday. The grief I'd bottled up for so long unexpectedly overflowed. My pain was almost too much to bear, leaving me seeking solace with counsellors and clairvoyants. The support from my husband not only proved his lifesaving skills but his abundant love. My decision to move forward with my life was made easier when I discovered my mother had always been by my side. It may have been in a spiritual sense but it was the healing I needed. She had been my guardian angel throughout the difficult years of my childhood. She watched over me as I transferred my love from one mother figure to another, always searching for her replacement. I feel her presence now as I write these words. I feel her warmth as her arms envelop my body. I still miss her.

My mother's body was cremated and, as an adult, I once asked Offla where her ashes were. He had kept them in a tin inside a larger container in the kitchen in Inala. The last he saw them was there in our family home. And so I can only assume that his loyal wife of ten years and my precious loving mother's final resting place was the local rubbish dump via the bus shed at Silky Oaks.

Since my father's death, both my brothers have been diagnosed with cancer. Firstly, Paul with an aggressive form of Non-Hodgkin lymphoma and just as it looked like he was in the clear Chris was diagnosed with throat cancer. It was such a shock as the boys were particularly fit and healthy for their age. Both brothers are now doing okay. Paul has recovered from a donor stem cell transplant due to a second cancer diagnosis. I couldn't imagine life without them, especially after surviving our unique childhood.

As siblings, I feel we are particularly close. Our story may have taken a different course if not for the early years of nurturing from our mother and the strength and determination of our father. Losing them both was, in a strange way, our saving grace. In the two months we spent at the Depot prior to going to Silky Oaks it was decided that we should be kept together given the tragedy we'd already experienced. Many sibling groups were not so lucky, and I can't imagine what my life would have become if we were separated.

At the beginning, the thread that bound us was tattered. But, over the years, it has twisted and woven into the strong fibre it has become. This binding thread was always there. It was the love and determination of our parents in times of adversity.

*

The government controlled our father and our family. Governments in general conspire with insurance industries, playing mind control games involving every individual on the planet. Our brains are connected to a main frequency through individual codes. Our family became victim to a triple insurance fraud between Hungary, England and Australia.

At least this is what our father firmly believed.

The 'power cuts' to Offla's body became more frequent as he aged. His body was frail but his mind remained active. Sometimes a small creature scurried on the wall beside his bed. It was gone by the time he pointed it out to me. A policeman, soldier, insurance salesman or government agent remained on watch in the corner. Often silent but with an occasional outburst meant for one person only. I knew they existed for they migrated with him from Europe to Australia. They travelled interstate from Tasmania to New South Wales and finally to Queensland. They were with him in each place of residence and had no intention of leaving him now. They had become frail but remained determined. Just like Offla.

Epilogue

Our father had many traits. He was stubborn, determined, sarcastic, obsessive and a hoarder. He was strong and caring. He was quirky and cultured. He had a sense of humour. He wished for a harmonious and peaceful world. He missed the joy of ice-skating and the snowfalls of the European winter. He loved the warmth of the Queensland sunshine baking his aching bones. He was unique.

He once told a story of riding into a Russian town on horseback with his cavalry unit. The sound of the horses' hooves on the road was loud and hypnotic. He was proud of being part of this regiment and felt on top of the world. Sometime later, after fighting with his unit, he was captured and sent by the Russians to work on the very same road. As he and his fellow prisoners hammered and chiselled away, it reminded him of the sound of the horses, when he was confident and free. He stopped to take in what had occurred since then and how his fortunes had changed.

It was winter with snow and ice everywhere. After he escaped from the prisoner of war camp, he headed for a river – he could hear it flowing, though not very strongly. When he found it, the bank of the river was more like a cliff. He could hear the water below but it was dark and he didn't know how deep the drop would be or what exactly was below. As he had no choice – he couldn't go back to where he had come from – he leapt forward and, after an eternity, he heard what he thought was breaking glass. It was the thin sheet of ice over the river. He went through it and in over his head. Then he swam to the shore.

Offla's courage and resilience has inspired and comforted us throughout our lives.

This is how we remember him.

Paul, Liz, Helena.

LIZ ENDNOTE:

My darling husband, Ed, passed away at home after fifteen months with Jazzy, Austin and I by his side. He was so gracious and inspirational in the way he dealt with his cancer and we were blessed to have the time to reflect on our life together as a couple and a family. I miss him daily and hold onto the many happy memories we shared throughout our thirty years together.

HELENA ENDNOTE:

My dear friend Shelley McCready died within weeks of Liz's husband Ed. She arranged a video to be shown at her funeral thanking everyone for their love and friendship. She didn't fear death and asked us not to grieve but to celebrate her life. I have lost many loved ones in my lifetime and remain forever grateful for all who have been a part of it.

"But where are the snows of yester-year" are words engraved on Offla's gravestone. This conclusion is a reminder that death claims everyone, even women immortalized by their deeds, just as the warming temperatures of spring melt the snows of winter. Offla quoted parts of this poem he liked to Paul in his later years, as it summed up his views on growing older.

The Ballad of Dead Ladies

Tell me now in what hidden way is Lady Flora the lovely Roman?
Where's Hipparchia, and where is Thais, Neither of them the fairer woman?

Where is Echo, beheld of no man, only heard on river and mere,
She whose beauty was more than human? But where are the snows of yester-year?

Where's Héloise, the learned nun, for whose sake Abeillard, I ween,
Lost manhood and put priesthood on? (From Love he won such dule and teen!)
And where, I pray you, is the Queen Who willed that Buridan should steer
Sewed in a sack's mouth down the Seine? But where are the snows of yester-year?

White Queen Blanche, like a queen of lilies, with a voice like any mermaiden,
Bertha Broadfoot, Beatrice, Alice, And Ermengarde the lady of Maine,
And that good Joan whom Englishmen at Rouen doomed and burned her there
Mother of God, where are they then? But where are the snows of yester-year?

Nay, never ask this week, fair lord, where they are gone, nor yet this year,
Save with this much for an overword, but where are the snows of yester-year?

Francois Villon (1431-1489)
French poet, thief and vagabond

www.ingramcontent.com/pod-product-compliance
Lightning Source LLC
Chambersburg PA
CBHW070728020526
44107CB00077B/2086